Winning Ingredients

For

Stock & Super Stock
Kit Cars

By
David Fulton

*All illustrations and photos
are by the author*

FIRST EDITION
12/31/2014

Published by
David Fulton, Indianapolis, Indiana USA

Copyright 2014 David Fulton
All rights reserved. No part of this book
may be reproduced without permission.

ACKNOWLEDGEMENT

With immense pleasure, I take this opportunity to thank the many people who generously gave advice and assistance while I was working on *Winning Ingredients*.

When I wrote my first book, "Winning Ingredient for Soap Box Derby Racers," I was fortunate in having several knowledgeable Derby people to advise me. Their advice has followed me to this new book. I want to thank Ollie Brower, Mason Bell, Harry Fuhrman, Pete Fuhrman, Derek Fitzgerald, Larry Hatfield, and Jerry Pearson, for all the time they spent answering my dumb questions.

I am grateful to the following for their contribution of their Derby knowledge, and their review of the manuscript in its early stages: Paul Abbott, Ollie Brower, Bruce Finwall, David Snetsinger, and Bob Snoddy. I want to thank them for their insightful comments and excellent suggestions.

For manuscript preparation, I am especially indebted to Susan Freeman for the immense amount of work she did on various drafts. In addition, a special thanks to my sons Michael, Christopher, and Nicholas for the time we spent doing Soap Box Derby and Winning Ingredients.

TABLE OF CONTENTS

Acknowledgment ---------------------------------- II
Table of Contents-------------------------------- III
Introduction ------------------------------------ XVIII

CHAPTER 1
AERODYNAMICS

Introduction---------------------------------- 1-1
    Most Important------------------------- 1-2
    Topics--------------------------------- 1-2
Importance Of Aerodynamics-------------------- 1-3
    Aerodynamic Information---------------- 1-4
Eleven Aerodynamic Topics--------------------- 1-5
    Streamlining--------------------------- 1-7
    Frontal Area--------------------------- 1-7
    Largest Cross-section Placement-------- 1-8
    Cusp Magic----------------------------- 1-8
    Teardrop Shape------------------------- 1-9
    Airfoils------------------------------- 1-10
    Symmetrical Airfoil-------------------- 1-11
    Typical Wing-Shaped Airfoil, And
    30%   Symmetrical Airfoil------------ 1-12
    Angle Of Attack At 0 Degrees----------- 1-13
    Important Note------------------------- 1-20
    Frontal Shape Misconception------------ 1-20
    Small Size----------------------------- 1-24
    Possible Misconception----------------- 1-24
    Rounding------------------------------- 1-24

AERODYNAMICS CONTINUED

From High Pressure To Low	1-25
Vortex Generator	1-27
Fillets	1-28
Types Of Drag	1-31
Wind Tunnel Test	1-33
Best Aerodynamic Shape	1-35
Fast Teardrop	1-37
Teardrop Deceptive Length	1-38
Axle Fairings	1-39
Axle Fairing Wind Tunnel	1-40
Race Condition, Air Flow Direction	1-40
Race Condition, "Bouncing	1-40
Interference Drag	1-40
Fairings With A Long Chord	1-40
Fairing Length	1-41
Fairing Shape	1-42
Kit Car Aerodynamic	1-42
Kit Car Floorboard	1-43
Sharp Edges	1-43
Hardware Installation	1-43
Body	1-44
Stock Car/Super Stock	1-44
Masters	1-44
Foam Installation	1-45
Brake System	1-45
Axle And Fairings	1-46
Axles	1-46
Steering Cable	1-46
Driver	1-46

CHAPTER 2 ENERGY

Introduction	2-1
Word Usage Throughout The Book	2-2
Types Of Energy	2-3
Potential Energy	2-3
Kinetic Energy	2-4
What Can Happen To Energy	2-4
Lost Energy	2-5
Energy Experiment	2-5
The Following Things Take Energy	2-7
Friction	2-7
Aerodynamic Drag	2-8
Wasted Motion	2-8
More Energy Usage	2-9
Wheels	2-9
Bumps	2-11
Loose Parts	2-11
Inertia	2-11
NeWt.on's First Law Of Motion	2-12
Maximize Your Car's Energy	2-13
Suspension	2-14
Weight Placement	2-14
Energy Tests	2-15

CHAPTER 3 SUSPENSION

Introduction	3-1
Loose, Tight, And Solid	3-2
Items In This Chapter To Discuss	3-2
What Is A Suspension System	3-3
Suspension And Energy Usage	3-4
Solid Suspension Track Test	3-4
Solid, Tight, And Loose Suspension	3-5
Similarities	3-6
Differences	3-6
Loose System	3-7
What Loose Does: Best And Worst	3-7
What Solid Does: Best And Worst	3-7
Solid, Loose, And Tight Combinations	3-8
Car Body	3-9
Rigid	3-9
Strong	3-10
Resilient	3-10
Axles	3-10
Axle Selection	3-11
Which Side Up	3-14
Pre-Bowing Axles	3-14
Changing Axles	3-15
Conclusion	3-15

WINNING INGREDIENTS FOR KIT CARS   VII

CHAPTER 4
CONSTRUCTION

Introduction	4-1
This Chapter Will Cover	4-2
Examine Your Level	4-2
Construction Rules	4-3
Install Kingpin Bushings Before Tung Oil	4-3
Bushing Installation Preparation	4-3
Evaluating Your Bushing, Floorboard, Axle level	4-6
Level The Remaining Axle	4-10
Leveling Your Axle With A Feeler Gauge	4-11
Shimming Your Axle	4-11
Bushing Hole Adjustment	4-12
Prepare The Bushing Hole For Epoxy	4-12
Adjusting The Bushing In The Floorboard To Level The Axle	4-12
Epoxy The Bushing Into The Floorboard That Was Adjusted	4-13
Epoxy All Bushings That Need No Hole Adjustment	4-14
Rear Axle Radius Rods Bushings	4-15
Recheck Axles Level To The Floorboard	4-16
Floorboard Preparation And Finish	4-16
Apply Tung Oil	4-17
Wax Your Floorboard	4-18
Install The Elevator Bolts In The Floorboard	4-19

VIII   WINNING INGREDIENTS FOR KIT CARS

Install The Forward And Aft Axles------------------ 4-20
CONSTRUCTION CONTINUED

Finish Installation Of Floorboard Hardware------- 4-23
    Steering Hardware Installation---------- 4-23
    Complete Steering/Brake Assembly---- 4-24
Install The Steering Cable-------------------------- 4-25
    Prepare To Install The Steering Cable-- 4-26
Install Brake Pedal--------------------------------- 4-29
    Brake Pedal Position And Driver-------- 4-29
    Install The Brake Cable------------------ 4-30
    Test Drivers Position For Braking------- 4-31
Cockpit Foam Installation-------------------------- 4-32
Weight Installation---------------------------------- 4-34
    Determine the Amount Of Added
    Weight Needed----------------------- 4-35

    Determine Where To Place Your-----
    Weight---------------------------------- 4-35
    Weight Material Most Used---------- 4-37
Install The Super Stock----------------------------- 4-37
    Install The Rear Axle Stabilizers -----
    Bushings-------------------------------- 4-38
    Assemble The Super Stock Aft Axle----- 4-39
Install The Body------------------------------------- 4-41
    Install The Stock Car Body-------------- 4-41
    Install Stock Car Body Screws---------- 4-42
    Install The Super Stock Body----------- 4-43
Car Body Paint-------------------------------------- 4-44
Construction Conclusion--------------------------- 4-45

CHAPTER 5 ALIGNMENT AND ADJUSTMENTS

Introduction	5-1
Tools Required	5-2
Tools And Other Items Needed	5-2
Prepare The Car	5-3
Prepare Your Scales	5-4
Make Your Level Board	5-5
Check The Car Total Weight	5-7
Prepare To Check Total Weight	5-7
Weight And Balance Adjustments Form	5-8
The Form Has Five Sections And Here Is How It Works	5-9
Weight And Balance Adjustments Form 1	5-10
Check Total Weight Of Car And Driver	5-10
Weight And Balance Adjustments Form 2	5-12
Check Lateral Weight	5-13
Items Needed To Check Lateral Weight	5-14
Place The Car On The Scales	5-15
Check Lateral Weight With Driver	5-15
Cross-Bind Adjustment	5-15
What Is Cross-Bind	5-15
Why "O" Cross-Bind Is So Important	5-16
Tools Used To Measure Cross-Bind	5-16
Cross-Bind Measuring	5-20

WINNING INGREDIENTS FOR KIT CARS

ALIGNMENT CONTINUED

Tools Conclusion --------------------------------- 5-20
Most Accurate Cross-Bind Tool System ----------- 5-20
Prepare For Cross-Bind Adjustment ------------ 5-21
Cross-Bind Measurement And Adjustment By----
Scales Using Two Scales And A Level Board   5-23
Stock And Masters Car Cross-Bind Measurement
And Adjustment   5-23
    Super Stock Car Cross-Bind ---------- 5-25
    Shim Forward Axle In Super Stock------ 5-25
Steering ------------------------------------- 5-26
    Steering And Brake Safety -------------- 5-26
Final Steering Adjustment --------------------- 5-27
    Adjust Steering Cable----------------- 5-27
Mark Car Body And Axle For Steering Straight   5-28
Axle Spindle Alignment------------------------- 5-30
    Where To Set Your Spindles-------------- 5-32
    Least Important Direction ------------ 5-33
    Most Important Direction----------------- 5-34
    Suggestion ---------------------------- 5-34
    Alignment Check List --------------------- 5-34
    Camber Adjustments --------------------- 5-35
    Toe-In Adjustments ------------------ 5-36
Conclusion------------------------------------- 5-37
    Kingpin Bolt Torque --------------------- 5-37

CHAPTER 6 TOOLS

Introduction	6-1
Tool List	6-2
Spindle Alignment Tools	6-3
Alignment Tool Construction	6-4
Alignment Tool Calibration	6-7
Professional Built Alignment Tool	6-9
Spindle Bending Tool	6-11
Axel Stands	6-14
Level Table	6-15
Track Slope Testing Tool	6-16
How Much Track Slop Is Needed	6-18
You Can Help Gain This Experience	6-18
Fisher Gauge	6-19
Steel Car Dolly	6-19
You Will Need To Build The Dolly	6-20
Building Your Car Dally	6-21
Trammel Tool	6-26
Steering Wheel Holder	6-27
Remaining Tools	6-29
Torque Wrench	6-29
Two Bathroom Scales	6-29
Feeler Gauges	6-29
Small Bullet Level (6" Long	6-29
Large Level For Cross-Bind	6-29
Alignment	

TOOLS CONTINUED

Tool Maintenance ------------------------------------- 6-30
        Checking Your Square ------------------- 6-30
Special Tool Manufacturers ------------------------ 6-31
Tool Conclusion -------------------------------------- 6-31

CHAPTER 7 PARTS INSPECTION

Introduction -- 7-1
Inspect Your Parts -- 7-2
Parts Inspection -- 7-3
Floorboard -- 7-3
        Floorboard Features To Look For ------- 7-5
        Floorboard Inspection ------------------- 7-6
        Check Your Floorboard Longitudinally
        For Warping ------------------------------ 7-8
Body -- 7-9
        Body Inspection -------------------------- 7-10
Axles --- 7-13
        Axle Inspection --------------------------- 7-14
        Solve Minor Problems -------------------- 7-15

PARTS INSPECTION CONTINUED

Axle Dimensions	7-13
Check Kingpin Hole	7-17
Check Axle For Bends	7-17
Check Axle Length	7-18
Axle Inspection In Suspension Chapter	7-21
Stock Car Radius Rods	7-21
Bent Radius Rods	7-21
Radius Rod Inspection	7-22
Drilled Holes	7-22
Size	7-22
Steering And Brake Assembly	7-23
Inspection	7-23
Miscellaneous Parts	7-26
Kingpin Bolts	7-26
Conclusion	7-27

CHAPTER 8 WEIGHT MANAGEMENT

Introduction	8-1
Weight	8-2
Weight Density	8-3
Metal Weight Chart	8-4
Weight Distribution	8-4
Metal	8-5
Weight Placement Experiments	8-6
High Weight Experiment	8-8
Inertia	8-9
Balanced Weight Experiment With Weights Near	

XIV WINNING INGREDIENTS FOR KIT CARS

The End Of The Poles -------------------------------- 8-11

WEIGHT MANAGEMENT CONTINUED

Balanced Weight Experiment With Weights
Placed Close To Pivot Point At Each Side Of
Your Hand-- 8-11
Application Of Vertical Weight Experiment-------- 8-12
Application Problems (Driver And Vertical Weight 8-15
Lateral Weight Placement Experiment-------------- 8-16
Balanced Weight Not Close To The Pivot Point
And Balanced Weight Close To The Pivot Point--- 8-17
      Car Body Lateral Experiment------------ 8-18
      Axle Lateral Weight Experiment--------- 8-18
      Lateral Weight Conclusion -------------- 8-18
Application Of Lateral Weight Experiments-------- 8-19
      Body------------------------------------ 8-19
      Placing Lateral Weight In A Kit Car----- 8-20
      Axles----------------------------------- 8-20
Longitudinal Weight Placement Experiment-------- 8-21
Application Of Longitudinal Experiments---------- 8-22
      Kit Car Considerations------------------ 8-22
Weight Placement Conclusion---------------------- 8-23
      High Weight---------------------------- 8-23
      Balanced Weigh------------------------ 8-24
Conclusion-- 8-28
      Making Lead Weights------------------- 8-29

CHAPTER 9 WEIGHT & BALANCE CALCULATIONS

Introduction -- 9-1
Weight & Balance Calculations---------------------- 9-1
    Weight------------------------------------ 9-2
    Arm--------------------------------------- 9-2
    Moment----------------------------------- 9-2
    Formula For Moment-------------------- 9-3
    Formula For Center Of Gravity (Cg) 9-3
    Vertical Cg------------------------------- 9-3
    Horizontal------------------------------- 9-7
Conclusion-- 9-10

Chapter 10 Practice

Introduction -- 10-1
Practice--- 10-2
    First Trip Down The Hill--------------- 10-2
Driver's Education---------------------------------- 10-3
    Communication------------------------- 10-3
    Derby Tech ----------------------------- 10-4
    Be A Good Sport----------------------- 10-4
    Keep Your Car In The Sun-------------- 10-5

WINNING INGREDIENTS FOR KIT CARS

PRACTICE CONTINUED

Keep Your Wheels On Dark Asphalt	10-4
Don't Shad Your Car It	10-5
Don't Drive On Painted Lines	10-5
Stop Your Car Smoothly	10-6
Don't Jerk Up At The Finish Line	10-6
Don't Turn Your Head	10-6
Brake Past The Finish Line	10-7
Don't Look Back At The Finish Line	10-7
Know What To Do If Your Steering Fails	10-7
If Your Brakes Fail	10-7
Know What To Do When Someone Drives Into Your Lane	10-8
Know How To Swap Wheels	10-8
The Driver Is Part Of The Team8	10-8
Pay Attention When Your Car Is Being Handled	10-8
Know When Your Steering Is Straight	10-9
Understand Why You Shouldn't Steer The First 20 Yards	10-9
Understand Why You Should Drive To The Steepest Part Of The Track As Soon As Possible	10-9
All Steering Movements Smooth	10-10
Ramp Alignment	10-11
Steering	10-11
Lining Your Car Up	10-11
Transition From Ramp To Track	10-12
Starting Gate Angle	10-12

WINNING INGREDIENTS FOR KIT CARS XVII

PRACTICE CONTINUED

Starting Gate Speed	10-12
Un-Level Ramp	10-13
Track Shape	10-13
Practice	10-14
Use Illustration To Teach	10-15
Ramp Alignment Conclusion	10-17
Testing	10-17
People Who Test	10-18
Tips On Testing	10-19
Pay Attention To The Elements	10-20
Wind And Shade	10-20
Test Equipment	10-20
Buddy System	10-20
What To Test	10-21

INTRODUCTION

The original idea for Winning Ingredients came while I was in Akron in 1989. My son was racing in the Masters division that year, and my friend, Paul Abbott had a son s racing in the Kit Car division. During race week, Paul suggested I write a book about what makes Soap Box Derby cars fast. Paul was a writer of aviation books and said he would help me promote my book if I wrote it. I did not feel qualified, but I felt a book could be helpful. I felt there were many Derby Families that had a disadvantage with their lack of Soap Box Derby knowledge. I felt that with more technical knowledge, those families would stay in Soap Box Derby and be more competitive. In June of 1993, I published Winning Ingredients for Soap Box Derby Racers.

POSITIVE RESPONSE
When I started this project, I was pleased with the positive response I received. Since the first publication, I have received positive feedback from those who have bought the book. I am extremely pleased that Winning Ingredients has helped Derby people even more than I had hoped. I am also pleased to announce that most Derby city libraries have copies of Winning Ingredients. This makes Winning Ingredients available to anyone for nothing.

INTRODUCTION OF THE KIT CAR
With the introduction of the kit cars in the early 1990s, it soon became apparent that a revision of Winning Ingredients was needed. With the success of "Winning Ingredients for Soap Box Derby Races," I knew a revision would be accepted and be very helpful.

WINNING INGREDIENTS FOR KIT CARS   XIX

WHAT IS NEW IN WINNING INGREDIENTS FOR KIT CARS

Chapter 6 "Tools," Chapter 7 "Parts Inspection," Chapter 8 "Weight Management," and Chapter 9 "Weight and Balance Calculations," are new Chapters. Chapter 2 "Energy," Chapter 4 "Construction," and Chapter 5, "Alignment & Adjustments," have had major revisions. The "Construction Chapter" has changed the most as it strives to help new and old families assemble their kit cars. Chapter 1 "Aerodynamics," Chapter 3 "Suspension," and Chapter 10 "Practice," have had minor revisions.

Winning Ingredients for kit cars contain the following Chapters and Subjects.

1. Aerodynamics and its importance
    a. This chapter explains the influence of aerodynamics in Soap Box Derby
2. Energy
    a. This chapter explains what produces the energy for Soap Box Derby and helps you manage it.
3. Suspension
    a. This chapter explains what a suspension system is and how to get the most out of your suspension system.
4. Construction
    a. This Chapter helps construct the car in the best practices available. Proper construction will aid final alignment and performance.
5. Alignment
    a. This chapter aligns the car for the best performance
6. Tools
    a. This chapter explains the special tools needed and shows how to make them.
7. Parts inspection

a. This chapter helps the family inspect the parts for defects and explains what to look for when inspecting.
8. Weight Management
   a. This chapter helps families understand where to place the added weight for the best performance.
9. Weight and Balance Calculations
   a. This chapter explains how to calculate the weight and balance of the racecar.
10. Practice
    a. This chapter includes Practice, driver's Training, and Testing. When you do one of these things, you are doing the others at the same time.

WHY I WROTE THIS BOOK

I wrote this book to help all Derby families be able to be competitive. Everyone deserves to have the knowledge to be competitive.

Derby people take their knowledge with them when they leave Derby. That knowledge takes a long time to acquire. Access to this book will give you a head start that only years of experience can buy. The basic physics contained in this book will not change even if the rules are changed.

RACING DIVISIONS TO USE THIS BOOK

The information contained in this book is for Stock, Super Stock, Masters, and the Ultimate Speed Division. The Construction Chapter is the only chapter that is not relevant to the Masters and Ultimate Speed car. Some of the information is relevant to the Masters, but the chapter is not focused on the "Masters" and "Ultimate Speed" car's specific construction. I have friends who build Masters cars and are very successful. They have a few secrets that you only learn from the repetitive building of Masters

WINNING INGREDIENTS FOR KIT CARS   XXI

cars. Until I build and learn these secrets, I will not write a construction chapter for Masters. The basic science of Soap Box Derby contained in Winning Ingredients is used for all Divisions. From that information, the Ultimate Speed builders will design and construct their cars, as they perceive to be the best.

HOW TO USE THIS BOOK

Start at the first chapter and read to the last. When you get your Soap Box Derby car and are anxious to start building, start with Chapter 7 "Parts Inspection," 8 "Weight Management," and continue with 4 "Construction," and then Chapter 5, "Alignment & Adjustment."

ILLUSTRATIONS

There are **Figures and photo** illustrations to aid you. The drawn Figures and photo references have a caption under them to identify them as a specific **Figure or photo**. Be cautious when reading the book so you do not mistake a **photo** reference for a **Figure** reference and vice versa.

TEXT CONVENTIONS

I use italics, underlining, and **bold** to emphasize something important to remember. I often use these to emphasize something important to be done in a specific order. The most important of the three is **bold, the** text is underlined, and the least is Italic. However, it is best if you just remember that they all are important to help you.

REPEATING IN WRITING

I remember from writing class that you should not repeat yourself in writing. I break that rule sometimes. If I am in one chapter and want to make a point that is relevant to the subject, I might repeat something I have written in another chapter.

MOST IMPORTANT INGREDIENT

The most important ingredient in any activity is work. All the Soap Box Derby experts I know put a lot of effort into whatever they do. Some of those experts are active local Derby board members. Some are active in the National Derby Rally, or All-American Soap Box Derby.

FAMILY SPORT

I feel Derby is a family sport. There are so many things that children can do without other family members. With Derby, you see families coming together. Families in Derby will learn to communicate and work together. Families that work as a team are always tough competitors.

I truly wish you the best of luck in your Derby efforts. I know it will give your family many rewarding moments, as it has mine.

CHAPTER ONE
AERODYNAMICS

INTRODUCTION

In this chapter, we will cover the basics of aerodynamic principles while dispelling the misconceptions caused by these aircraft-based theories. We will also discuss the types of aerodynamic drag and how to reduce them. We will also look at the results of wind tunnel tests performed by the **Massachusetts Institute of Technology (MIT)**.

The All-American Soap Box Derby decided on switching to kit cars in the early 1990s. In 1992, the Stock car came out, and in 1995 the Super Stock. With the inception of the Kit cars, the car body shape is already determined. With all the bodies shaped the same, you might think this chapter is not needed. I started to make a major revision to this chapter eliminating parts needed to build your car from scratch. However, aerodynamics is a very important part of Soap Box Derby racing, and the Ultimate Speed division can use this information. A small improvement in

Aerodynamics often will give you greater gains than you would expect.

By reading this chapter, you will get a better understanding of what to do to make your car parts go through the air while producing the least drag. Some of you may find it interesting to find out what is required to make an aerodynamic race car. Everything on your car that is exposed to the air affects your car's aerodynamics and affects your speed. At the end of this chapter, I am more specific about what you can do to affect the aerodynamics of your Kit Car. See Kit Car Aerodynamics on page 40.

MOST IMPORTANT

Everyone always wants to know what the most important part of aerodynamics is, and that is *streamlining*. With good streamlining, a car with a large cross-section can be as fast as a small car. This was proven in 1992 when the second and third place cars were large compared to the competition present that day at the National Derby Rally Championship race. It has often been thought drivers over 120 pounds cannot compete against smaller drivers. This is untrue; the second and third place cars were driven by larger than average drivers. The second place driver was about 135 pounds.

TOPICS

An understanding of the eleven topics presented will give you the foundation to build a competitive Ultimate Speed car of your own.

AERODYNAMICS 1-3

IMPORTANCE OF AERODYNAMICS

The aerodynamic drag on a Soap Box Derby racer increases with the square of its speed. That means that if the speed of a Soap Box Derby Racer is doubled, the drag becomes four times greater. Table 1-1 is a comparison of speed to units of drag. The numbers in the **UNITS OF DRAG** column are for comparison only. This table shows how speed affects the drag of an object. A small improvement in aerodynamics can make a significant increase in speed.

Speed is only one of three factors used to determine the drag of an object. The actual drag of an object depends on Airspeed, Cross-sectional area, and Shape.

TABLE 1-1

SPEED	UNIT OF DRAG
5 MPH	25
10 MPH	100
15 MPH	200
20 MPH	400
25 MPH	600
30 MPH	800

The table above illustrates the effect of speed on drag. Derby people spend a lot of time working on aerodynamics because it can be a major factor in winning. Aerodynamics is only one of several ingredients needed to build a winning car.

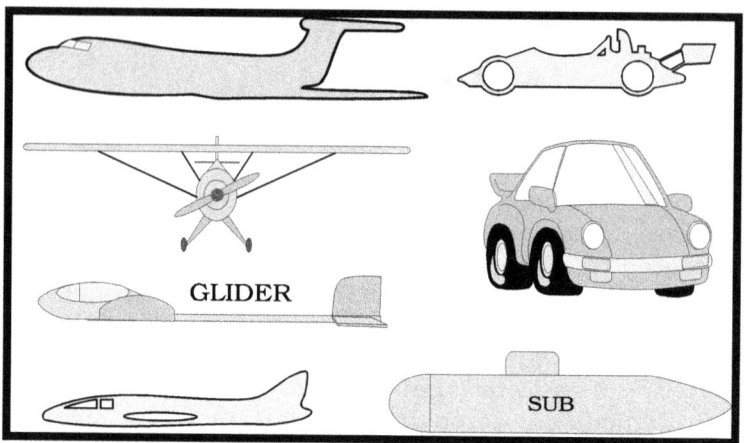

Figure 1-1

AERODYNAMIC INFORMATION

It is difficult to locate information on aerodynamics as it applies to the Soap Box Derby. Some aerodynamic books are filled with formulas. Formulas are great for people who know how to work them, but most of us cannot. I find illustrations more helpful, and I hope you will find the illustrations in this chapter helpful to you.

Figure 1-1 shows several items whose shapes you might have considered for your Derby car. These items are shaped to do a specific job under specific rules. None of these is trying to do the same job, and none operates under the same rules. It is impractical to copy any of their shapes until you understand a lot more about the reason for their shape and rules. Only then could we decide if the shape can be applied to Soap Box Derby. Some of the aerodynamic terms we are going to discuss are tied to a specific purpose. An understanding of these terms will help you decide if they can be applied to Soap Box Derby.

ELEVEN AERODYNAMIC TOPICS

In the original *Winning Ingredients*, I divided the Aerodynamic chapter into 11 topics as listed below. I used these topics because they were the subjects, I heard discussed by Soap Box Derby people everywhere. These topics are familiar to most of us, and their definitions can be found in most dictionaries.

1. **Streamlining**
2. **Symmetrical**
3. **Cross-section (largest)**
4. **Frontal Area Shape**
5. **Trailing-Edge Shape**
6. **Size (Cross-section, the number of square inches going through the air)**
7. **Rounding (The more the better)**
8. **Fairings (A device to streamline something sticking out in the air)**
9. **Airfoils (Covered under Streamlining)**
10. **Vortex**
11. **Fillets**

The above topics bring all kinds of images to our minds. When you hear talk about *Streamlining*, what picture does it bring to your mind? Do you have visions of an airplane, a submarine, or maybe a new RX7? We all differ on what is the best representation of streamlining. The other topics may also give you some strange visions. Even experienced Soap Box Derby people do not agree on the meanings and applications of these topics. You will have a better understanding of what these words mean to you after reading this chapter. You will also be better prepared to use that knowledge.

Some ingredients of aerodynamics interfere with one another. As an example, if you build the smallest cross-section into your car, it will not be the most streamlined. This is because the smallest cross-section has too many sharp curves. If you build the most streamlined shape, you will not have the smallest cross-section. This is because the increased rounding of a streamlined object increases its cross-sectional area. See that comparison in Figure 1-2.

Streamlining and small cross-sections are both important, but you cannot do one very well without interfering with the other. In Derby, this is called a trade-off. You must decide which ingredient is the most important.

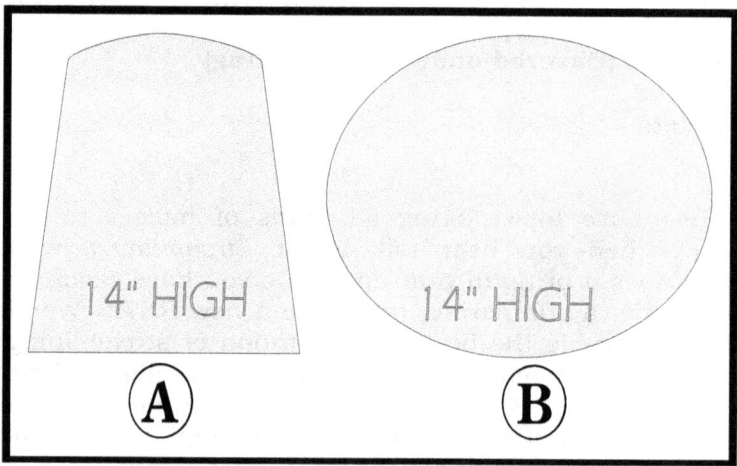

Figure 1-2

AERODYNAMICS   1-7

n Figure 1-2, you see two cross-sections. The round cross-section of "B" is best for streamlining. The smallest allowable cross-section of "A" is best for making a small hole in the air. Both of these shapes have been used successfully. I feel the most desirable shape lies somewhere between these extremes.

Below is an explanation of each topic as you might find it in a dictionary or encyclopedia. I will expand on this and explain some of the misconceptions that we get from this information. The shapes above were used by the Soap Box Derby when I wrote the original *Winning Ingredients*.

STREAMLINING

To streamline something is to shape it to reduce its resistance to the fluid it travels through. Under **Streamlining**, we will discuss details of the teardrop and airfoil shape.

FRONTAL AREA

In this chapter, I often refer to the *frontal area*. By *frontal area*, I mean the front half of the car, and especially that area from the largest cross-section to the nose.

The teardrop, and airfoil shapes refer to *specific shapes* that have been built from a combination of sound aerodynamic principles. These shapes have been tested in wind tunnels for years. The main purposes of these tests have been to reduce drag and increase lift in aircraft wings. Derby people have adopted these shapes and their aviation name, and have applied them to their racers

Most of the airfoil and teardrop shapes will give your racer an adequate streamlined shape; however, I want to disclose some misunderstandings these shapes have caused. <u>Below are listed three possible misunderstandings people have gotten from these shapes.</u>

1. Large frontal areas are the best for streamlining.
2. The largest cross-section should be no farther back than 33 inches from the front. (40% airfoil or less)
3. There's magic in the cusp tail of the teardrop shape.

Different percentages of airfoils represent the placement of the largest width and height of your car body. To find the location of a 30% airfoil, take the length of your car body in inches and multiply by (.30). The answer is measured from the nose of your car in inches.

FRONTAL AREA

A large frontal area does not make your car faster. (Do not design the front of your car like an actual teardrop.) The height and width of your car should never be larger than rules dictate, or needed because of the size of the driver.

LARGEST CROSS-SECTION PLACEMENT

A 30% airfoil is not the best placement for your largest cross-section. That placement depends on the size of the driver, weight placement, rules, and suspension. *A 40, 50, and 60% airfoil can be used successfully with an average size driver and proper streamlining.* The largest cross-section is needed where the driver's hips are located.

CUSP MAGIC

Figure 1-3 shows two teardrop shapes. The way the tail comes in quickly is called a cusp. The cusp magic is in its smallness in the back, and the way it releases the air off its tail. This can be incorporated into an Ultimate Speed racer. Ultimate Speed Competitor Derek Fitzgerald uses a cusp on his cars.

AERODYNAMICS   1-9

TEARDROP SHAPE

There is a theory that the teardrop is the most streamlined shape. The teardrop shape is a good shape. It is especially good for aircraft applications. Some people get the impression that the large frontal area of the teardrop shape is the secret to aerodynamics.

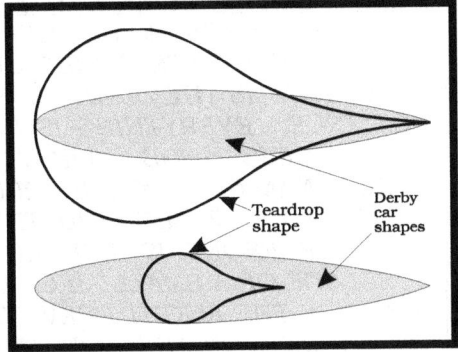

Figure 1-3

TEARDROP PROPORTIONAL SHAPE

Figure 1-3 shows two shaded Derby car shapes with teardrop shapes over them. As you can see, the shape of the teardrop does not conform to the Soap Box Derby dimensions. It is either too wide or too short when its dimensions are changed proportionally.

The shaded shaped Derby cars in Figure 1-3 above are best. They are wide enough to fit the required dimensions and placed where they are needed the most, and that is at the driver's hip and shoulder area.

Most Derby people do not use a large frontal area teardrop shape like the one in Figure 1-3.

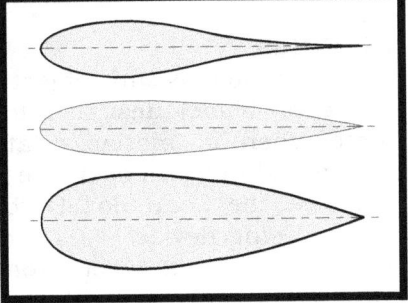

Figure 1-4

Instead, they stretch it out like the shapes in Figure 1-4. These shapes when used on aircraft have been nicknamed Teardrop, or polliwog shapes.

> ### TEARDROP SHAPE
> *WE SEE WINGS AND THE AIRCRAFT FUSELAGE SHAPED LIKE A STRETCHED OUT TEARDROP AND WE THINK THAT IS THE ULTIMATE SHAPE. WELL, THAT IS NOT TRUE. EVERYTHING IS DESIGNED TO PERFORM A SPECIFIC JOB FIRST, AND THEN THE AERODYNAMICS IS CONSIDERED. AN AIRCRAFT WING MUST PRODUCE LIFT AND THE THICKNESS OF THE WING UP FRONT IS NEEDED TO DO THAT. THE FUSELAGE OF A SMALL AIRCRAFT IS LARGE UP FRONT BECAUSE THE FLIGHT CREW NEEDS TO BE UP FRONT TO SEE OUT. IN ADDITION, THAT IS THE BEST SHAPE FOR SOMETHING THAT CHANGES ANGLES OF ATTACK AT HIGH SPEEDS.*

> DESIGN YOUR CAR BODY SHAPE TO FIT YOUR <u>REQUIRED DIMENSIONS</u>. DO NOT INCREASE YOUR CAR DIMENSIONS TO FIT A SPECIFIC BODY SHAPE.

AIRFOILS

An airfoil is an object (like an airplane wing or propeller blade) designed to provide a desired reaction force when in motion relative to the surrounding air. Today and in years past, the word **airfoil** has been used to describe the Soap Box Derby racer's body and the axle streamlining devices. As the definition above states, "An airfoil is designed to get a **reactive force** from the air." In Derby, you do not want any reactive force from the air. You want your car's body to disturb the air as little as possible, and the air to disturb your racer as little as possible. The air says, **"IF YOU DON'T BOTHER ME, I WON'T BOTHER YOU."**

AERODYNAMICS 1-11

I do not want to change the words used to describe items in Derby, but I want you to be aware of the proper meaning. This will allow you to make an intelligent investigation into the shape to use for your Soap Box Derby racer. The use of the word "airfoil" in Derby is simply a reflection of the influence of people with aviation backgrounds.

> WHEN AN AIRFOIL IS DESIGNED IN AVIATION, THE PRIMARY GOAL IS TO PRODUCE LIFT WITH LOW DRAG CHARACTERISTICS.

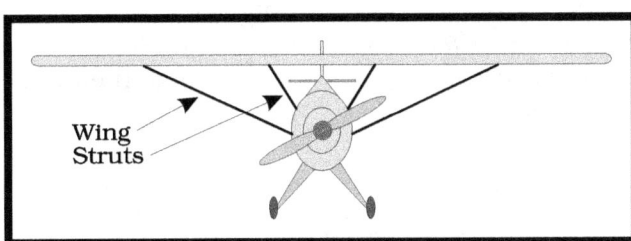

Figure 1-5

SYMMETRICAL AIRFOIL

A symmetrical airfoil is shaped the same above and below the horizontal center of the airfoil. All the airfoils in Figures 1-4 and 1-6 are symmetrical airfoil shapes. The symmetrical airfoil shape is the one Derby people should use. Symmetrical airfoils are used on acrobatic aircraft.

30% SYMMETRICAL AIRFOIL

Although airfoils are usually wings on aircraft, some are used to streamline items on the aircraft. Figure 1-5 shows an aircraft with wing and landing gear struts that need to be streamlined. Struts are support structures for wings, landing gear, and other items. Figure 1-6 shows some airfoil shapes used over landing gear and wing supports. *Besides streamlining the struts, the airfoils can provide a reactive force.* Note that if the aircraft increases its angle of attack, the strut airfoils change their angle and will produce lift.

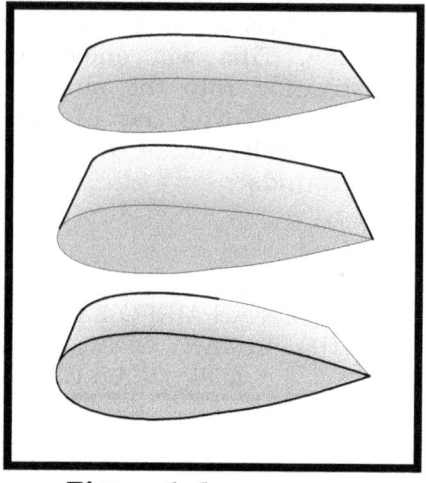

Figure 1-6

> SYMMETRICAL AIRFOILS DO NOT PRODUCE LIFT DURING LEVEL FLIGHT.
> (0-DEGREE ANGLE OF ATTACK)

TYPICAL WING-SHAPED AIRFOIL, AND 30% SYMMETRICAL AIRFOIL

The airfoil in Figure 1-7 (A) is used on aircraft wings to produce lift while flying at a 0-degree angle of attack. ("0" degree angle of attack is when the air is flowing parallel to the airfoil.) Airfoil 1-7 (B) is symmetrical on top and bottom. It <u>will not</u> produce lift when at a "0" degree angle of attack.

AERODYNAMICS 1-13

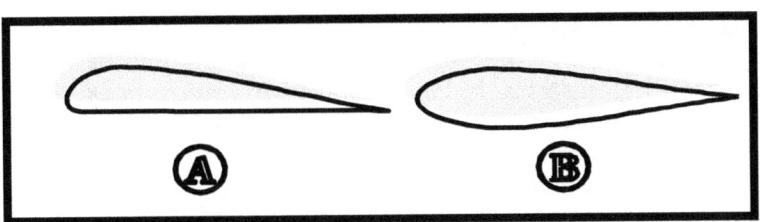
Figure 1-7

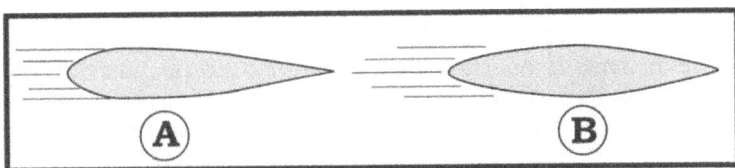
Figure 1-8

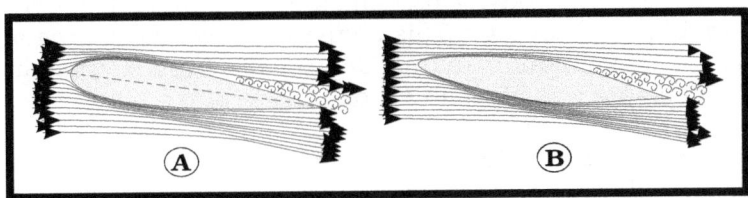
Figure 1-9

"0" % AND 50% AIRFOIL TESTS

ANGLE OF ATTACK AT 0 DEGREES

The airfoils in Figure 1-8 are at a 0-degree angle of attack. The disturbance of the air is a little greater by airfoil (A), causing more drag. *(In wind tunnel tests, the 50% airfoil shape has less drag than the 30% airfoil)* See "Wind Tunnel Tests, Body Shapes," page 1-36.

ANGLE OF ATTACK AT 10 DEGREES

In Figure 1-9, the same two shapes are placed at 10 degrees angle of attack. *The rounded frontal area of airfoil (A) creates lift with less drag than shape (B).* Airfoil (B) creates more drag than (A), because it did not have a rounded frontal area. A sharper leading edge will cause an airfoil to move abruptly as the angle of attack is changed.

In Figure 1-9 (A), the air meets a rounded frontal area, even at a 10-degree angle of attack. The large rounding of the frontal area has less drag at angles other than 0 degrees. *This large rounded frontal area will prevent abrupt movement as the angle of attack is changed.*

The airfoil in Figure 1-9 (B), has little rounding to its frontal area and body. This makes it more difficult for the air to follow its contour. This shape will have more drag at angles of attack other than 0 degrees. The top of this airfoil will create less lift than airfoil (A).

You can see the virtues of the two shapes in Figures 1-8, and 1-9. If the shape in 1-9 (B) was used on an aircraft, it would stall at low speeds and at low angles of attack. What this means to us is that the round frontal area of the 30% airfoil is great for changing angles of attack. The 50% airfoil gives us the least drag at a 0-degree angle of attack. It can be said that Derby cars run at zero angle of attack most of the time and do not need large frontal areas like an aircraft airfoil. That makes the smaller rounded frontal area more advantageous.

Do not make the mistake of thinking I am suggesting anything pointed. On the contrary, rounding is important. The large forward frontal areas are not necessary. A 1.25" radius nose is small enough for Soap Box Derby.

AERODYNAMICS

1-15

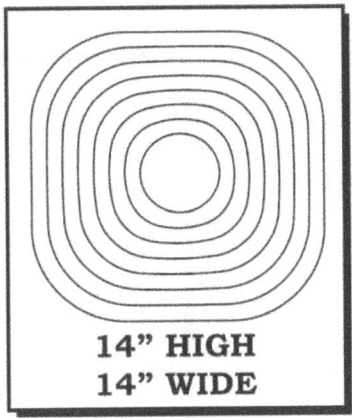

14" HIGH
14" WIDE

Figure 1-10

SYMMETRICAL

A symmetrical object is capable of division by a longitudinal plane into similar halves. That definition was found in Webster's Dictionary. You may find the following definition easier to understand. **A symmetrical object can be divided into two identical mirror images.** Figure 1-10 shows us the individual bulkheads of a symmetrically designed Soap Box Derby racer's body. The top, bottom, and sides are equal in shape and dimension. Each circle represents a bulkhead that might be used in forming the Soap Box Derby racer. (Number of bulkheads used is a personal preference) Figure 1-11 shows a design that has a symmetrical top and bottom, and symmetrical sides.

The objective of a symmetrical design is to keep the airflow over opposing sides the same. This creates equal forces on opposing sides using equal amounts of energy. When the force on one side is greater than its opposing side, drag increases. As the air flows over a non-symmetrical object, it exerts a force on that object and wastes valuable energy.

14" HIGH
13" WIDE

Figure 1-11

Figure 1-12 shows a Soap Box Derby racer that is symmetrical on its sides, but is not symmetrical top and bottom. The air will exert a greater force on the top of the racer than on its bottom. This downward force increases the drag.

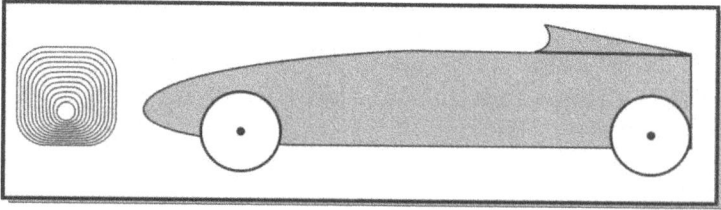

Figure 1-12

AERODYNAMICS   1-17

To be symmetrical does not mean you have two sides, and the top and bottom shaped the same. It is not necessary to have all four sides symmetrical. Figure 1-11 shows both sides symmetrical, and the top and bottom symmetrical. **This satisfies what we are trying to accomplish, and that is to have equal air drag on opposing sides.**

CROSS-SECTION (LARGEST REQUIRED)

A cross-section is a cutting or piece of something cut off at right angles to an axis. Figure 1-13 is a representation of different cuttings. The cross-section we are discussing refers to the largest width and height of a Soap Box Derby racer. The size of the largest cross-section determines how big a hole your racecar will punch in the air. A small cross-section would make a smaller hole through the air, and produce less drag. Soap Box Derby rules once required a 49" minimum circumference at some point on the car. Nowadays they may require a minimum height on the body shells in the Stock and Masters division. To get a small cross-section using the 49" rule, you had to make several sharp corners in the car body circumference. The sharp corners increase drag and possibly nullify any gain from punching a smaller hole in the air.

Figure 1-13 shows several cross-sections that have been used under the 49" rule. Each has 49" around its circumference. The square inches of the cross-sections shown here is an average; you may have more or less. The more curves you have around your cross-section, the larger the cross-section.

The point of cross-section discussion is to help you understand that the smallest cross-section is the best for your speed. You want to punch the smallest hole in the air. <u>With the Kit Car</u>, you must consider this when you make your headrest on the masters car. However, make sure the driver can see. I have seen my share of cars that were built without the proper consideration of the driver's ability to see. In some of the cars, they would have won the championship if the driver had been able to see properly.

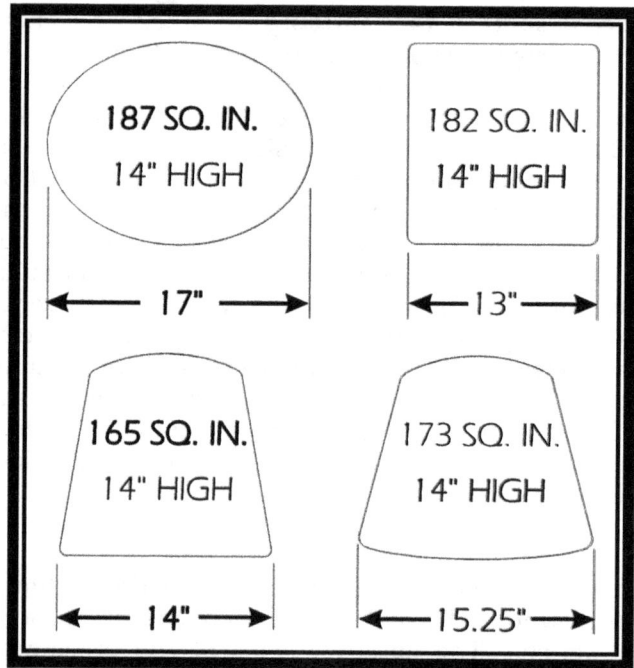

Figure 1-13

There has always been a question of the importance of a small cross-section. Many Soap Box Derby Experts feel *streamlining* is more important than a small cross-section. *I think you should treat small cross-section and streamlining as equal in importance.* Some have built

AERODYNAMICS

1-19

streamlined cars without consideration of their cross-section. Others have built the smallest cross-section without consideration of streamlining. Even the smallest cross-section shaped car should pay attention to streamlining. Even the best streamlining must consider the smallest cross-section. These two go together.

FRONTAL AREA SHAPE

Here is a theory about frontal area design that you might have heard. The best frontal area shape is a radius equal to 1/2 the diameter of the item being streamlined. I heard this for years, just like the teardrop theory. Let us look at what the theory means

In Figure 1-14 (A), we see the item to be streamlined with the frontal area shaped as described above. The item has now taken on the appearance of a submarine. The front rounding is like the teardrop frontal area.

To reinforce the above theory, the following is added. It is said that if the nose were extended, as in Figure 1-14 (B), the increased surface area would produce more drag than Figure 1-14 (A). It's also stated that it's best to get your car body shape up to the largest cross-section as fast as possible to have the least drag.

IMPORTANT NOTE:
The theories in the previous paragraph are wrong.

More surface area will increase drag, but the shape in Figure 1-14 (B) reduces drag overall when going at a 0-degree angle of attack. This is a tradeoff. We gain a little surface drag, but reduce the drag overall by going through the air with a sharper frontal area. Air does not like to be bothered, and the more gradually you start going through the air the less the air is bothered and that produces the least resistance from the air.

FRONTAL SHAPE MISCONCEPTION
Following the above-underlined theories on frontal area, Derby people have shaped their cars like the one in Figure 1-15 (A). This makes for a large frontal area. View (B) shows a smaller shape over shape (A). The length of the cars is the same. Only the shape from the largest cross-section forward has been reduced.

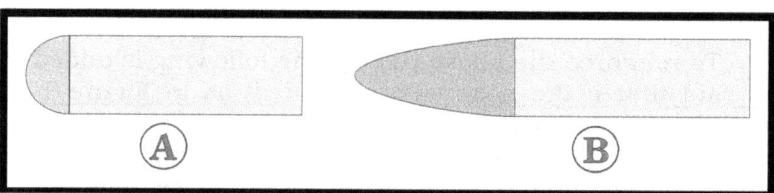

Figure 1-14

AERODYNAMICS

1-21

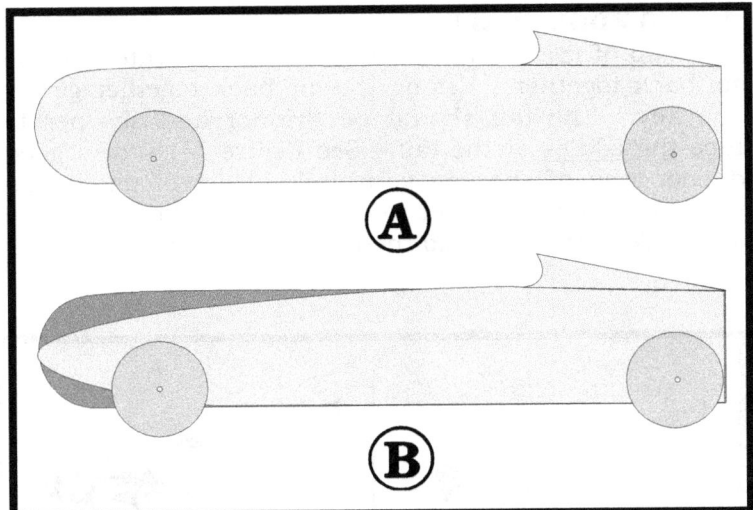

Figure 1-15

The above-underlined theory does not apply to Soap Box Derby Cars. The Derby car is designed to go straight and rarely changes its angle of attack more than a few degrees. The above theory applies to ships that turn and change their pitch. In addition, the Derby car that tapers its frontal area is not extending its nose and adding square inches. The square inches would be reduced by tapering your frontal area.

> Derby cars do change their angle of attack very much. A small radius of about 1.25" to 1.5"
> is best for your aerodynamics. Rounding must be maintained in the frontal area to reduce drag, but a large frontal area like an aircraft wing shape would produce more drag.

TRAILING EDGE SHAPE

The job of the tail is to bring the air separated by the nose, back together. Easing the air back together gently is the key. The tail should be thinner and sharper to reduce the eddies at the tail. See Figure 1-16 for a good and poor way of shaping your tail. Most of us do not have a small enough driver to cusp the tail like a teardrop shape. We just have to do the best job we can.

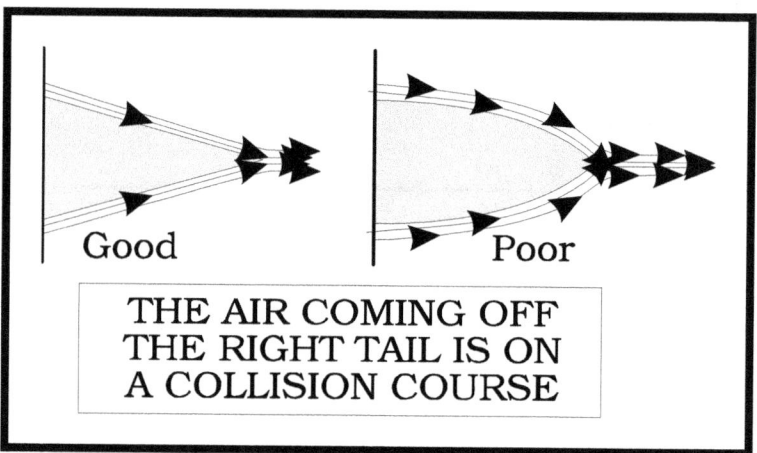

Figure 1-16

When sticking your car, do not let the stick flare way out to the sides. Instead, curve it at the body's widest part and bring it straight back to the point of the tail. See Figure 1-17.

AERODYNAMICS 1-23

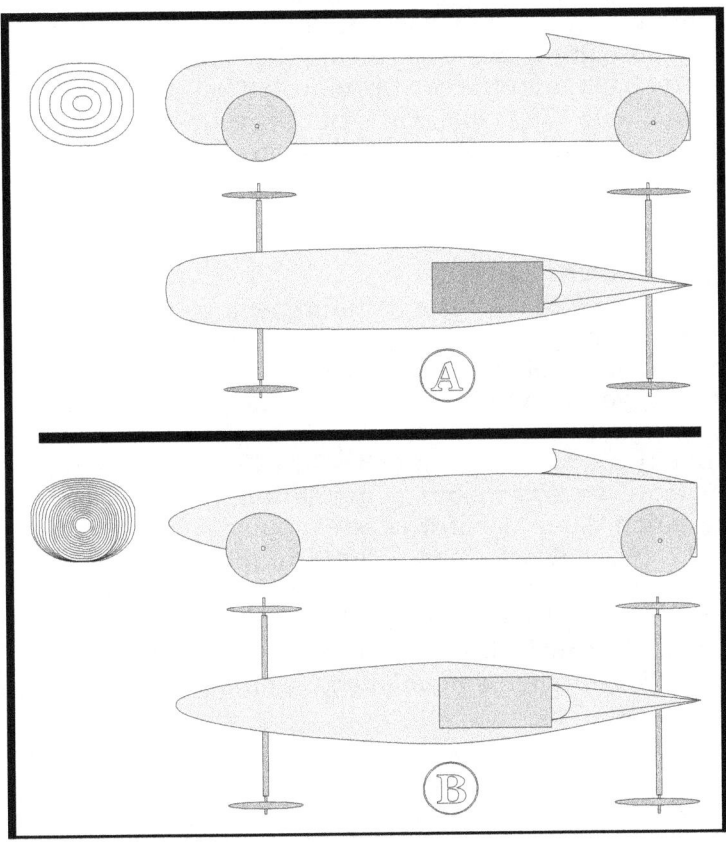

Figure 1-17

SMALL SIZE

Small size refers to the total area, expressed in square inches of an object going through the air. In Figure 1-17, we have two Soap Box Derby body designs that reflect the same cross-section. Racer (A) has a large number of square inches going through the air. When building your car, eliminate any square inch that does not have a purpose. You can do this by bringing the bottom of your car up in the back, and the top down in the back. Do not make a tall tale for your car unless you know the weatherman personally, and he will guarantee a strong tailwind!

POSSIBLE MISCONCEPTION

The importance of total body square inches is small as long as the size of the cross-section is not increased. Sometimes because of the rules, strength considerations, or driver size, you may not be able to make your racer as small as you would like. If the racer is kept streamlined, you will not be giving up that much. In a Soap Box Derby racer, 15 more square inches going through the air will not make much difference if it is streamlined. The car in Figure 1-17 (A), not only has a large number of square inches, but also has long straight sides. It also has a large blunt nose. In this case, the square inches are going to hurt, but more because of improper streamlining than size. *With proper streamlining, a large car can be fast.*

ROUNDING

Rounding is important for streamlining your racecar. Rounding is in two directions, from front to back, and around the circumference of the car. As the air flows over your car from front to back, it should not contact any sharp directional changes.

AERODYNAMICS

1-25

FROM HIGH PRESSURE TO LOW

As the air flows over your car, it is always going from a high-pressure area to a low-pressure area. Because of this, the air is not just going from front to back; it is also going up, down, and around your car. Do not impede the air going around the car body with a sharp ridge.

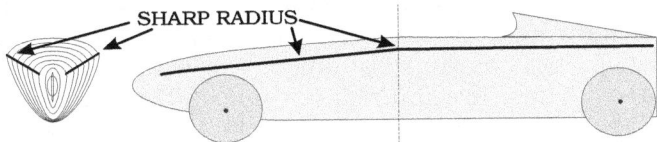

Figure 1-18

In Figure 1-18, we have a car with a sharp radius near the top on both sides. It runs from the front to the back of the car. As if that is not enough, the radius is slanted down as it comes forward. It also has a little change in direction at the car's largest point. This car was built for drag.

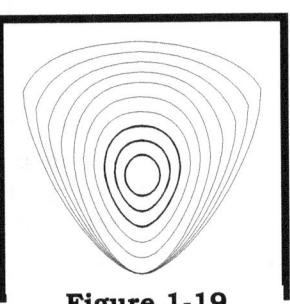

Figure 1-19

The car in Figure 1-18 should not have continued the sharp radius the entire length of the car. The largest bulkhead influences the shape of the rest of the car. The largest bulkhead seen in 1-18 should have never been used. However, working with that shape, you could round the car body sooner as you go forward. Figure 1-

19 shows the possible shape of bulkheads to bring the car to a more favorable frontal area. Do not shape your largest bulkhead as this one was.

FAIRINGS

A fairing is a member or structure whose primary function is to produce a smooth outline and to reduce drag or air resistance. Fairings are used on aircraft to ease the air around objects that stick out. In addition, fairings are used to streamline the area where two objects meet, like the wing and fuselage. There *are wing-to-body fairings* where the top and bottom of the wing attach to the fuselage. There are fairings for *pylons* that hold the engine to the wing. These fairings help to *guide the air* around objects protruding from the main body of the aircraft. The most obvious place fairings are used on a Soap Box Derby car is where the axles and body meet. Sometimes the fairings on the axles are incorrectly called airfoils. *Airfoils* are designed to get a specific reaction from the air. Fairings are used to reduce the drag of an object going through the air.

Design your Soap Box Derby Racer with the thought of producing a fairing around the dimension requirements. This means the largest cross-section will be determined by the size and position of the driver, or other protruding object and not based on a predetermined shape.

VORTEX

A vortex is a mass of fluid, with a whirling or circular motion that tends to form a vacuum in the center of the circle. The words, "vortex" and "eddy" are sometimes used interchangeably. When the air coming across a wing begins to change from <u>laminar flow</u>, it begins to vortex.

AERODYNAMICS 1-27

LAMINAR FLOW

In <u>fluid dynamics</u>, **laminar flow** (or <u>streamline</u> flow) occurs when a fluid flows in parallel layers, with no disruption between the layers. At low velocities, the fluid tends to flow without lateral mixing, and adjacent layers slide past one another like playing cards. There are no cross-currents perpendicular to the direction of flow, nor <u>eddies or swirls of fluids</u>.[1]

The air flowing across your racer will attempt to follow the shape of the car. Your car is increasing in size, as the air contacts the car's nose. As the car shape increases in size, the air is under pressure and has a laminar flow. When the air reaches the widest part of your car, it is going its fastest and is at its lowest pressure. When the car shape starts decreasing in size, the air tries to follow the car's shape. When the shape of the car starts reducing in size, the air is susceptible to breaking away from the car. Some separation does occur. The amount of separation depends on the size of the car and abruptness of the reduction in shape.

VORTEX GENERATOR

A vortex generator is something that stirs up the air. On large aircraft, there are metal angles that protrude into the air to stir it up. Aircraft designers have found that a vortex is sometimes beneficial to flight. Vortex generators are placed forward of flight controls to make them more responsive.

Model aircraft builders have experimented with placing a small wire across the front of the wing. This causes a vortex forward of the wings. This improves the speed of the aircraft. Therefore, sometimes the vortex can be helpful.

Soap Box Derby Builders have also known about the benefits of a vortex. The fairings, or airfoils, on your front axle are more important than the aft ones. This is because the vortex produced by the front fairings helps the rear axle and its fairings get through the air.

This Aerodynamic Principle was used by Greg Kitchum in 1979. (Axle fairings were not allowed by the All-American Soap Box Derby that year) To vortex the air in front of his bare axles, a cable was run from the car body in front of his axles and attached near the end of the axles. Greg was the 1979 Senior Division Champion in The All American Soap Box Derby. Very few cars were close to Greg in speed that year.

FILLETS
The formation of eddies always increases air resistance. In designing an aircraft, great care is taken not to have sharp edges, projections, and corners that will tend to produce eddies. When one surface intersects another, a large fillet (gentle curved surfaces to fill in sharp corners) is placed at the intersection to prevent eddies.

I wondered if there was a formula for the size of fillets, so I asked Bruce Finwall if he could help. Bruce is a Derby Enthusiast and late 1980s Editor of *Derby Tech.*. Bruce is a supporter of Soap Box Derby and an Aerospace Engineer. I could not think of a better person to give us this information. *Derby Tech* was a quarterly publication that gave technical tips on Soap Box Derby Racing.

AERODYNAMICS 1-29

Bruce says fillets can reduce axle fairing drag by 20 to 30%! The fillets are forward and aft of the axle fairings. The fillets above and below the axles are often called fairings. It is like the wing-to-body fairings on an aircraft. **See Figure 1-20 and 21.**

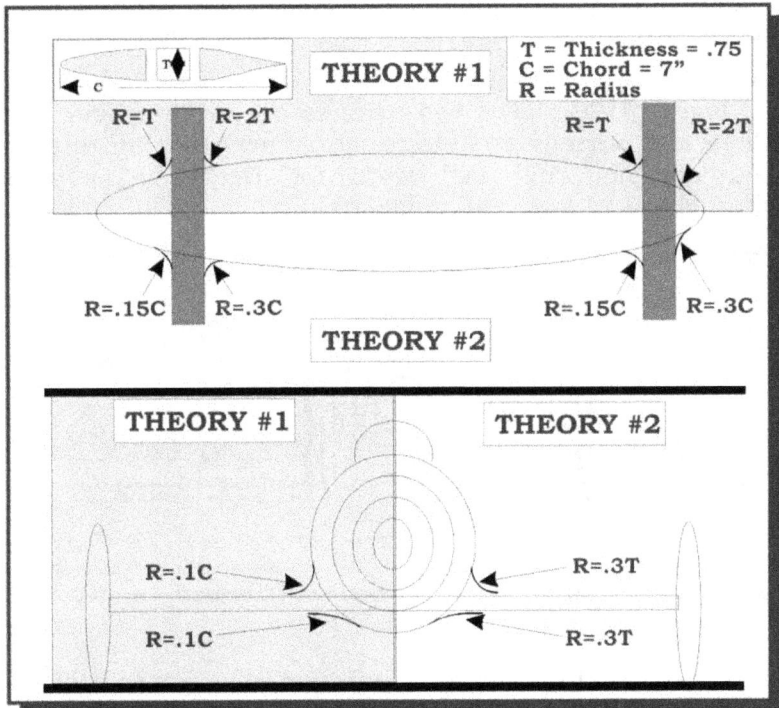

Figure 1-20

☺ *The "T" represents the *thickness of the axle fairing*. You do not want your axle fairings thicker than your axles, so we will use .75 inches.

☺ The "C" represents the Chord of the axle foil. The chord is from the leading edge of the forward axle fairing to the aft end of the aft axle fairing. See the end view of the axle fairing in the top left corner of Figure 1-20.

☺ The "R" represents the fillet radius.

Figure 1-20 shows two theories on the dimensions of fillets and fairings. These formulas are used on aircraft and are not the final word for Derby. Use this information as a general guideline.

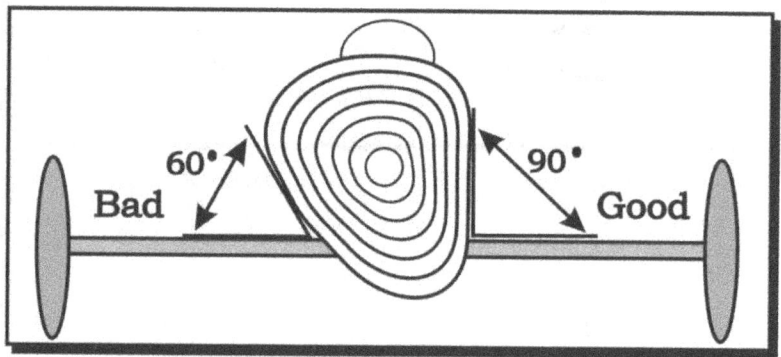

Figure 1-21

Figure 1-21 shows a frontal area of a car that has a 60-degree angle between the body and axles on the left side. A small angle like 60 degrees or less causes more drag. On the right side of the car, there is a 90-degree angle between the axle and the body. On the bottom side of the body, the angle is more than 120 degrees. With an angle less than 120 degrees, increase the radius of your fairing, or fillet.

AERODYNAMICS 1-31

TYPES OF DRAG

The following are the different types of drag with information about what causes it, and how to reduce it.

SKIN FRICTION

Skin Friction is proportional to the amount of exposed surface area and its roughness as well as its speed. Making your car as small as possible will help reduce drag. However, do not sacrifice streamlining. When sanding your car body, make sure it is smooth without bumps or dents. Wet sand, paint, and polish your car to a slick finish. A good slick polish job *is said* to make your car up to two inches faster. I do not know about two inches, maybe one inch. Whatever amount it is, you want it.

INTERFERENCE DRAG

In an aircraft, this is caused by the breakdown of smooth airflow because of such things as landing gear struts, dowels, open cockpits, etc. These objects disrupt the smooth flow of air over the car body, behind the objects that cause the disruption. You can reduce this by placing fairings over these items. Cockpit gaps should be kept to a minimum. Cut cockpit openings parallel to the airflow. Shape items sticking out in the air to reduce drag. Use fillets where the axles meet the body. This will decrease drag where the fairings intersect the body.

SEPARATION DRAG

An example of this is a lower wing on a round fuselage. The air has to expand from a high point of the wing to the trailing edge and fills the reentrant corner formed at the trailing edge and lower fuselage. In Soap Box Derby, this would be the axle fairing where it attaches to the car body. The air expands from the high point of the axle to the aft fairing trailing edge, and fills the reentrant corner formed at the trailing edge and the lower part of the car body. The resultant turbulent flow causes high drag. Body to axle-foil fairings helps this condition. Fillets are also helpful.

INDUCED DRAG

Induced drag results from the production of lift. The amount of drag is dependent on the amount of lift. You also have induced drag when the car top is flat like the one in Figure 1-15 (B). The top of the car is pushed down by the airflow, inducing drag.

UPWASH AND DOWNWASH DRAG

In level flight, air does not flow horizontally onto the wing's leading edge. Ahead of the wing, the air flows upward to the leading edge (called upwash) and downward off the trailing edge (called downwash). This also applies to Soap Box Derby. I often wondered what that does to the long axle fairings. When we test shapes in a wind tunnel, the air is horizontal to the object being tested. Remember, this only happens during a wind tunnel test.

There are other types of drag, but they are characteristic of aircraft and do not apply to Soap Box Derby.

WIND TUNNEL TESTS

MASSACHUSETTS INSTITUTE OF TECHNOLOGY
Small projections coming from an otherwise streamlined object can produce lots of drag. To demonstrate this, examine the wind tunnel tests performed by the Massachusetts Institute of Technology, at their Aeronautical Laboratory. These test results were found in the *Model Airplane News*, January 1992. The original article for *Model Airplane News* was written by Hewitt Phillips and Bill Tyler of MIT. The original article title was "Cutting Down the Drag."

These tests were performed at model airplane speeds of 15 to 40 mph. The test models were 48 inches long. Figure 1-22 summarizes the test results in drag coefficients (C_D). The actual drag in ounces depends on three factors: 1. Air Speed, 2. Cross-section area, and 3. Shape. The C_D for each reflects the drag value of that shape in ounces. When used in a formula that includes cross-section area and speed, it will accurately provide the drag in ounces. For our purposes, the C_D provides the relative drag value of each shape. These are for comparison only.

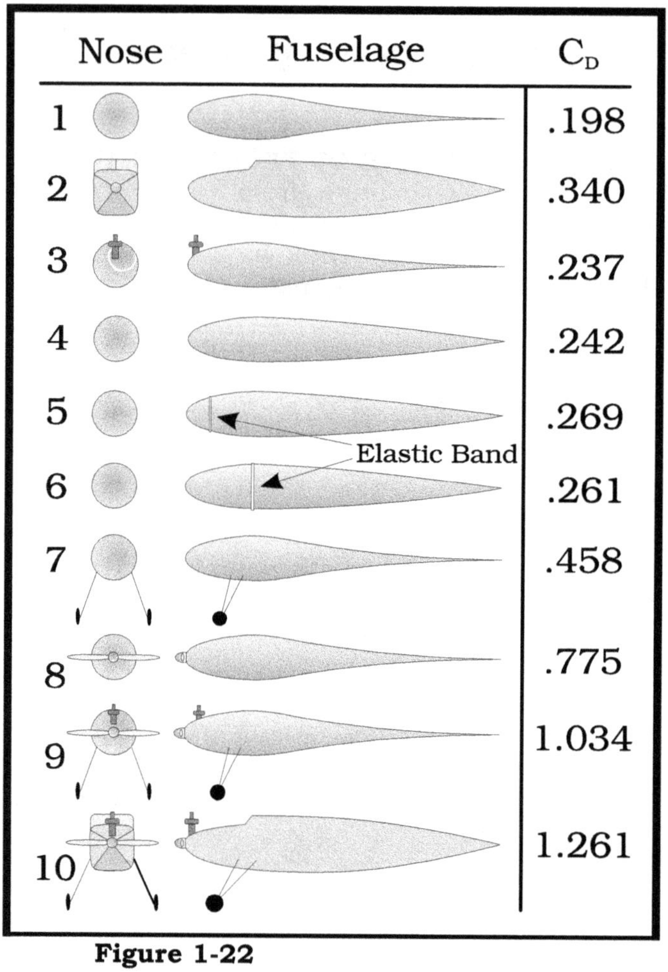

Nose	Fuselage	C_D
1		.198
2		.340
3		.237
4		.242
5		.269
6		.261
7		.458
8		.775
9		1.034
10		1.261

(Elastic Band indicated between shapes 5 and 6)

Figure 1-22

In Figure 1-22, fuselage shape 1 has the least drag. Subtracting the C_D of shape 1 (.198) from the C_D of shape 7 (458), gives us a C_D of .260 for the drag of the landing gear. **This indicates how a small wire and two tires can cause a lot of drag.** (*The gear will have more or less*

AERODYNAMICS 1-35

drag depending on the effect the gear and body have on each other). The landing gear is a 1/8-inch wire. The wheels were thin and symmetrical.

Subtracting the .198 C_D of shape 1, from the fuselage 8, (.775) gives us a C_D of .577 for the stationary propeller. We see that it is not just the square inches of an object that is important, but also its shape. That is why streamlining is the most important aerodynamic ingredient. Number 1 fuselage has more square inches than the gear or the propeller by themselves, but the fuselage is *streamlined*. (The propeller will have an adverse effect on the drag of the fuselage, so the .577 C_D for the prop is only approximate).

BEST AERODYNAMIC SHAPE

The shapes in Figure 1-22 look as if they were written by believers in the teardrop theory. We see this shape so much; could there be something to it? Well, there is. These shapes were chosen because they represent the shape of a model aircraft or normal-size aircraft. The rule for designing a full-size, or model aircraft, is the same. The person who flies the airplane must be able to see out the front. That is one reason. The other reason is that a rounded frontal area is best for objects that change angles of attack at fast speeds like an aircraft. (See "Airfoils" on pages 1-9 through 1-13.) During aircraft design, the required dimensions must be known first, and then the aerodynamic design can be added around those size requirements. Have you noticed that a passenger and freight aircraft fuselage is not shaped like a teardrop? Their purpose requires the fuselage to be large enough to carry people and freight. In a Derby car, the front does not have to be very big to carry two feet!

BODY SHAPES

I performed several wind tunnel tests to examine the teardrop shape. A "Teardrop Shape" has its largest width and height near its front. In Soap Box Derby, this means having your largest cross-section at 25% to 40% of the body length. I chose to test the top three shapes shown in Figure 1-23.

They were all one-quarter scale and had the following specifications.

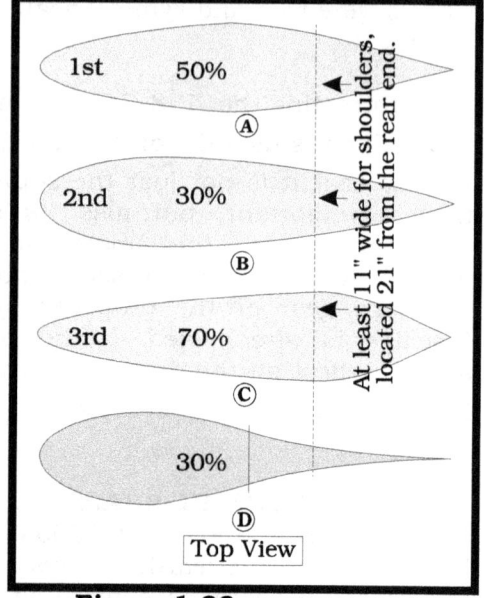

Figure 1-23

1. All models were 15 inches wide.
2. All models were 14 inches high.
3. All models were the same length.
4. All models were the same weight.
5. All models were 11 inches wide, at 21 inches from the tail to locate the drivers' shoulders. The shoulder location was 5 inches below the top of the car.
6. All cross-sectional shapes were round, except the tail area.
7. Body shape (A) had its largest cross-section at 50% of its length.
8. Body shape (B) had its largest cross-section at 30% of its length.

AERODYNAMICS   1-37

9. Body shape (C) had its largest cross-section at 70% of its length.

A fair test could not be conducted unless the same size driver was considered in each model. So, I calculated in an 11-inch shoulder width at 21 inches from the tail. This car is for an average size driver. The driver's weight could be 80 to 120 pounds. The driver's height could be 5 feet 5 inches or smaller.

THE WINNER

The shape with the largest cross-section at 50% had the least drag. The 30% position was second, with the 70% position coming in third. **Although the 50% position had the least drag, placing the largest cross-section at 40 to 60% should have little difference.** I used 30% and 70% airfoil sizes as my extremes to get a difference that was easy to see. When testing small models, it can sometimes be difficult to come to an unequivocal conclusion. This is caused by the inaccessibility of sensitive measuring tools and inexperience in wind tunnel testing. I tested these models several ways before I felt confident about the results. The differences among the three shapes were close, and that is why I feel confident that placing your largest cross-section at **40 to 60%** would not result in a big difference in speed, provided it is streamlined properly.

Shape (D) was not used in the tests. It had the same cross-section, but the shoulder area was about 5 inches across. This shape would be faster than the other three. It is also obvious that only a very small driver could get into this car.

FAST TEARDROP

There are two main reasons (D) would be faster. First, the car is smaller. It is as if the car does not exist after the first 55 inches of the car. Second is the way it discharges the air at the tail. The air's transition from the car is good. Compare body shapes (D) to shape (C). The air coming off (C's) tail is going to have a collision. Its tail has poor air transition characteristics.

> **DO NOT PLACE YOUR LARGEST CROSS-SECTION BASED ON THE PERCENTAGE OF AN AIRFOIL.**

TEARDROP DECEPTIVE LENGTH

The position of the largest cross-section of shapes in Figure 1-23 (D) is deceptive. I feel shape (D) has its largest cross-section positioned at about 50% of its largest portion. Imagine the car did not exist aft of the solid line going across the body. If the car only extended to that line, it would have a 50% airfoil design. It is misleading to think of shape (D) as a 30% airfoil. The aft 40% of the car is so thin; it is as if it is not there.

Figure 1-24 is like (D) in Figure 1-23, except the tail has been stretched. This gives us a 14% airfoil! The last 70% of Figure 1-24 may as well not be there. Does this mean we should run a 14% airfoil? *No, you should not position the largest cross-section of your car's body based on a percentage of an aircraft airfoil.*

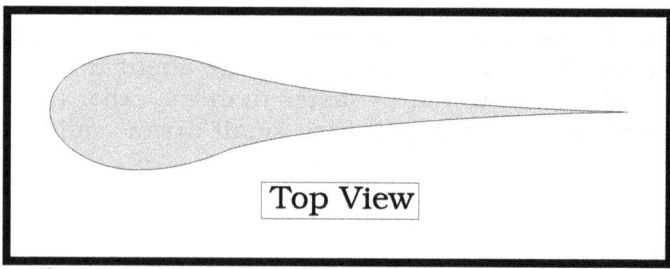

Figure 1-24

AXLE FAIRINGS

Axle foils, airfoils, or axle fairings are all the same name for ways of streamlining an axle. Whatever you choose to call it, we are designing a fairing for an axle. **A fairing is a member or structure whose primary function is to produce a smooth outline and to reduce drag or air resistance. The fairing streamlines the axle!**

The axle fairings are easy to test. They fit in a small wind tunnel with no reduction in the size required. The people in Derby that do any testing at all will eventually test axle-fairing shapes. The results from these tests have been varied, as well as the method of testing. Amateur tests, as well as sophisticated wind tunnel tests, have been run. Some people mount the axle on their automobile or bicycle. Some suspend shapes from strings and blow on them with a shop-vac. Whatever methods you use, avoid the following pitfalls.

- ☺ Do not mount the axle close to an automobile surface or stick it through a sunroof, unless it is mounted high enough to get into clean air. The air near an automobile is moving in directions that may compromise your test.

- ☺ If you test two shapes on opposite sides of an axle at the same time, the side with the most drag will turn the axle on a pivot point. Turn the axle end to end and try the experiment again. The axle may have a tendency to turn in one direction. Also, test the axle with no fairings on both sides to see if it has a tendency to swing one way or the other.

☺ If you perform your test in a wind tunnel, remember that the wind does not come straight at the axles during a race.

☺ Do not waste your time testing during windy conditions.

AXLE FAIRING WIND TUNNEL TEST

Wind tunnel tests show long axle fairings reduce drag. (For the purpose of this section, long fairings are 7 inches or more front to back including air space and axle.) In a wind tunnel, your air comes at your fairings at a 0-degree angle of attack. Fairings that have a long gradual increase of size, and long gradual decreases of size toward the tail, have low drag. See Figure 1-25.

RACE CONDITION, AIR FLOW DIRECTION

During a race, the air flows relatively straight toward the front axle. The aft axle has air coming up from under the car. This causes the aft fairings to catch an upwash of airflow.

RACE CONDITION, "BOUNCING"

You have constant bouncing of the car during a race. When large bumps are hit, the bouncing is more intense. This will affect the angle of attack of the fairings if they are the least bit loose. The longer fairings will be affected the most.

INTERFERENCE DRAG

Fairings with a long chord have more interference drag. However, the difference in drag should be too small to be concerned.

AERODYNAMICS

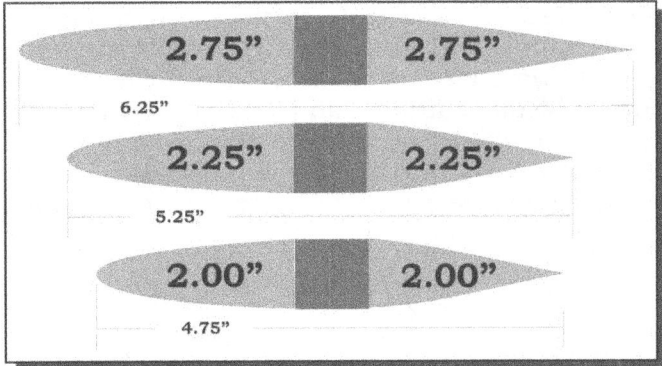

Figure 1-25

FAIRING LENGTH

I do not think anyone has tested axle fairings under their operating conditions. That would be difficult to do. There would be only small differences, and they can be caused by the environment. Wind Tunnel tests I performed point to the 6.25" long axle fairings in Figure 1-25 as the best. Although you might use the 5.25" fairings in Figure 1-25, or make one as long as 7", you will not be able to measure a difference without using a wind tunnel. I am concerned about the upwash and bouncing of the fairings at their leading edge if you use a long fairing. I do not like any over 7 inches. The air comes toward the front axle mostly at a 0-degree angle of attack. This is best for a long fairing. I would consider making the aft axle fairing shorter. You still have the bouncing to contend with, so do not make your forward fairings too long. The aft fairing also has the advantage because of the vortex from the forward axle and the car body.

FAIRING SHAPE

Noting the results of our tests on page 1-8 through 1-10, I think a shape like the ones in Figure 1-25 are good. (I like the first two shapes and sizes) Do not make the leading edge of your fairings any sharper than those above. Sharper fairings that work well in the wind tunnel tests react differently during a race because of the bouncing and wind pressure on an improperly secured axle faring.

KIT CAR AERODYNAMIC

Pay attention to the following when building your Kit Car. These items can often improve your car's speed by improving your aerodynamics.

1. Floorboard
2. Body
   a. Body foam installation
   b. Body where it attaches to the floorboard
   c. Sharp edges
   d. Damage
   e. Brake Plunger, Pad and Rubber
3. Axle Fairings
4. Axles
5. Steering Cables
6. The driver should be down as low as possible

KIT CAR FLOORBOARD

The bottom of your Kit Car, as of this writing, is made of Aspen Pine. It is a soft wood and easy to work with. However, it makes it hard to tighten things without causing indents where you do not want them

SHARP EDGES

The floorboards will come with rough edges where it was cut out. You will also note that the cut around the outer edges of the floorboard is rough from the saw that cut it. You cannot do anything about the rough cut of the side of the floorboard. However, you can sand the top and bottom edges of the floorboard where you will find sharp splinters. Do not be carried away and make a large radius on these edges. Just sand the edges enough to knock off the rough edge.

HARDWARE INSTALLATION

When you install your hardware, you do not want to draw your elevator bolts into the floorboard any further than flush. The holes come predrilled and often are too big to prevent the elevator bolt from drawing into the bottom of the floorboard too far. See the Construction Chapter for elevator bolt installation. Some elevator bolts may get tight before you draw the head of the bolt flush with the bottom of the floorboard. In this case, you will be concerned with your pulleys pulling into the top of the floorboard causing misalignment of your steering cable. More information on this is given in the Construction Chapter.

BODY

If your body has minor scratches, they can be sanded and or buffed out. The car bodies are often of different sizes. Make sure your car body is one of the smaller ones. The Stock Car measures about 10.75" to as much as 11 1/8" at the nose. Most of the Stock Cars I have measured run around 10 ¾" 10 7/8" range. Measure this by hooking the end of your tape measure over the top of the nose and pulling it down to the bottom of the nose to read its height. The All-American is not making an effort to make all Stock Shells the same size.

The round shape of the Super Stock body makes it hard to determine just by looking at it, if it is a larger or smaller body. Even having two Super Stock cars next to each other is difficult to see any difference in size.

STOCK CAR

The Stock Car body comes with sharp edges around its bottom edge. You can knock the outer edge off, but here again do not get carried away. It is best to look at other Stock cars and see how they look. Most will have this edge knocked off for safety.

MASTERS

The Masters Car is more difficult to build, but you are given more leeway in construction. You are allowed to cut the body to fit. Here again, sand edges for safety and check the rules so you are not carried away with your rounding of lower edges.

AERODYNAMICS

FOAM INSTALLATION

When installing the Stock, Super Stock, and Masters Car cockpit foam, make sure it is as aerodynamic as possible. Often two or more tries are required before you get it correct. Check with your local experts to give you help in this area.

BRAKE SYSTEM

The brake parts often cause a lot of drag. The plunger may not actuate vertically making the brake pad not level. This can make the brake pad have more cross-section going through the air causing a lot of drag. Often shimming of the brake mount can fix this; however, check the rules before doing this.

The brake pad attaches to the bottom of the plunger which has a 3" X 3" metal plate welded on the bottom. That is the minimum size. Cut your brake pad to the minimum size to prevent air drag. When you install the brake pad, the bolts will make the rubber swell over the outer edges of the brake plate. Take a blade and cut the extra rubber back to the 3" X 3" plate.

Make sure your brake return spring is good enough to pull the plunger up tight when racing. Each time you have the brake plunger out of your car, stretch your brake return spring. Make sure the plunger moves in the outer tube easily. Clean and lube before important races.

AXLE AND FAIRINGS

The axle fairings as of this writing are made of molded plastic. You will have to cut the length to fit some race divisions. Cut to the longest you can. Polishing these fairings is very important. Knock off rough edges at the trailing edges for safety.

AXLES

Knock the edges off the axles for safety.

STEERING CABLE

If your steering cable is bent, replace it with a new one. Attach the cable as close to the axle as possible.

DRIVER

The driver should be down in the car as much as possible. As the driver gets more experience and more determination, you will be surprised how good they can get down. The driver is the most important for gaining an aerodynamic advantage. The driver and the foam are very important.

Wax all items outside of your car before each race to get a slight gain aerodynamically.

AERODYNAMICS

CONCLUSION

You can often gain a lot with aerodynamics by doing a small amount of improvements. Engineer Bruce Finwall felt quite strongly about the effects of good aerodynamics and Soap Box Derby. He once said that (in Soap Box Derby) it is all aerodynamics. Of course, it is not all aerodynamics, and he knew it. However, his point is well taken that aerodynamics is very important. This chapter is an overkill of information in aerodynamics for the kit cars, but I had the information from the first *Winning Ingredients* book and felt it should be included for your interest and positional benefits. If you get into Ultimate Speed, racing at Akron, this book and chapter will come in handy.

1. Make sure all parts that are exposed to the air are rounded to the legal limit.
2. Your brake plunger should be a minimum size with a minimum brake pad.
3. Your body should have all sharp edges removed for safety and any extra material from the mold removed.
4. A painted Super Stock is best; however, a smooth unpainted shell can be very good. The Super Stock Shell can be difficult to paint, so be careful.
5. Position your shell on the nose of the car so the floorboard forward end is not sticking below the nose of the shell.
6. The driver's position is very important for the Stock and Super Stock division where the driver sets up in the car. Positioning the head and helmet down and back is very important for your aerodynamics.

The driver should exercise and stretch his or her muscles to become more flexible.

AIRFOILS

Axle airfoil is one area where you can do something about aerodynamics. Your airfoils should be free of damage and be polished.

Good Luck
And
Keep Everything Streamline

CHAPTER TWO

ENERGY

INTRODUCTION

The purpose of this chapter is to get you thinking about how energy is used and wasted on your Soap Box Derby racer. I will start by giving you a short introduction to energy and explain some of the principles it follows. Related subjects we will look at are Drag, Inertia, *Potential Energy*, and *Kinetic Energy*. You will find the information contained in this chapter useful for all divisions of Soap Box Derby racing.

Derby racing is different from most other racing because of the absence of an engine. When an engine is used in racing, there is the tendency to concentrate our focus on the engine to regulate the energy. In Derby racing, proper management of energy is everything.

Listed are ways energy is used in your car and some ways to reduce that loss. Again, I want to get you thinking. As you read this chapter, see if you can think of ways to reduce energy consumption. I may not have listed all the ways energy is lost or ways to prevent that loss. Put on your thinking cap.

There are experiments in the book to help you understand where to place your car's weight. They are described in Chapter 8, "Weight Management." These experiments will give you a better understanding of energy usage. Once you see how easy these experiments are and how they can show you the answers to your Derby questions, you will repeat these experiments often to discover new and different ways to conserve energy.

WORD USAGE THROUGHOUT THE BOOK

In the original *Winning Ingredients*, the terms **tight solid, and loose** were used when talking about the suspension systems. A **tight suspension** system refers to a suspension run **tight**, but **tight** allows for axle vertical movement at the wheels. When referring to a *solid suspension* **system**, I am talking about an axle and its mount that is as tight as you can get it. The **solid suspension system** is on hard steel mountings so you can keep from losing energy. **If allowed** to run a small contact area, it allows flexing to reduce cross-bind without losing energy. With the advent of Kit Cars, there are different requirements for the suspension systems in each division and these requirements often change each year. The All-American's desire is for everyone to have the same suspension set up for each respective division. This topic will be covered in more detail in Chapter 3, "Suspension."

ENERGY

TYPES OF ENERGY

In Soap Box Derby, we are concerned about potential energy and kinetic energy. **Potential energy is energy at rest. Kinetic energy is energy in motion.**

POTENTIAL ENERGY
The potential energy of your car is determined by its weight and its position. Think of your potential energy as **Weight times Height**. Potential energy is also called energy at rest. The further your racer's center of gravity is up the hill, the more Potential Energy is available. Since Soap Box Derby racers are started from their noses, your racecar must be as long as allowed, have the wheels as far aft as allowed, and with the shortest wheelbase. The wheelbase should be moved as far aft as possible. This will position the racecar's center of gravity where it will have the most Potential Energy.

With the Soap Box Derby kit cars, the position of the kingpin is fixed on all cars in their respective division. This means you cannot move your axle kingpin hole to move your center of gravity further up the hill by repositioning your axle's position. So why question where you position your axles if it is not allowed? Desired axle position is mentioned because there is an Ultimate Speed Division that is less restrictive with the axle positions.

KINETIC ENERGY

Kinetic energy is energy in motion and it increases with the speed of your racer. You want to get your racer up to speed quickly to take advantage of the kinetic energy.

At high speeds, you will lose little speed from a small steering correction or rolling over an object in your path because of the higher kinetic energy. At low speeds, and low kinetic energy, you lose a lot of speed from a small steering correction or rolling over a small imperfection on the track.

WHAT CAN HAPPEN TO ENERGY

Energy cannot be destroyed; however, it can be transformed. Below are examples of ways energy is transformed. Heat energy can be used to boil water, changing it into steam energy. A steam engine can convert steam energy into mechanical motion. That mechanical motion can be used to drive a generator creating electrical energy. While energy is being transformed, it produces some heat energy that can be lost into the atmosphere. Even here, the energy is not lost; it is heating the atmosphere. A machine that wastes little energy for its specific purpose is said to be energy efficient. That is what we hope to be with our racecars, energy efficient!

LOST ENERGY

Once energy is in the form of heat, it is difficult to control efficiently. As we have all experienced, not all the heat produced by a stove is used to cook. Some heat escapes into your kitchen. Not all the heat produced by the automobile engine is used to drive the pistons. Some escape into the atmosphere.

When we say energy is lost, we mean it is lost for the purpose it is intended. Energy is sometimes used to perform unnecessary tasks. That energy is lost for the purpose of driving you to the finish line.

LOOSE PARTS
Loose parts are responsible for energy loss. Perform the following experiment to understand how parts in contact with each other lose energy when they are loose. This experiment demonstrates how energy can be lost in your suspension system.

ENERGY EXPERIMENT

For this experiment, you will need two Soap Box Derby axles, a hammer, and a "C" clamp. See Figure 2-1. Overlap the square stock of the axles about three inches and clamp them together at this point. Use a good strong "C" clamp so you can clamp the axles together very tight. Now, hit one end of one axle while holding the opposite end of the other axle. You will feel the vibrations. Try this several times, noting the amount of vibration you feel, and the length of time it vibrates. You will also hear a sound produced when you hit the axle. Note the intensity and length of time of the sound.

Loosen the "C" clamp just a little. Hit the axle again and note the difference in vibration. Was the vibration as strong? Did it vibrate at a shorter duration? Perform the experiment with the "C" clamp at different degrees of tightness.

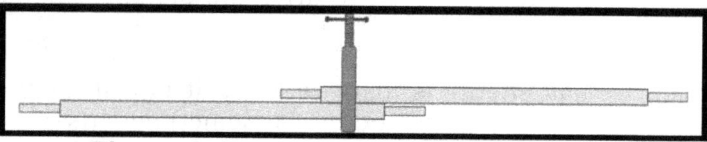

Figure 2-1

From the above experiment, you will find that the energy will dissipate faster with the clamp loose. This is shown by the shorter duration and less intensity of the vibration and sound with the clamp loose.

The following text is intended to explain how energy is lost to a loose suspension system. In the experiment above, when the two axles are loose, they have to do more work to pass on the vibration from one axle to the other axle. This extra work reduced the amount of energy that is transmitted from one axle to the other. Less energy is passed to the other axle because of the extra work required with the loose parts.

Let us explain this once more in a slightly different way for clarity. When the energy got to the axles held loosely together, the loose parts vibrated against each other. The rapid vibration of parts together dissipates the energy. The energy is used to vibrate the axles between one another. It is as if one part is trying to pass on the energy, but it is not accepted by the other. Instead, it has

ENERGY 2-7

passed right back. The passing back and forth wastes energy. The experiment shows the rapid dissipation of energy when the axles are held loosely together. The "C" clamp is responsible for the most energy used. This is because the threads of the "C" clamp have a large contact area that vibrates and wastes more energy than the vibration between the axles themselves.

This principle is true for other parts of your car. Make sure you assemble all parts of your car so there is good continuity. Continuity is what we want in all your car parts.

THE FOLLOWING THINGS TAKE ENERGY FROM YOUR CAR

LOOSE PARTS
Loose parts are responsible for energy loss. Performing the previous experiment will help you understand how parts in contact with each other lose energy when they are loose. This experiment demonstrates how energy can be lost in your suspension system. However, it can be applied anywhere two parts come in contact.

FRICTION
Friction is the force that resists motion between two bodies in contact with one another. Friction takes its share of energy and dissipates it in the form of heat. Small amounts of friction may not produce noticeable heat, but energy will escape. The solution to friction is to eliminate it wherever possible. If contact cannot be eliminated, reduce the contact area of objects rubbing together. After the contact has been reduced to its minimum, try making the rubbing parts out of a slippery material. Last, use lubricants or bearings where needed.

An example of friction is when the wheels slide on the spindles. This causes friction between the wheel bearings and the spindle.

AERODYNAMIC DRAG

Aerodynamic Drag is another way to lose energy. See the Aerodynamics Chapter.

WASTED MOTION

An example of wasted motion is elaborate suspension systems. When numerous parts move up and down against each other to absorb a small bump, they can lose more energy than they save.

When my son Chris won the All-American in 1980, and they kept his car. That fall he did not have a car to race in the local fall races. A friend came to the rescue and let Chris use their Master car. The car had a long metal bar with the front and aft axles mounted on each end. It was attached to the body near its center lengthwise. This made for a springing action as the car rolled down the hill. At the time, it was a superior car, but the bouncing up and down did nothing for the speed of the car. This was an example of wasted energy! We will discuss this more in Chapter 3, "Suspension."

A brake pedal, brake plunger, hatch cover, or inspection panel can also use energy if they are allowed to move. These four parts may not use much energy by themselves, but taken together they are measurable.

ENERGY 2-9

> **PEOPLE WHO PAY ATTENTION TO THE SMALL THINGS ARE LESS LIKELY TO NEGLECT THE LARGE ONES. BY PAYING ATTENTION TO SMALL ENERGY USERS, WE CAN ACCUMULATE AN ADVANTAGE OVER OUR COMPETITION.**

MORE ENERGY USAGE

On its way to the finish line, your Soap Box Derby racer uses energy in many ways. Listed below are some ways your racer uses energy and suggestions on how to reduce it.

WHEELS

Energy is used to start your car rolling. If you have cross-bind in your car, or the starting ramp has cross-bind, more energy is used. Usually, the starting ramps are smooth and offer the best surface for your racer during the race. Much energy is used to get over the smallest imperfection when your racer is going slow. That is why you will see people wipe off the starting ramp in front of their wheels before each race. This may not be allowed at some races. If the starting ramps are dirty, ask the race director to clean them for all the contestants.

There is friction where the wheels contact the pavement. Keep this friction to a minimum by aligning your axle and spindles. We will discuss axle and spindle alignment in more depth in Chapter 5, "Alignment & Adjustments." In addition, unnecessary steering increases energy loss where the wheels contact the pavement. The wheel bearings use energy, but in a photo or timer swap race, this is of little importance. Both racecars will have a turn on each set of wheels.

Some energy is lost when the wheel slides on the spindles during steering and crosswind conditions. This can be reduced by lubricating your spindles. Wheels should be free to slide on the spindle. Do not try to eliminate the sliding by placing washers to take up the space between the wheel and axle. It is better for the wheel to slide on the axle than to have the wheel attempt to slide on the pavement. <u>There have been families that placed washers on the spindle to prevent the wheel from sliding on the spindle. They claimed their driver could steer better when the wheels were not allowed to slide on the spindles.</u> Perform your own testing before you use these washers. Others have told me that when they put washers on, the car slowed down. Polish the spindles only at the contact area of the wheel bearings; polishing the entire spindle can reduce its size.

Sometimes it is necessary to steer when starting a race to get to a specific place on the track. Another exception would be when you are steering to avoid an imperfection in the track. This will be discussed more in Chapter 10, "Practice." The decision to steer or not steer at slow speeds needs to be weighed very carefully. Testing each track can help you decide where to drive. People who do not test follow where the local racers drive.

BUMPS

Energy is lost as your wheels roll over imperfections in the track. The wheels contact bumps not at a vertical angle, but at an upward and back angle. See Figure 2-2. As the wheel hits the bump, it must convert its forward motion into an upward motion. The amount of energy

ENERGY

2-11

lost is determined by your speed, size of the bump, weight distribution, and suspension.

LOOSE PARTS

Now, let us focus on items that come into contact, but cannot be tight. The loose brake pedal or brake plunger is an example. Your hatch cover and the nose inspection panel are two more examples. Do you have lucky items in the car that can rattle around? These items use the energy you need to win the race. This is a minor thing, but it will get you thinking about energy usage. Remember, the weight and its position is what determines your usable energy. Do not waste it

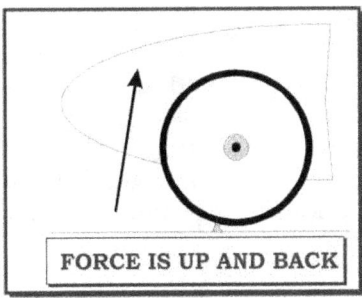

Figure 2-2

INERTIA

To understand energy usage better we need to understand the connection of energy to inertia.

NeWt.on's first law of motion states that "An object at rest stays at rest and an object in motion stays in motion with the same speed and in the same direction unless acted upon by an unbalanced force." Objects tend to "keep on doing what they're doing." It is the natural tendency of objects to resist changes in their state of motion. This tendency to resist changes in their state of motion is described as **Inertia**

NEWT.ON'S FIRST LAW OF MOTION

NeWt.on's conception of inertia stood in direct opposition to more popular conceptions about motion during his life. The dominant thought prior to NeWt.on's day was that it was the natural tendency of objects to come to a resting position. Moving objects, so it was believed, would eventually stop moving. It was thought that a force was necessary to keep an object moving. However, if left to itself, a moving object would eventually come to rest and an object at rest would stay at rest; thus, the idea that dominated people's thinking for nearly 2000 years.

Now we know that objects at rest stay at rest and those in motion stay in motion. That tells us that things that do not stay in motion have something slowing them down and stopping them. **In Soap Box Derby, we have to Figure out what those things are and reduce them to win.**

MAXIMIZE YOUR CAR'S ENERGY

The following are a few basics you should remember as you prepare to win the race. Just these six things will help you maximize your car's energy and be in the hunt for first place.

- ❖ A trained driver is number one for winning. Excessive steering can cost you. See Chapter 10, "Practice," for tips on driving.

- ❖ Low weight placement will help your car go the fastest. See Chapter 8, "Weight Management."

ENERGY   2-13

- ❖ A short wheelbase will position your car further up the hill and give you more potential energy.

- ❖ A small car body and or a small frontal area on the body will give you an aerodynamic advantage.

- ❖ Properly aligned axles and spindles will give you less starting and rolling resistance.

- ❖ A **solid suspension** loses less energy as it goes down the track. The only exception to running a solid suspension is if you have an excessive cross-bind on the starting ramps or have an excessively rough track.

SUSPENSION

Suspensions use energy to save energy. This is a delicate balance and will be covered in more depth in Chapter 3, "Suspension."

WEIGHT PLACEMENT

See Chapter 8 "Weight Management" to help place your weight and why. You will also find out more ways to preserve your energy by placing your weight properly.

CONCLUSION

There is a lot of information packed in this chapter. I am not going to repeat it all here. You might get a tablet, read this chapter, and write down all the ways to save energy in one column and all the things that you use energy in another column. This way you will be more likely to remember it and have a reference for the future.

You need to have your axles aligned and your spindles aligned to prevent the loss of energy. Cross-bind check is also very important to perform at least before each race weekend. See Chapter 4, "Construction" to start your alignment with the assembly of your car. Continue with Chapter 5, "Alignment and Adjustments" for the final adjustments.

ENERGY TESTS

In *Chapter 8, "Weight Management,"* there are some experiments to help you determine where to place your weight. These tests will refocus your thoughts on energy conservation. These tests are easy to perform and can be performed by the Soap Box Derby Driver! Soap Box Derby is a learning experience for all involved. Take advantage of it.

CHAPTER THREE
SUSPENSION

INTRODUCTION

The kit cars have changed the way we look at the suspension systems. When we had the liberty to design our own suspension system we ideally wanted to have a *solid suspension system* (a suspension that has its parts as tight to each other as possible). We tempered that with a suspension that was flexible enough to prevent cross-bind from slowing us down at the starting gate. We accomplished this by designing a small contact area in the solid system or used the isolated steel plate system. Now we are limited in what we can do to the suspension system in the Kit Cars. However, all Divisions can make use of this chapter.

This part of your car is more important than you may realize. How many times have you seen streamlined-looking cars that do not run? In many cases, they have a suspension problem.

In the original *Winning Ingredients for Soap Box Derby Racers,* there is a large chapter on suspension. It details the type of suspension systems that were used when you built your suspension system. In *Winning Ingredients for Kit Cars,* the suspension system is limited. In the masters division, there is some allowance for the axle mount. In the Ultimate Speed Division, your options are numerous. If you are interested in building an Ultimate Speed car, get a copy of *Winning Ingredients for Soap Box Derby Racers,* at www.winningingredients.com

IN THIS CHAPTER, WE WILL DISCUSS THE FOLLOWING:

1. What is the Suspension System
2. Suspensions and Energy Usage
3. Energy Usage Experiment
4. Track testing of the Solid Suspension System
5. Solid, Tight, and Loose Suspension, and how they work together
6. Car body and Axles role in the Suspension System

WHAT IS A SUSPENSION SYSTEM

Webster says a suspension is a device (such as springs) supporting the upper part of the car. The **suspension** holds the upper and lower portions of your car together. **A suspension system** is a specific way to attach your upper and lower car. Besides attaching your upper and lower car together, your suspension system is responsible for getting you over imperfections in the track with the least energy loss. It is sometimes necessary to

SUSPENSION 3-3

use more than the axle mount to accomplish this. The rigidity of the floorboard and body is also important.

The floorboard and body of the car often play a part in the suspension of your car. If you have a weak floorboard with a lot of weight in the center of your floorboard, you could produce on a rough track a bouncing throughout your floorboard that consumes a lot of energy. In addition, if your body is weak and or attached loosely to the floorboard, the rigidity of the floorboard and body combination can be compromised, causing you to waste energy.

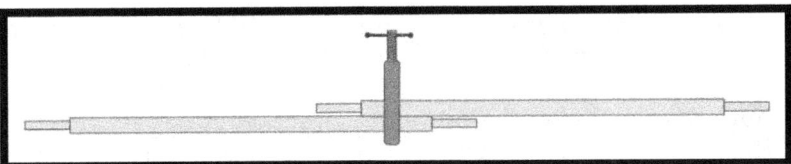

Figure 3-1

SUSPENSION AND ENERGY USAGE

Having your suspension parts **Solid** generally makes your car go faster. It saves more energy than running loose. There are exceptions, which were explained in Chapter 2, "Energy" and other places throughout the book. Perform the **Energy Experiment** found in the Chapter Energy on page 2-5 for more information on energy usage.

SOLID SUSPENSION TRACK TEST

In 1983, I was experimenting with the rear axle radius (stabilizer) rods.

I wanted to know how it affected the speed of the car if the axles were pulled tighter forward with the two radius rods. I had a turn barrel on each radius rod. The radius rods were attached to the floorboard and the axle. The radius rods and turn barrels together were a total of about 8" long. I was using two aircraft-type turn barrels. See the turn barrel in Figure 3-2.

After the car was driven down the hill several times to get a consistent time, I began tightening the turn barrels. I tightened each turn barrel about 1/8 of a turn. We noticed no change in our next practice run. I tightened them another 1/8 turn. This time the timer showed a .050 of a second faster than before. When I saw this time I Figured it was a fluke and we ran another practice run down the hill. *Again, it showed .050 of a second faster than we had before the adjustments. I was very excited then.* Next, I tightened the turn barrel another 1/8 turn. To my surprise, it showed a .050 of a second slower. I was now back to square one. I loosened the turn barrels until I regained the .050 faster time. This is the setup we used to run our local race.

I did not know what I had done, but later I realized that I was removing the slop in the threads. The turn barrels did not have jam nuts at each end to tighten after adjustment. This experiment and other similar experiments helped clarify how important it is to keep suspension parts tight against each other.

SUSPENSION 3-5

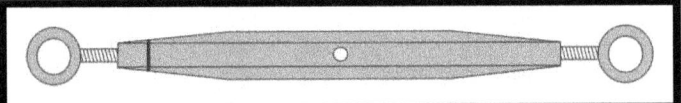

Figure 3-2

SOLID, TIGHT, AND LOOSE SUSPENSION

The **solid system** only has movement from the flexing of the attached components. The **loose system** is designed to move without causing much friction. Its movement is at or near the axle mount.

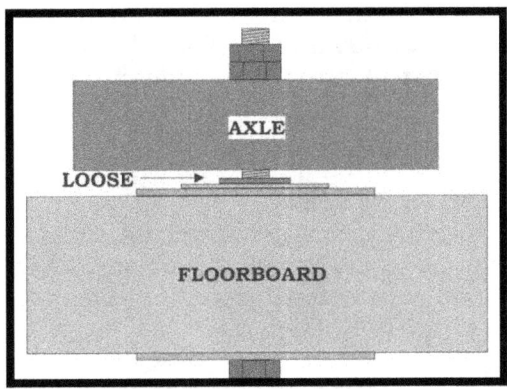

When I say **loose,** I mean extremely loose, loose so the friction is reduced to zero. The parts that must make contact are designed to minimize friction and vibration. The kingpin is loose letting the floorboard hang

Figure 3-3

from the axle as shown in Figure 3-3. When I say **solid**, I mean extremely solid, so there is no movement between the attaching parts. Often kingpins are over-torqued to achieve the desired tightness. Be careful not to strip the threads on your nut and or bolt.

Very few people use the loose system in the past and today, but I felt it should be used in this book for comparison if nothing else. Ted Ayers had great success with running loose with his *junior cars* that ran until the early 1990s.

SIMILARITIES
Both systems strive to save energy and realize the importance of reducing friction and vibration.

DIFFERENCES
The difference between loose and solid systems is their approach to getting over the imperfections in the track. **Those running loose** feel they save energy with their ability to get over track imperfections. They feel the amount of energy loss to friction is less. Their cross-bind is "0" at the start and throughout the race, which is the greatest advantage of the loose system. **Those running solid** feel they save energy because of no friction or vibration and good continuity.

LOOSE SYSTEM
With a loose system, an unleveled starting ramp will not pose a cross-bind problem. A quick start off the ramp is one of the most important parts of the race.

WHAT LOOSE DOES: BEST AND WORST
The loose system gets over imperfections in the track better than the solid system. The biggest problem is the loose system has more friction and vibration. The drivers of the loose cars have said that moving side to side in the

SUSPENSION 3-7

car can influence the steering of the car. *The best thing a loose suspension system does is eliminate any cross-bind.*

WHAT SOLID DOES: BEST AND WORST

The solid system is less efficient getting over bumps, but it has the least friction and vibration in its system. The solid system does not lose energy due to moving parts' friction or vibration. A solid system can lose energy to cross-bind. This is very important consideration on unlevel starting ramps.

SOLID, LOOSE, AND TIGHT COMBINATIONS

The solid and loose systems are rarely combined. Most often, it is a solid rear with a tight front axle. In addition, you rarely hear of a solid front axle with a less-than-solid rear axle being used. That does not mean it has not been tried. The rear axle has radius rods of some sort to keep the rear axle aligned and does not lend itself to being loose without giving up a lot of energy. This is especially true for the Super Stock rear axle mount. You should never run the Super Stock rear axle mount and alignment bolts loose.

The front axle is often loosened to reduce the cross-bind that is encountered with a solid front and rear axle that has a wide mounting area at the kingpin. Now days with the rules allowing only one large 1.25" washer with a normal size ¼" washer on top of that and then the axle, you get a rigid suspension. This makes up and down movement of the wheel very hard and it can use a lot of energy from cross-bind. This is why some elect to loosen up the front kingpin. Even if you have your cross-bind adjusted to "0," you can still benefit on some tracks by running your front axle less than solid.

> In July of 1984, Derby Tech printed the results of restricted axle movement tests. Their conclusion was that restricted axles perform poorly.

CAR BODY

RIGID

Most Soap Box Derby cars go faster when warm. The warmer they get, the faster they run. The wheels are affected the most by the heat, but the axles and car body are also affected to a lesser degree. This lets me think that flexibility or resilience is important, so how rigid is rigid? **The rigidity we are talking about in a Soap Box Derby car has no movement between parts, no movement between each wood strip, fiberglass, and floorboard.** Movement between parts loses energy to friction and vibration. The floorboard is the heart of the rigidity and strength needed. **Most of the experts, at this time feel super rigidity is the key to more speed**.

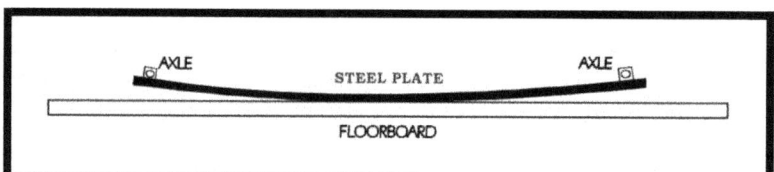

Figure 3-4

STRONG

When your car's nose hits the starting gate, it should not break. Your car should be strong enough to take normal track abuse and go on ticking. You want your car body to be strong, but resilient. **Flexing is not using much energy. The movement between parts uses energy.**

SUSPENSION 3-9

RESILIENT

Something that is resilient may lose its shape briefly when force is applied, but immediately returns to its original shape when the force is removed. A resilient Soap Box Derby racer is flexible and does not lose its shape. If you construct your car so there is *no* movement between parts, you will have flexibility, without a major loss of energy

AXLES

Axles are important in winning a Soap Box Derby Race. When you purchase your axles, get more than one pair, if you can. That way you can select the two you like and sell the others. Below are listed items to check on your axles. You may have to accept some imperfections listed below. There are not many perfect axles out there. Be sure to leave a protective coating on your axles at all times to prevent corrosion. See Chapter 7, "Parts Inspection" for axle dimensions.

AXLE SELECTION:
1. Your axle should not twist, as viewed from one end. **A twisted axle should be rejected.**
2. Check the spindles' diameter throughout their length with a micrometer. See Figure 3-5 (B) (2). **An axle that is tapered is undesirable. The difference between the inner and outer bearing surface should not exceed .005". Tapered spindles make alignment difficult.** If you accept an axle like this, the taper would have to be taken into account when aligning your spindles.

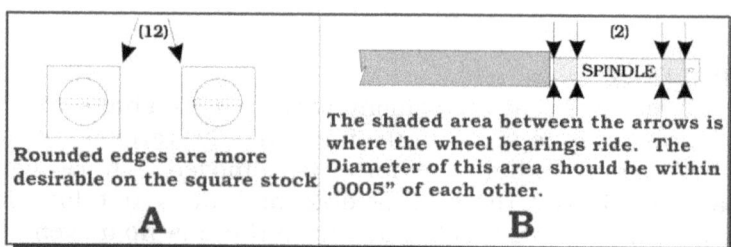

Figure 3-5

3. Spindle diameter should be .496" or larger. See Figure 3-6. **Anything loose associated with the axle wastes energy.**

4. Check the spindle for roundness. See Figure 3-7 (D) (4). Check the spindle where the inner and outer bearing of the wheel will ride for roundness. Be careful when polishing your spindles. You could remove too much material and make your spindle out of round and or tapered!

5. Check spindles for a smooth finish. **A smooth finish reduces the friction when the wheel slides on the spindle. Unless it is very bad, most finishes can be polished satisfactorily.** The underside of the spindle is the area where the wheel bearing rides.

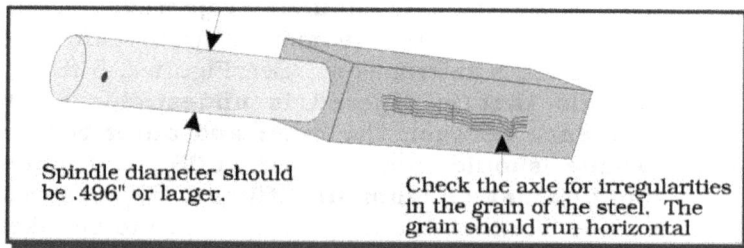

Figure 3-6

SUSPENSION 3-11

6. The dimensions of the spindles should be the same on each end of an axle. (These dimensions are outlined in items 2, 3, 8, and 9)

7. Axle hardness should be 10 to 18 on the Rockwell "C" scale. The hardness should be the same throughout the length of the square stock. Experts do not agree on whether the axles should be more toward the harder or softer side. Go with the harder side. *It might be noted that it was once legal to make your axles in the National Derby Rally, and no one came up with a superior axle.*

8. Select the axles that are the shortest. *Longer axles generally have longer spindles. Longer axles create more drag.*

9. Select axles with the longest spindles. See Figure 3-7 (C) (9). *Longer spindles give the wheel more spindles to slide on, reducing wheel-to-track drag.*

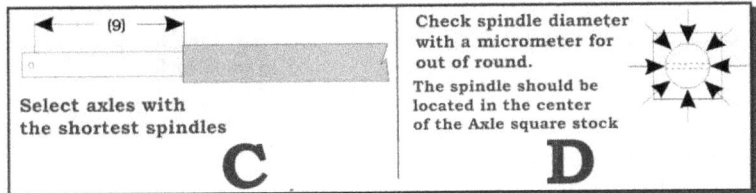

Figure 3-7

10. The spindles should be in the center of the square stock. See Figure 3-7 (D). **The bad news is most spindles are not in the middle of the square stock. You should check this, but it should not be a problem unless one spindle is off-center over .005". You would not want a large difference between two spindles on the same axle. Checking this is very difficult, especially if the spindles or axles have been bent.**

11. Axle grain should run horizontally. See Figure 3-6. Check the axle for a flaw in the grain. If it is flawed, in most cases you will see it. If you do

3-12   WINNING INGREDIENTS FOR KIT CARS

suspect a problem but are not sure, check with a good machinist. Most likely, you will not see any axles with a grain problem.

12. Square stock edges are best if rounded. (Do not alter the edges of the square stock, because it is against the rules.) See Figure 3-5 (A) (12). **Rounded square stock edges reduce drag. This is especially true when axle foils/fairings are not used.**

13. Small square stock is desirable within legal limits. **Small square stock will offer less drag when axle foils/fairings are not used. Place the thinnest square stock in line with the airflow.** It is unlikely you will find an axle like this.

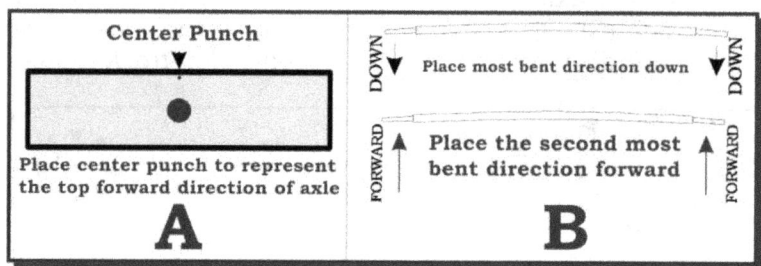

Figure 3-8

WHICH SIDE UP

There are two things to consider when deciding which side of the axle should face up: (1) The spindle wheel pin drilled hole direction and (2) the direction of the axle's natural bend. The drilled hole in the spindle should be horizontal, to reduce drag. The axles should come drilled so that when installed the spindle wheel pinhole is horizontal. With that in mind, place the axles on a flat surface to determine their bow. All axles are bowed to some extent. Most are bowed in two directions. Place the largest bow with the ends of the axles pointed up; this gives you a little more low weight. The second largest bow should have the axle ends pointed aft; this moves

SUSPENSION 3-13

your wheels aft giving you more time on the hill. Mark your axles so you will be able to tell their position and direction. Put a punch mark on the top square stock, forward of where the kingpin hole will be. See Figure 3-8 (A). The forward and aft axles can be identified by the steering or radius rod hole.

PRE-BOWING AXLES

Pre-bowing the axle down at the ends is the practice of bending your axles before they are installed. With a pre-bow, your axles will be straight when the weight of the driver and car is applied. The bending is best when performed before you drill your axles, otherwise, the axle will bend at the drilled hole.

Pre-bowing was used when the axle square stock was five-eighths of an inch. Those axles were weak. They bowed so much that the fairings (airfoils) would not line up with the axle. Running the fairings through the body aggravated the axle and fairing alignment. To align the axles and fairings, the axles were pre-bowed. The current three-quarter-inch axle bends less and today most axle fairings are not run through the car body. This eliminates the need for axle pre-bow. The All-American still lets you pre-bow your axles in the masters division; this is because the weight limit is high and causes your axles to bend quite a bit.

A small number of people still pre-bow their axles. There is no benefit from doing this, except to lower the center of gravity of your car. After the axles are bowed, they are installed on the car upside down. This lowers the car and its center of gravity.

CHANGING AXLES

Some change their axles frequently. It is thought that the axles get work-hardened and lose their elasticity. The frequency of axle changes varies. Some do it as often as before every race. *This is something people were doing in the past, not recently.* Keep your same axles unless they have obviously been damaged; changing your axles before every race is too expensive and a waste of time.

CONCLUSION

The same suspension principles apply to all divisions. However, there are several differences of application because of the rules in each division.

The **Stock and Super Stock Divisions** are similar in their axle mount rules. The major difference is the radius rods used for the rear axle in the Stock and Super Stock divisions. Check with the All-American Construction Rules for the latest updates.

The **Masters Division** gives you some leeway in your axle mount. You are allowed several ways to stabilize your rear axle and you are allowed to determine the number of washers to use under and on top of your axles. **Use the long stabilizer rods for your rear axle in the masters**. Check with the All-American Construction Rules for the latest updates.

In all divisions, when the starting ramp or track condition requires you to run loose, _leave the rear of the car as tight_ as you can get it and loosen the front axle. That way you get the benefits of a tight rear suspension system while reducing, or eliminating cross-bind.

The **Super Stock** rear axle mount is vulnerable to misalignment from movement and bumps. Often families move their car by lifting the aft end to keep from rolling it on the aft axle. Check your aft axle mount before each weekend of racing.

GOOD LUCK
AND
KEEP IT SOLID

CHAPTER FOUR
CONSTRUCTION

INTRODUCTION

You should have already read Chapter 7, Parts Inspection, and are satisfied with the parts. As we go through this chapter, if you see a part that is not going to be acceptable, make plans to repair or replace that part before you go forward with the assembly of your car.

Follow your All-American Kit Plans and Rules as you go through this chapter. In this here we will go through the assembly of the Stock and Super Stock kit cars. This chapter is not in the same order as the Kit Plans. The Super Stock Aft Axle mount installation will be addressed at the end of the chapter.

This chapter will cover some things that are in the Kit Plans and some things that are not covered in the Kit Plans. As an example, the Kit Plans do not cover how to Epoxy something. This may be thought to be common knowledge; however, most need a little guidance to get it right. Epoxy is like gluing, the preparation is the most important part. We will cover more on epoxy in the following pages.

THIS CHAPTER WILL COVER
- Kingpin Bushing Installation
- Bushing Hole Adjustment
- Floorboard Preparation And Finish
- Leveling Your Axle To The Floorboard During And After Bushing Installation
- Elevator Bolt Installation And Floorboard Hardware
- Installation Of Forward And Aft Axles
- Installation Of The Steering And Brake Assembly
- Installation Of Steering Cable
- Installation Of The Brake Pedal And Cable
- Installation Of The Added Weight
- Installation Of The Super Stock Aft Axle
- Body Installation
- Super Stock Paint

EXAMINE YOUR LEVEL

Before starting the construction, take a minute to make sure your level is giving the correct readings. Place your level on a table that is as level as you can find. Shim under one end of the level until it shows level like the **top level** in Figure 4-2 on page 4-6. (Where you now have your level, we will call **the level area**) To check the accuracy of your level just turn it around 180 degrees so the ends of your level are now opposite. If your level does not show level after you turn it 180 degrees, adjust it so that when you place it on **the level area** it shows level no matter which direction you place it.

CONSTRUCTION RULES

Make sure you consult the All-American plans for your division as you build your racecar. **If there are any differences between the instructions in this book and the All-American, the All-American rules and instructions shall prevail.** The All-American rules are often changing; it is up to you to keep up with the latest changes. Talk with your director and check on the All-American website for the latest changes. http://www.aasbd.org/

INSTALL KINGPIN BUSHINGS BEFORE TUNG OIL APPLICATION

We install the bushings before applying Tung Oil because you do not want to get Tung Oil in the <u>floorboard bushing holes</u>. After installing the bushings, we will place tape over the bushings to prevent Tung Oil from getting into the bushings.

BUSHING INSTALLATION PREPARATION

The bushing installation is the foundation of your car's Alignment and elimination of cross-bind. In the following, we will check your floorboard for level longitudinally and

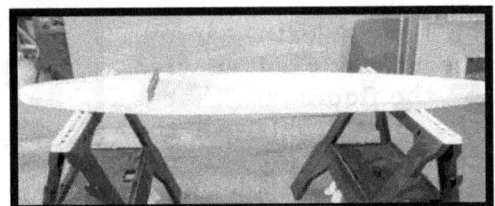

Photo 4-1

laterally. Then we will check the axle level to your floorboard. We will then examine why things are not level and fix them starting with the simplest and progressing to the most difficult.

You can shim one of your axles and eliminate Cross-Bind, but you should strive to use no shims. When your kingpin bolt is forced to one side of the bushing and washers, the bolt will have a more restricted movement on one side than the other. It is best to have everything symmetrical.

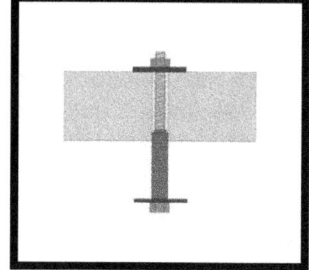

Figure 4-1

Start by leveling your floorboard as in photo 4-1. After leveling the floorboard the best you can, place a level laterally in several places to see if the floorboard checks level its full length. *Note: if the front kingpin area is mostly level with the rest of the floorboard or is the aft kingpin area most level with the rest of the floorboard?* This is important because you may have to adjust one bushing hole that is out the most. **Find an area on the floorboard that is the most level with the front and or aft axle and use that position when doing any floorboard and axle leveling from now forward.**

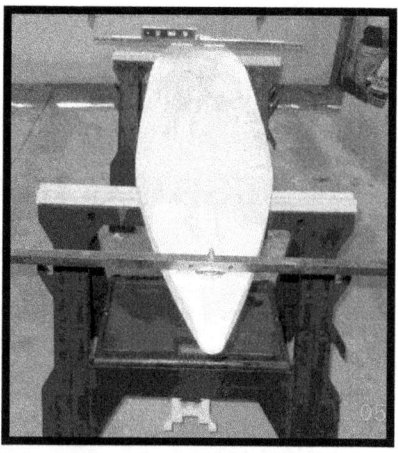

Photo 4-2

CONSTRUCTION 4-5

To help evaluate your bushing installation and the car's cross-bind you need to **install your bushings and axles per the Soap Box Derby Plans**. <u>The installation of your bushings and axles is temporary. Do not epoxy the bushings at this time.</u> Figure 4-1 shows the bushing being drawn into the floorboard as described in the Soap Box Derby Plans. Torque your kingpin bolts to 150 to 200-inch lbs.

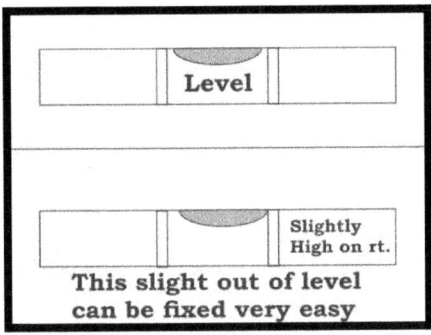

Figure 4-2

After the bushings and axles are installed, level your floorboard using the same place you used on Page 4-4. Photo 4-2 shows your floorboard with the axles installed per the construction plans. <u>With your floorboard level, check the axles and floorboard to see which axle is nearest to **level** with the floorboard and which axle is most **unlevel** with the floorboard.</u> **We will work on the axle that is the most level with the floorboard first**. A view of the level might appear greater than it is. In Figure 4-2, the lower level shows a small amount of out-of-level. This is not a lot and can often be leveled by rotating the washers under the axle. More on this later.

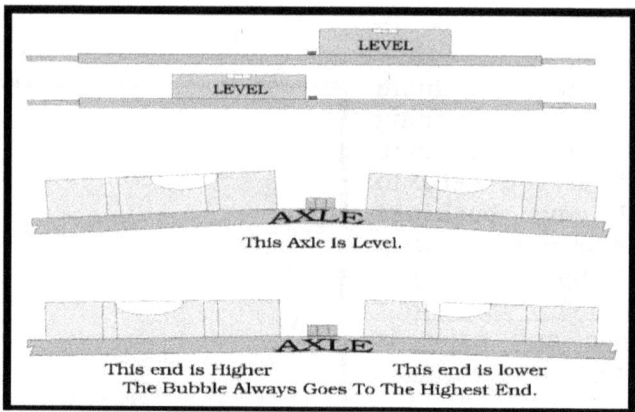

Figure 4-3

You might have an axle that is bent. This will make it more difficult to check the level and make your floorboard and axle level. See Figure 4-3.

Take your time and Figure out when the axle is level with the floorboard. In Figure 4-3 note the axle in the middle that is bent. Your levels will look something like these when the axle is level. If it is out of level, it will look like the lowest axle and levels.

EVALUATING YOUR BUSHING, FLOORBOARD, AND AXLE LEVEL

To evaluate the correct position of your Bushings, Floorboard, and Axle, read the following listed things that affect their alignment. Depending on what we find, we will go through how to correct any problems found. Some items you have already checked in Chapter 7, "Parts Inspection," however you might want to revisit the inspection of some of these items depending on what we find. We are working on the most level axle at this time.

CONSTRUCTION 4-7

1. The floorboard hole might not be drilled square.
2. The hole in the bushing can be drilled at an angle to the outside of the bushing. See Figure 4-4 for an exaggerated example.
3. The floorboard could be soft on top of the floorboard on one side under the washer. This can cause the washers to draw into the floorboard more on one side than another.
4. Your *floorboard could be* twisted
5. Your *washers are often physically higher on one half than the other.* This can be caused when manufactured, or from damaged. (**This is not a problem at all, because all you have to do to fix it is to rotate your washers until the axle is level with the floorboard.**)
6. The *kingpin hole in your axle* could be drilled incorrectly.
7. Your axle *kingpin could be bent.*

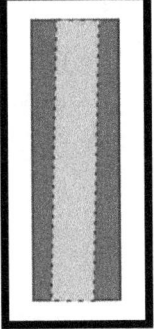

Figure 4-4

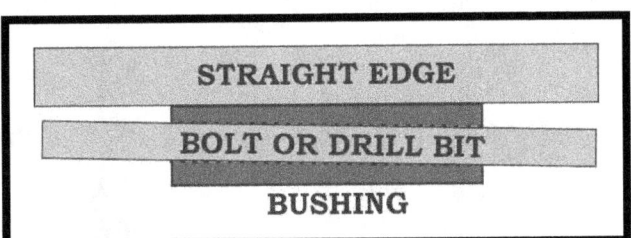

Figure 4-5

CORRECTING THE 1-7, PROBLEMS LISTED ABOVE.

The following solutions are matched to the listed possible problems listed above.

1. *The bushing hole in the floorboard is most likely drilled straight into the floorboard.* The problem comes when the floorboard is twisted from being

warped. At this time, *we are working on the least out-of-level floorboard end and axle*, so no adjustment of the hole will be needed unless it is so far out you cannot adjust it in one of the following ways. See Figure 4-6 for checking the bushing hole.

2. *If a bushing is drilled incorrectly* as in Figure 4-4, you can check it by placing a bolt or drill bit in the bushing and placing a straight edge alongside the bushing. See Figure 4-5. **This is a possible problem, but unlikely to happen**. Replace any bad bushings, or use them to position them to help in a badly warped floorboard.

3. *The floorboard is often softer in one area than another.* Because of this, the top large washers can be pulled into the floorboard more on one side than the other side. This is a common problem and to correct it you will put a clamp on the high side of the large washer to make it compress the same as the low side. This takes time and effort to make the washer level. Take it slow as you adjust it. You do not want to overdo it.

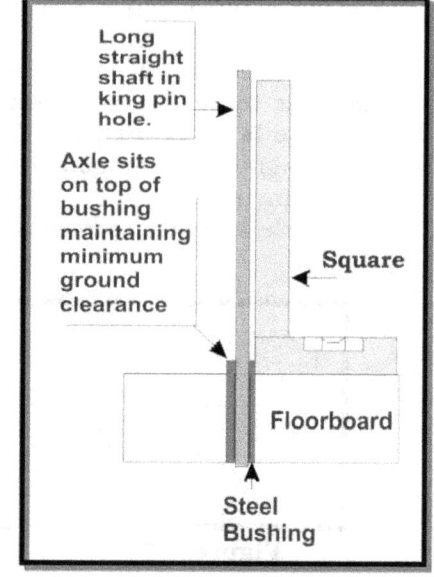

Figure 4-6

4. *The floorboard could be warped.* The floorboard might be warped causing the axle to be unlevel with the floorboard. *However, we are working*

CONSTRUCTION 4-9

with the axle and floorboard that are the least unlevel with one another. You should be able to compress the washer more into the floor on one side or turn the position of the washers to level the axle with the floorboard.

5. *The washers under the axle could be higher on one side than the other.* You can most likely rotate the washer to correct the problem, or replace the washer. Each washer will be different because of manufacturing or damage. Just by changing the washer and or turning it, you should be able to adjust out minor unlevel axles.

6. *The kingpin hole in the axle could be drilled at an angle.* To check this, turn your axle around 180 degrees and see if it helps make the axle more level. Replace this axle if the hole is excessive.

7. *Your kingpin could be bent.* Often these bolts are bent. To check this, roll the bolt on a level surface. Install the kingpin bolt and torque it to about 150 inch-lbs. to 200 inch-lbs. Then place a level on the axle and turn the bolt to see if the level changes as you turn the bolt. Replace the bent bolt.

Items 3, 5, 6, and 7 above are most likely to level your axle the small amount you need. Try rotating your axle first, then compress your washer if not level, then check your kingpin bolt, and last, position your washers to level your axle.

Photo 4-3

LEVEL YOUR AXLE

Everyone positions his or her washers for the final level adjustment. That is why you see them marked with a permanent marker to mark their placement for a level axle. See photo 4-3 for an example of marked washers. This one is marked on the aft side of the axles. It is recommended that you mark the front and aft side of the washers so you can see them from inside the car with the body installed.

If you would like to keep a kingpin bolt that is bent, you can do so and mark the head of the bolt so you can make sure it is in the proper position. In Akron at the All-American Championship race, they make you turn your kingpin. Make sure you get to move the bolt back to your mark or you will change your cross-bind.

Once you have the easy axle leveled, install the bushing before trying to level the next axle. Follow the epoxy instructions on page 4-14 under the title; **EPOXY ALL BUSHINGS THAT NEED NO HOLE ADJUSTMENT**.

LEVEL THE REMAINING AXLE

Once you have one axle leveled with your floorboard, level the remaining axle with that axle and floorboard. Once again, go through the 7 things that can cause the axle to be unlevel on page 4-7 and correct what you can. Make every effort to correct the level of the remaining axle before you decide to adjust the bushing hole. If you will need to adjust the bushing hole, go to the **BUSHING HOLE ADJUSTMENT** heading on page 4-12.

CONSTRUCTION 4-11

Most often, after the first axle is leveled you can also get your other axle to level. Remember you are allowed to use a feeler gauge to place between the two biggest washers to level your axle. If you can use a feeler gauge to level your axle, you do not need to adjust the bushing hole in the floorboard. If you feel you have to use a feeler gauge larger than about .007" then you might consider adjusting the bushing hole.

LEVELING YOUR AXLE WITH A FEELER GAUGE

The All-American rules allow you to use one feeler gauge to shim one axle to eliminate cross-bind. <u>Check the All-American rules before you shim an axle in case the rules have changed since the writing of this book.</u>

SHIMMING YOUR AXLE

There are things about shimming your axle for the final time that you need to know now.

- When shimming the axle for the final adjustment, you will do it with your car assembly complete, the shell installed and all weight adjustments complete.
- In the **Super Stock**, it is best to place the shim between the two largest washers under the **forward axle.** This is because the rear axle mount in the Super Stock is difficult to adjust. When you do get the rear axle mount adjusted, you do not want to be loosening and retightening it with the shell installed.
- The **Stock** car is easiest to shim between the two largest washers under the **aft axle**. The Stock car rear axle mount is not complex. Just loosening the kingpin bolt a small amount will allow you to slip the feeler gauge between the two large washers under the axle. The Stock front axle could be shimmed instead of the aft if needed.

BUSHING HOLE ADJUSTMENT

The following is the procedure for adjusting your floorboard-bushing hole. It includes several steps of bushing hole preparation for the epoxy process.

PREPARE THE BUSHING HOLE FOR EPOXY

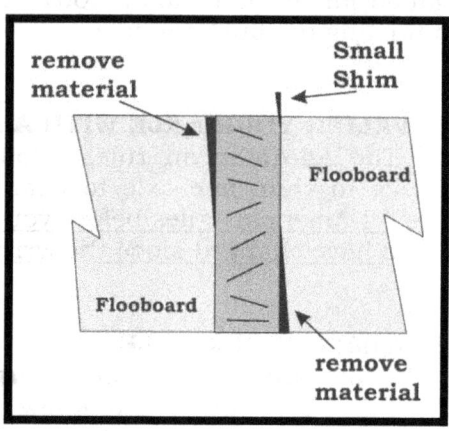

Figure 4-7

Before you get started adjusting the floorboard-bushing hole, take the time to prepare the floorboard's hole for the epoxy of the bushing in place. We do this first because if done afterward it could change the fit of the bushing. To prepare the hole we want to rough up the hole and drill some 1/8" holes in the bushing hole to receive the epoxy. After you have done this, you can continue with the next paragraphs to adjust the hole for bushing position adjustment.

ADJUSTING THE BUSHING IN THE FLOORBOARD TO LEVEL THE AXLE

First, you must know in which direction you want your bushing to go. Take some time to make sure you are relieving the bushing hole so the bushing will go in the correct direction.

In Figure 4-7, you see a bushing in the floorboard. As you view this, the problem you would be correcting is an axle that is too low to the right of Figure 4-7, and an axle that is too high to the left of Figure 4-7.

CONSTRUCTION 4-13

Correct this by removing floorboard hole material from the dark areas in Figure 4-7. These dark areas are exaggerated to direct you to the area needing material removed. Remove just enough material to where you can move the bushing into position with just a little prying or shimming as shown in Figure 4-7. Install the bushing dry to test if the material removed is sufficient. Continue removing material until you can install the bushing dry and get the axle level. Position the bushing exactly with a small shim if needed. Taking your time, you can get it into position. When you have the bushing where you want it, epoxy it in position per the following instructions.

EPOXY THE BUSHING INTO THE FLOORBOARD HOLE THAT WAS ADJUSTED

Your preparation will determine the quality of your bushing installation.

- Recheck the roughness of the bushing hole without changing your bushing position.
- Rough up your bushing. The edge of a file or a hacksaw can be used. See Figure 4-7 and note the marks on the bushing. This is the roughness so the epoxy will have something to grip.
- Lubricate the inside of the bushing with a thick grease or Vaseline. This keeps epoxy from getting in it. Clean the bushing hole after the glue sets with some alcohol.
- **Prepare to install the bushing by getting the tools you will need to put epoxy in the hole and on the outside of the bushing, filling the file marks in the bushing.** You will need small sticks to work the epoxy into the floorboard hole and on the bushing. The epoxy dries fast and does not give you a lot of time to find your tools if they are not already collected for the job. **The bushing is installed with the top flush with the top of the floorboard.**

- Mixing the epoxy is very important. **Make sure you thoroughly mix the epoxy.** Both parts of the epoxy are clear and it is hard to tell when it is properly mixed.
- <u>As soon as you mix the epoxy, apply it to the bushing hole and bushing</u>. Get the tools and install the bushing. If you used a shim to hold the bushing in place on the dry run, put it in to hold the bushing in place while the epoxy dries.
- Clean up the excess epoxy after it has dried. The epoxy will dry hard, but can be removed with a chisel or putty knife.
- Use alcohol to clean the grease from the inside of the bushing.

Now you are ready to install your axle and see if you can level it.

If you have just installed the easy axle bushing with the above epoxy steps, return to Page 4-10 and continue at **"LEVEL THE REMAINING AXLE"**.

EPOXY ALL BUSHINGS THAT NEED NO HOLE ADJUSTMENT

Your preparation will determine the quality of your bushing installation. Install all bushings not needing hole adjustment, including the Rear Axle Radius Rod bushings. See special instructions for Radius Rod installation after the following eight steps to install the bushings.

CONSTRUCTION 4-15

1. Rough up the inside of the bushing holes. Use a small drill bit to drill holes in the bushing hole that will hold epoxy.
2. Rough up your bushings. The edge of a file or a hacksaw can be used. See Figure 4-7 and note the marks on the bushing. This is the roughness so the epoxy will have something to grip.
3. Lubricate the inside of the bushing with a thick grease or Vaseline. This keeps epoxy from getting in it. Clean the bushing after the glue sets with some alcohol.
4. **Prepare to install the bushing by getting the tools you will need to put epoxy in the hole and on the outside of the bushing, filling the file marks in the bushing**. You will need small sticks to work the epoxy into the hole and on the bushing. The epoxy dries fast and does not give you a lot of time to find your tools if they are not already collected for the job.
5. Mixing the epoxy is very important. **Make sure you thoroughly mix the epoxy;** this is one of the most made mistakes. Both parts of epoxy are clear liquid and it is hard to tell when it is properly mixed.
6. **The bushing is to be installed flush with the top of the floorboard.**
7. As soon as you mix the epoxy, apply it to the bushing hole and the bushing outside. Get the tools and install the bushing.
8. Clean up the excess epoxy after it has dried. The epoxy will dry hard and can be removed with a chisel or putty knife.
9. Use alcohol to clean the grease from the bushing.

REAR AXLE RADIUS RODS BUSHINGS

The "rear axle radius rod bushings" should be epoxied in position so they are level with the top of the floorboard. Also, later when you install the Stock radius rods, use the thickest ¼" washers you can find to get the radius rods closer to level with the axle on the Stock car. The All-American has used at least 5 different types ¼" washers since the kit car came out. The grade 8 washers are the latest and the thickest.

AXLES LEVEL TO THE FLOORBOARD RECHECK
Reinstall your axles without the radius rods and recheck the axles and floorboard for level. Go to page 4-7 and go over the list of level corrections. Items 3, 5, and 7 should get your axles level. Remember you can still use a feeler gauge to shim one axle later. A final adjustment will be made after the car is finished with all weights installed and the car body is installed.

Remove axles and hardware in preparation for the floorboard sanding, apply Tung Oil, and Wax. The axles will be reinstalled and level checked again after some of the hardware is installed on the floorboard.

FLOORBOARD PREPARATION AND FINISH

PREPARING FLOORBOARD FOR TUNG OIL
Lightly sand the top, bottom, and sharp edges of your floorboard. You can sand the rough edges off the top and bottom edges of the floorboard, but do not make a large radius. Before applying Tung oil, remove all loose dust with a brush, dry rag, and an air compressor if available. Next, wipe the floorboard with a warm wet rag to lift the wood fibers. Let dry before applying Tung oil.

CONSTRUCTION 4-17

APPLY TUNG OIL

Recently the All-American Soap Box Derby has allowed the application of Tung oil on your floorboard. It also allows the use of wax. <u>Remember to recheck the rules for changes since the writing of this book.</u>

The amount of Tung Oil that you apply is up to you; however, for best results apply 4 to 8 coats and more if you wish. You may coat the bottom of the floorboard more than the top. The following gives you a guide to applying Tung Oil. Do not apply tung oil to the sides of the floorboard.

- Install the bushings before the Tung oil is applied. After the bushings are installed, cover them with tape before applying your Tung Oil.
- Tung Oil is applied before any other hardware is installed.
- When using pure Tung oil, you need several coats. It is important that you thin each coat with the first coat being the thinnest (recommended 70 percent solvent). This will help you rub the Tung Oil deep in the wood. Each successive coat should be thicker (less thinning), and the last coat must be the thickest. Your thinner needs to be an organic solvent, one that is carbon based like turpentine, mineral spirits, or the newfangled "citrus solvent."
- Apply the oil liberally with a soft cloth and then wipe it off. Rub the first two coats into the floorboard, for the rest you can use a brush.
- Allow to dry completely to the touch. If it is tacky, it is not dry. With thinned Tong Oil, you will be able to sand and reapply in 12 hrs. The longer you wait between coats the better. You might

place a fan blowing toward the floorboard to speed up the drying process.
- Every layer except the last must be sanded, so that the next layer of Tung oil will bond to the previous layer. Three hundred and twenty-grit sandpaper creates the "tooth" that grips the next layer.

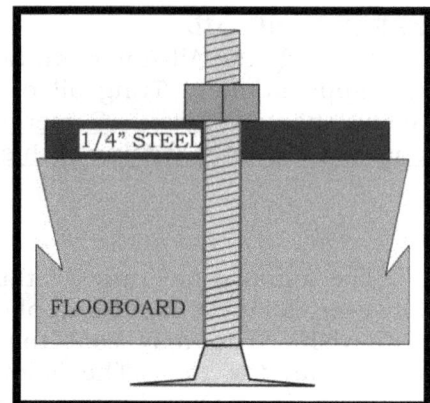

Figure 4-8

- Make sure you get plenty of Tung Oil in the Elevator bolt holes. This will help to keep the bolts from pulling too far into the floorboard. This will allow you to put torque on the bolts that you need without pulling the bolt into the floorboard. The floorboard is very soft and the bolts will often pull deep into the floorboard before they will tighten enough.

For more information on Tung oil application, check out some of the You Tube videos. Some of the videos are quite good and some of them are quite bad.

WAX YOUR FLOORBOARD

Before you start the installation of the hardware at the top of the floorboard, you should wax the floorboard. S C Johnson Paste Wax is good for the floorboard. Be careful when lifting the car by the front floorboard. The wax can make you drop the car.

CONSTRUCTION   4-19

INSTALL THE ELEVATOR BOLTS IN THE FLOORBOARD

The floorboards are very soft and because of this, you may find your elevator bolt drawing deeper into the floorboard than you want. Make sure you get plenty of Tung Oil into those bolt holes so you will not have this problem. After the Tung Oil is dry, install the elevator bolts and attach the floorboard hardware **per the Soap Box Derby Stock Car Plans.** The All-American construction plans list the installation steps we will use on the next page. Read the following on the problem of drawing the items on top of the floorboard into the floorboard. **See Figure 4-8 for a view of using a steel plate to prevent dents in the top of the floorboard**.

When you install your elevator bolts for the first time, pay attention to the position of the bolt head as the bolt is tightened. You want your elevator bolt head to be flush with the bottom of the floorboard. Different bolt positions will require greater torque than others. Be careful not to pull the bolt head deep into the floorboard where the bolt hole is too large or the wood is soft.

Install the Elevator Bolts for the following items as directed by the All-American Soap Box Derby Stock Plans. Often when you install the elevator bolts, they will require a lot of torque to pull the head of the bolt flush with the floorboard. **This could cause things on the top of the floorboard to pull into the top of the floorboard. You do not want this to happen.**

In Figure 4-8, you see a cutaway of the floorboard with an elevator bolt being installed. **Note the ¼" steel plate on top of the floorboard to prevent something from sinking into the top of the floorboard.** The steel plate should be at least 2" X 3" to keep it from making a dent in the floorboard. Install all elevator bolts using something like this steel plate. It spreads out the load on the floorboard and prevents dents in the top of your floorboard. **As an example, this can prevent your steering pulley and washer from being sunk into the floorboard, which can change the position of your steering cable.** After you get all of the bolt heads flush with the bottom of the floorboard, you can replace the steel plate on top with the item that goes in that position.

- Install steering stop per AA Plans 1
- Install adjustable weight bolt per AA Plans step 9 front and aft position
- Install the foot brace per step AA Plans 2
- Install the steering pulleys in AA Plans step 5

Do not install the optional weight bolts at this time. If a weight is not installed, the bolts will fall out. You will install the weight bolts when the required weight is determined and installed.

INSTALL THE FORWARD AND AFT AXLES AND RADIUS RODS.

Before you finish the installation of the rest of the floorboard hardware, install your axles and level them to the floorboard. **See Page 4-37 for Super Stock Rear Axle installation.**

CONSTRUCTION 4-21

Remove the tape you put over the bushings for the Tung Oil application.

1. **Install the forward axle** and level it to the floorboard.
2. **Install the aft axle** and level it to the floorboard and the forward axle.

   a. If you are having trouble leveling your two axles to the floorboard, you can use a shim. The All-American rules allow you to shim one of your axles to get the floorboard and both axles level with one another. **See Page 4-11 "SHIM YOUR AXLE" for the shimming instructions.**
   Remember, it is advisable to shim the rear axle on the Stock car and shim the forward axle on the Super Stock car. **You will recheck the cross-bind of the axles after the car is finished with the shell attached in Chapter 5, "Alignment & Adjustments."**

   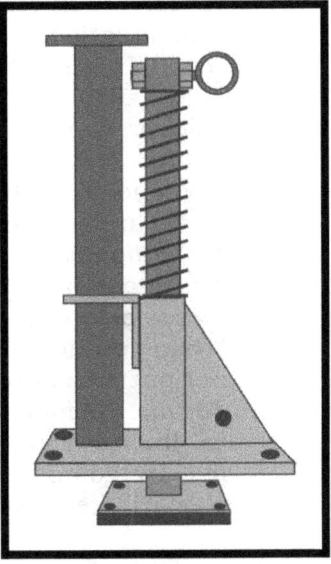

   Figure 4-9

   b. Install the aft axle radius rods and leave them loose for adjustment. **When installing the aft axle radius rods, use the thickest ¼" washers on the forward end.** At this time, that is the grade 8 ¼" washers in your kit.
   c. **Triangulate Align the rear axle** per the All-American Soap Box Derby Plans. The All-American alignment instructions for this are very detailed and easy to follow at this time.

d. You can align the rear axle in several ways, all of which involve measuring between the forward kingpin bolt and the ends of the aft axle square stock. This is referred to as rear axle Triangulation.
e. Use a Trammel Tool to help align the rear axle or tape measure. Photo 4-4 shows a Trammel Tool that you can purchase at your local hardware store or on line.

Photo 4-4

f. *When tightening the radius rods, be careful with the aft screws in the axles. They will not take much torque* before they strip or brake.
g. When you tighten your forward radius rod bolts, do not put a forward or aft load on them.
h. Torque the forward radius rod attach-points to 100 in. lbs. or 150 in lbs. Try to get it up to 150 in lbs. by going very slow from 100 to 150. Going slow will keep you from breaking a bolt.

FINISH INSTALLATION OF FLOORBOARD HARDWARE

STEERING HARDWARE INSTALLATION

Install the steering and brake hardware per the All-America Stock Plans. In Figure 4-9, you see the steering and brake assembly. You should be aware of several possible issues with these assemblies:

CONSTRUCTION 4-23

1. The mounting plate could come bent
2. The assembly may not be welded square. Replace
3. The inner brake shaft may be excessively loose in the outer square tube
4. The inner brake shaft may have too little space between the inner brake shaft and the outer square tube. Some light filing or sanding can often cure this.
5. The brake pad steel mounting plate could be welded at an angle or not square. Replace
6. *When the brakes are applied as shown in Figure 4-10 the eyebolt for the brake cable can come in contact with the steering shaft preventing the brakes from being applied. This is combined with the driver pulling back on the steering while stopping.*

Because of the above possibilities, the brake can contact the pavement at an angle that will cause the brake to chatter. This can give the driver an unpleasant feeling in his hands as the steering wheel vibrates. This may only happen when a new brake pad is installed. After the new brake pad has some wear on it, the vibration/chatter may no longer appear. *To prevent the brake shaft from being at an angle,* place a washer under the two front mount bolts of the Steering & Brake Assembly. This will cause the brake to go down at a lesser angle and not chatter. **Please check with the All-Americans for the rule that applies to this**.

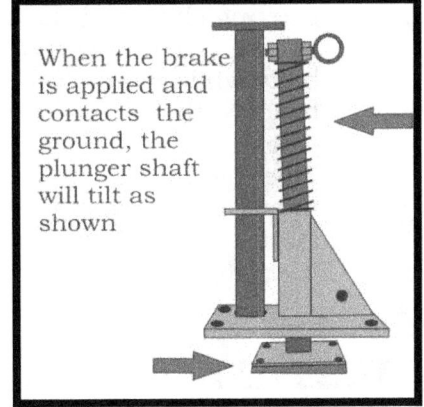

When the brake is applied and contacts the ground, the plunger shaft will tilt as shown

Figure 4-10

As noted in item 6 on page 4-23, the brake can be kept from going down because the Brake Eyebolt contacts the steering shaft when the brakes are applied. The excessive tilt of the brake shaft or the excessive length of the "brake cable eyebolt" can cause this. In addition, the steering shaft being loose in its brackets can contribute to this.

In Figure 4-10, you might notice the brake pad is wearing at an angle. As you might have guessed, this is desired for better aerodynamics.

COMPLETE STEERING/BRAKE ASSEMBLY INSTALLATION
- Install elevator bolts as previously described.
- When you bolt the assembly to the floorboard the steering shaft may be loose. This may be because the hole it sits in is too deep. A thin washer under the quarter could solve this problem.
- Remember to examine the clearance between the steering shaft and the brake shaft eyebolt.
- Secure the Steering/Brake Assembly mounting bolts while maintaining a flush position of the bolt heads with the bottom of the floorboard.
- Often the brake cable **pulley** on the Steering/Brake Assembly is installed with improper hardware. Follows the All-American Plans and use the proper hardware.

INSTALL THE STEERING CABLE

Installing the steering cable can be one of the most time consuming and frustrating jobs in the construction of the kit car. *Below are some tips to consider before you start installing the Steering Cable.*

CONSTRUCTION 4-25

1. The steering cable will stretch, so tighten it a little tight with the initial installation, and check it often and before each race day.
2. The white plastic tube adjusters are difficult to adjust and take an 11/32" wrench that most of us do not have. Start by adjusting them about halfway as seen in photo 4-5. Most Derby people use the *axle eyebolts* for the <u>final adjustment on the steering cable</u>. A final adjustment of the steering will be made in Chapter 5, Alignment & Adjustments.

Photo 4-5

3. Put some tension on the steering cables with the plastic adjusters whether you use them or not for adjusting the steering cables. You do not want these items to be loose.

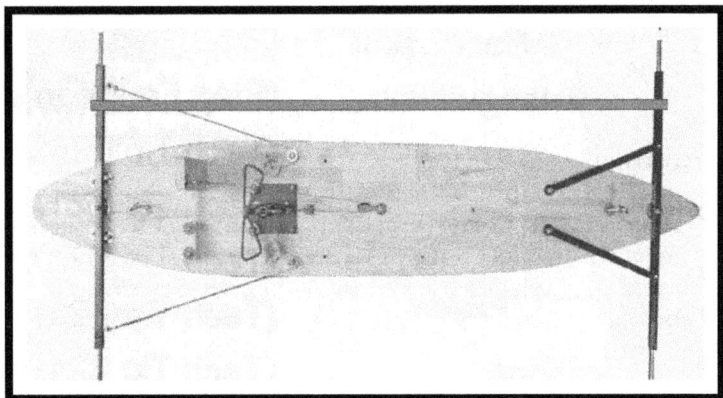

Photo 4-6

4-26 WINNING INGREDIENTS FOR KIT CARS

4. The cable should wrap around the steering shaft without the cable wrapping over each other when the steering wheel is turned. See item 11 on page 4-28 for how to accomplish this. See photo 4-7 to see how the **Stock Car** cables should look on the steering shaft.
5. **Stock car** *photos are used in this chapter, See the All-American instructions for the* **Super Stock and Masters** *for Steering Cable routing.*

Install the steering cable by following the 2014 All-American Soap Box Derby Plans. The following are some steps to make the job a bit easier.

PREPARE TO INSTALL THE STEERING CABLE

1. Before installing the steering cable, take your Spindle alignment tool and adjust the Toe-in to about .000" on both Spindles at this time.

Photo 4-7

2. You have the rear axle aligned on a previous page. To align the front axle to the aft axle, measure equal distance from the aft axel square stock ends to the forward axle square stock ends. When your measurement is the same on each side, clamp a small board to the axles as seen in photo 4-6 to keep the front axles aligned while you install the steering cable.

CONSTRUCTION 4-27

3. Install the cable on the steering shaft as shown and described in the 2014 Soap Box Derby Stock Plans. The objective is not to cross any cables on the steering shaft. See *photo 4-7*. <u>The Stock and Super Stock steering cable installation and routing has changed over the years Make sure you are following the latest All-American Plans.</u>
4. Make sure the axle eyebolts are installed and adjusted to extend aft of the axles so you have room to tighten the cable for the final adjustment. The final adjustment will be made in Chapter 5 "Alignment and Adjustments".
5. Route the cable and attach it loosely to the axle eyebolts. Use two cable clamps on each end.
6. **Before you get too far along, make sure the steering turns right when the steering wheel is turned right, and left when turned left.** <u>The cable will come off the back of the steering shaft to turn the axle in the correct direction for the Stock car photo shown. See photo 4-7</u>
7. In **Chapter 6," Tools," photo 6-11** there is a tool to hold your steering shaft while you install and adjust the steering. Use this tool or someone to hold the steering straight while you install the steering cable.
8. Loosen the cable clamps and use a vice grip to grab the end of the cable. Pull the cable ends until you have the left, and right cable ends the same tightness, and the steering wheel stays in the center position. This will take a few tighten on one side and then the other before you get it as even as possible.
9. Use the axle eyebolts to tighten and adjust the steering straight. If you do not have enough travel on your eyebolts, tighten the plastic tube adjusters more.
10. To get the Steering Cable tight enough check your Spindle alignment Toe-In reading. We are looking for a negative Toe-out of .003" to .005" reading. We will readjust this in Chapter 5, "Alignment and Adjustments."

11. <u>In photo 4-7, you see what the cables should look like when tension is applied</u>. When you turn the steering wheel, you do not want the cables to wrap over one another. **The end of the cable on one side of the steering shaft should be coming off the top of the cable wrap and the cable coming off the other side of the steering shaft should be coming off the bottom of the cable wrap.** See photo 4-8 for Stock Steering routing at the time of this books publishing.

Final adjustments will be made in the Chapter 5, "Alignment and Adjustments." At that time, we will also Figure out how to make sure the driver is starting out straight in the starting gate.

INSTALL BRAKE PEDAL "SAFETY"

BRAKE PEDAL POSITION AND DRIVER
The driver needs to be comfortable with the position of the brake pedal. <u>If the driver is out of positioned where the pedal is **out of reach** the driver will feel stress as they come to the finish line.</u> As they reach the finish line, they may start getting into position to stop too soon causing their head to rise up. In addition, in order to feel in control for stopping they may start applying the brake early. <u>Other times the driver is so close to the brake pedal that they do not have enough room for their foot as they drive down the hill.</u> The driver will strain to pull his or her foot back or inadvertently rest their foot on the brake pedal causing the brake to extend under the car. Often the brake pedal position is not addressed because no one thinks of the above possibilities.

CONSTRUCTION 4-29

ONE THING THAT CAN HAPPEN

There was a race where a boy was complaining to his dad that his brake would not stop him. His dad went over, checked it, and told his wife that there was nothing wrong with the brake, the driver was just too lazy to push hard enough. An examination of the brake found that the brake cable had too much slack in it and when the brake was applied, the plunger traveled just to the pavement, but had no travel left to put pressure on the pavement. Removing the cable slack took care of this.

POSITION THE BRAKE PEDAL FOR THE DRIVER

It is best to start with the brake pedal positioned where the holes in your floorboard are already positioned. You do not want any more holes in your floorboard than needed. If you have a driver that weighs between 50 to 70 lbs., the drilled position for the brake pedal will most likely work. See photos in 4-9 for brake pedal positions while mounted at the same position on the floorboard.

INSTALL BRAKE PEDAL TEMPORARILY

In case you might move the brake pedal, do not mess up the floorboard holes by installing elevator bolts at this time. Instead, use regular ¼" bolts and a large flat washer on the bottom of the floorboard so you leave no marks. Tighten the brake pedal bolts just enough to hold them in place for a few tests.

INSTALL THE BRAKE CABLE

Install the brake cable per the All-American Plans. Tighten the 4 cable clamps and leave 6 inches of extra cable at the end of the brake plunger eyebolt on the Brake/Steering Assembly. Tape the ends of the cables at the ends to protect the driver's legs. The cable should be snug at its full length, but not tight enough to pull down on the brake plunger. See photo 4-8 for brake cable installation with little slack in the cable.

Photo 4-8

TEST DRIVER'S POSITION FOR BRAKING

As noted previously, communication with the driver can be difficult because of the difference in word definition. What is tight to some is not tight to others. A new driver will not know what distance from the brake is best. A new driver will not know what a good position for the pedal is. Take the time to experiment with different positions before you decide on one based on the driver getting in and saying it is OK.

The best position for the brake pedal is when the driver has room between his foot and the brake pedal. During their trip down the hill and they can comfortably reach the brake pedal and put on the brake when sitting up. The driver should not contact the brake pedal while driving.

1. Install the car body with 6 to 10 screws to test the brakes. <u>Place the driver in the car to test the brakes with the car on the ground.</u>

CONSTRUCTION 4-31

2. The brake pedal can have a small piece of wood (Popsicle sticks) placed under it aft of the hinge to change its position. When you find the best brake pedal position, glue the wood shim or shims in place. Check with the
3. See photo 4-9. *Check to make sure the All-American rules have not changed and you can still adjust the brake pedal for the driver's safety. They have allowed this since I have been in Derby in 1978.*

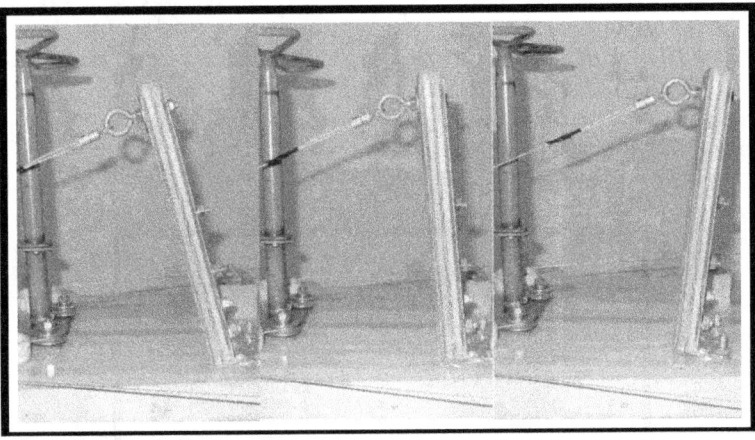

Photo 4-9

4. Once you find the brake pedal position needed for the driver, glue the sticks in place and install the elevator bolts per the plans.
5. Make sure the brake cable is routed correctly.
6. Tighten all 4 cable clamps, allowing very little slack in the cable.
7. The bolts in the brake pad will sink into the bottom of the floorboard changing the tension on the cable. *Allow for this.*

8. Cut extra brake cable and tape the ends of the cable for the safety of the driver. See photo 4-8 and 4-9.

COCKPIT FOAM INSTALLATION

Preparation is the most important part of any kind of bonding. If you are gluing new foam to a new car body, sand the shell where the foam will attach. For previously installed foam, remove the old foam and any loose material as best you can. Use Contact Cement to attach the foam to the car body, it will do the best job. Do not use any of the spray glues to attach the foam to the car body. They do a very poor job.

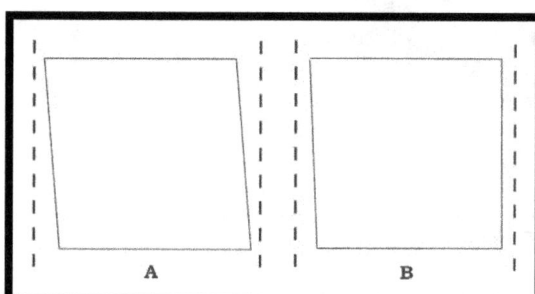

Figure 4-11

In order to get your foam to attach to the cockpit edge and be level with the top of the shell, you may need a slight angle cut on one side of the foam. In Figure 4-11 above you see two foam ends. Figure 4-11 foam end "A" has been cut at an angle on two sides. Foam end "B" has just one side cut at an angle. <u>Examine the foam that came with your kit to find the angle you need to keep the</u>

CONSTRUCTION 4-33

top of the foam level with the top of your car. You will find some variation in the foam you receive.

Often the aft foam is installed at more of an angle down as it goes forward. This is thought to help with the airflow. This has not been proven an advantage or disadvantage. See photo 4-10 for an example of the aft foam slanted down.

Photo 4-10

The foam does not last more than 8 to 12 races before it starts to get loose and torn. You will want to replace it before an important race. Teach the driver to hold the leading edges of the aft foam when getting in and out of the car to reduce wear and tear.

WEIGHT INSTALLATION

If you have not read **Chapter 8, "Weight Management"** and **Chapter 9, "Weight and Balance Calculations,"** it is suggested you read them. The following section will deal with calculating the added weight, and figuring where to best place it. Most of us do not have access to four scales. I have always found it adequate to do all the weight adjustments with just two scales. The process of using only two scales to weigh the car and balance your weight can be found in Chapter 5, "Alignment and Adjustments." All final weight adjustments will also be in Chapter 5.

DETERMINE AMOUNT OF ADDED WEIGHT NEEDED
Weigh the complete assembled car including the wheels and fairings. Below, table lists the max weight for all divisions at this time. Also in the table are examples of the car's weight and the driver's weight. Subtract the car's weight and the driver's weight from the weight of the division to find the amount of weight you are allowed to add.

Table 4-1

Division	Stock	Super Stock	Masters
Car Wt. limit	200	240	255
Subtract Car Wt..	-65	-65	-70
Total	135	175	185
Subtract Driver Wt..	-61	-103	-120
Total Weight you need to add	74	72	65

DETERMINE WHERE TO PLACE YOUR WEIGHT
From the experiments in Chapter 8, "Weight Management," we learned that it is best to have your weight in the center-left and right and forward and aft. However, many race families choose to spread their weight out forward and aft, because they do not have any pitching of their track. By spreading your weight out you

CONSTRUCTION 4-35

will get more low weight. Wherever you want to place your weight, the process is the same.

You have a center, aft, and forward weight placement area. Weight spread out evenly will keep your tail weight about even. That is a good place to start. Now you need to determine the center of gravity of the driver. See Figure 4-12 and perform the following to get an idea of where the driver's center of gravity will be located.

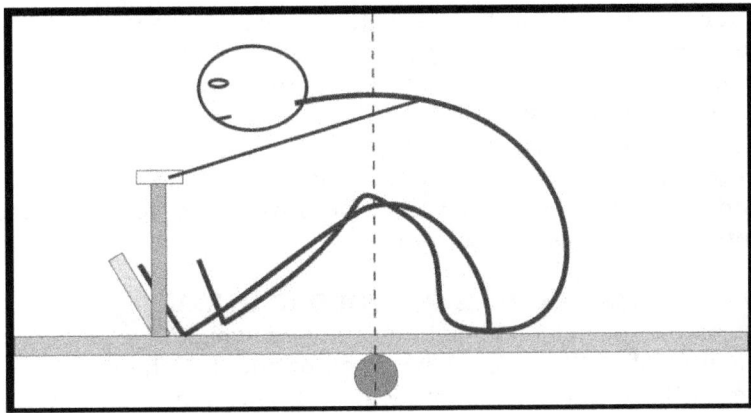

Figure 4-12

1. Use a Soap Box Derby floorboard, or other board that you have handy and balance it on a round broomstick or something similar. See Figure 4-12
2. Position the driver in the driving position as shown in Figure 4-12 lined up with the center of the board and a round broomstick.
3. When the driver is balanced, make a mark on the driver above where the board balances on the stick. See the dotted line in Figure 4-12.
4. Position the driver in their car in the driving position and transfer the mark on the driver to the car. This is where his or her center of gravity is in the car.

Now you know where the driver's center of gravity is located in the car. If it is forward between the axles, you will need a little more weight in the aft to balance out the car. If the driver's center of gravity is more aft, you will have to add a little more to the forward end to balance out your weight.

Add the weight to the car until you reach the total weight of the division. Distribute the weight to keep the car balanced as well as possible without weighing it. After you reach the total weight, determine the tail weight you want to run. Move your weight to get the desired tail weight. Your local Director or fellow competitors will be able to tell you what tail weight is best to run at your track. However, practicing and determining the tail weight yourself is always best. See Chapter 8, "Alignment and Adjustments" if you need help weighing your car and determining your tail weight.

WEIGHT MATERIAL MOST USED IS STEEL.
If you select steel for your added weight, your center weight will be restricted because of the 1.5" high rule for weight between the driver's legs. If you plan to spread the weight out this will not be a problem. Use lead weight for the center weight if you plan to load up the center weight. Check the latest rules to determine what material is allowed for weight. See **Chapter 8, "Alignment & Adjustments"** for further and final weight adjustments.

INSTALL THE SUPER STOCK AFT AXLE AND AXLE MOUNT

The Super Stock rear axle installation and its means of alignment need special attention. This Axle mount can be difficult to adjust. It can also be difficult to maintain the alignment and cross-bind.

CONSTRUCTION 4-37

The following are things to remember about the Super Stock Rear axle mount. This will be expanded on in the following pages.
A. Difficult to adjust alignment and maintain same.
B. Lengthen the Alignment Bolts to full length allowed. This gives the bolts more room to move.
C. Push the steel "L"-angle forward to the limit. This is how you lengthen the Alignment bolts and get good continuity with the axle mount assembly.
D. Do not tighten the bolts too tight and stripe, or break them.
E. Do not attempt to use a shim between the aft mount to adjust cross-bind. The final cross-bind is checked and adjusted with the body attached to the floorboard. If you shim the rear axle, you will have to recheck the rear axle alignment and this is difficult to do with the body on the floorboard.
F. Check the rear axle mount alignment before all race weekends and before any important races.

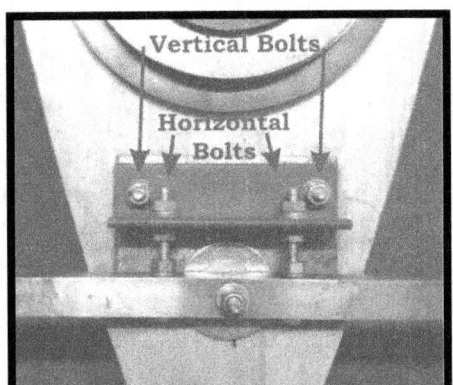

INSTALL THE SUPER STOCK REAR AXLE STABILIZERS BUSHINGS

Install the rear steel bushings in the floorboard as described earlier in this chapter, if not previously completed. Epoxy the bushings in place with the top of the bushing flush with the top of the floorboard. See Page 4-3, 4-13, and 4-14.

ASSEMBLE THE SUPER STOCK AFT AXLE

I will be referring to the bolts in photo 4-12 as either Horizontal bolts, or Vertical bolts.

Install the steel plate and make sure the kingpin bolt and the two **vertical bolts** will align and go into the steel plate. It is all right for them to have a tight fit in the plate, as long as you can get them all three in the steel plate. Next, install the "L" angle and tighten the *Vertical Bolts finger tight.* Install the axle and its washers per plans. *Loosely tighten the kingpin bolt.* Install the two **horizontal bolts** (radius bolts) in the axle and place the nuts and washers per plans. T*ighten the nut against the axle* only at this time. Align (triangulate) the rear axle and tighten the kingpin down at this time to about 100 in lbs. You may loosen the kingpin later when you have the "L" angle secure and are doing the final alignment. The **vertical** bolts remain finger tight. The **horizontal** bolts are only tightened to the axle.

Now we will try to get as much horizontal bolt length as we can. **First, tighten the vertical bolts just to make contact on the "L" angle.**

Photo 4-13

The "L" angle hitting the Vertical bolt holes is what will stop the extension of the Horizontal bolts. See photo 4-13. **Slowly turn the nuts on the Horizontal bolts**

CONSTRUCTION 4-39

against the "L" angle. **Tighten the nuts until the "L" angle can no longer go forward because of hitting the vertical bolts in the "L" angle.**

You might have the "L" angle hit one of the Vertical bolts before hitting the other Vertical bolt. Ideally, we would like to be able to force the "L" angle against both Vertical bolts at the same time. **This is because we want the "L" angle to remain parallel to the Axle.**

Sometimes you can just knock off some steel burs on the "L" angle drilled holes and help the alignment of the "L" angle. Other times you can torque one side of the "L" angle against the Vertical Bolt and that will allow the opposite Vertical Bolt to make contact with the "L" angle. If the Parallel alignment between the "L" angle and the axle is off too much, proceed as follows. See photo 4-13.

Make sure the rear axle is still aligned and the kingpin bolt is tight. Realign as needed. With the steel "L"-angle against the first Vertical bolt, adjust the opposite end of the "L" angle so it is parallel with the axle *and tighten the Vertical Bolts going through the "L" angle.*

<u>With the two nuts on the horizontal bolts, aft of the "L" angle holding the "L" angle forward, install the washers and nuts. Adjust the nuts forward and aft of the "L" angle until the rear axle is aligned, - Triangulated, and the axle and the steel "L"-angle is parallel.</u> You want all nuts and bolts as tight as possible without stripping the bolts and nuts. 100 to 150 lbs. of torque is adequate. You are dealing with non-precision hardware and they can break at an unregulated torque. You might want to practice torquing your nuts and bolts to see just where they will fail. This will give you the knowledge to do a better job of tightening the nuts and bolts to the torque you want. You want the maximum torque allowed without failure.

INSTALL THE BODY

This section will describe the installation of the Stock and Super Stock car body, or sometimes call the car **Shell.** The Stock and Super Stock body offered different installation situations.

The Stock Body has numerous attach screws that contribute to body and floorboard rigidity. The Super Stock Body uses few screws and offers little support for the floorboard.

Photo 4-14

INSTALL THE STOCK CAR BODY

Gently set the Stock car body on the floorboard. When placing the Stock body on the floorboard, be careful going over the steering cables. Some of the car bodies do not come with a drilled hole in the nose of the shell. If this is the case, measure between the first screw holes on each side of the body and drill a hole in the nose at the same height as the others.

The car body must maintain 39.5" dimension as measured in *front of the cockpit, from the bottom of the body on one side, over the top of the body to the bottom of the body on the other side of the body.* This measurement must include part of the side of the floorboard if the body alone does not meet the minimum of 39.5" dimension. In some cases, this measurement will

CONSTRUCTION   4-41

require you to raise the car body above the floorboard bottom on each side of the shell to reach the 39.5" dimension. See the Measurement in photo 4-14.

The All-American Stock inspection sheet says, **"Shell circumference 39.5 inches."** It does not mean **circumference** of the car body and floorboard, it just means the Shell left side, the right side, and the top. The All-American Stock inspection also says, **"Shell Flush with the bottom of the floorboard, but can be up to ½" high in the back.** Some Stock cars have the Shell flush with the floorboard at the front and bring it up gradually if needed at the circumference measurement location This can make the aft of the shell above the bottom of the floorboard ½". See the Stock Body in Figure 4-13. However, even if you need to elevate the body at the measurement point, you can make an effort to keep the body level from there back.

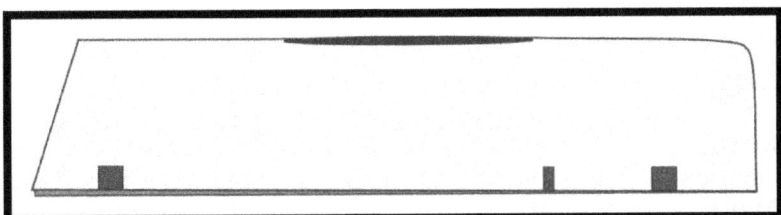

Figure 4-13

INSTALL STOCK CAR BODY SCREWS

When installing the Stock Body start at the front and work your way back alternating side to side. Keep the car body pulled back slightly to keep the sides tight so they keep flat against the floorboard. If you are doing this by yourself, make two wedges to place between the aft axle and the body on each side to keep the body pulled back.

As you install the screws, you can pull up or push down on the body to help keep it positioned in relationship with the bottom of the floorboard. Also, by position the saw horses, you allow the weight in the car let the floorboard sag or be supported to assist in positioning the floorboard with the car body.

Positioning the car on saw horses spread apart will make the center of the floorboard flex down and affect the installation of the car body. Some racers purposely stress their floorboard and car body. It is believed that this prevents the loss of energy.

When you are finished screwing the body to the floorboard, go over the screws again with a screwdriver and make sure that all the screws are tight. Between races, it is a good idea to check all your body screws for tightness.

INSTALL THE SUPER STOCK CAR BODY

The Super Stock body has few screws and adds little in the way of support to the floorboard. Often it comes with extra pieces on the lower body edges from the mold. Make sure these are removed and sanded smooth.

Lower the Shell on the floorboard <u>making sure you get the steering cables in the body slots.</u> Align the nose of the body with the front of the floorboard left and right. Put in the forward screw with the bottom of the body <u>even with the bottom of the floorboard.</u>

With the Super Stock, you can experiment with pushing it around and making it fit better to your findings. Recently a local family started pushing the shell forward after installing the nose screw, or the first two screws. The advantage is to move the nose forward and flare out the side of the body forward of the forward axles. As you can see, both of these things are advantages. With the nose pushed forward you get the car pushed further up the hill giving you more energy to use, and with the sides of the car forward of the axle you get more coverage of your front axle with the body.

After you install the screws aft of the front axle, you will want to keep some aft tension on the body to keep the body pulled against the floorboard as you progress aft installing the screws. If you are doing this by yourself, make two wedges to place between the aft axle and the body on each side. Continue installing the screws along the body, while keeping the body even with the bottom of the floorboard.

> Recently a friend said he found his Super Stock ran better with his body screws a little loose! Who knew? That would be something to test.

CAR BODY PAINT

The Stock shell is not allowed to be painted. The Super Stock and Masters can be painted on the exterior. Super Stock Shells often do not take paint well and the paint may peel. Do a search on the web for the best instructions for painting the Super Stock Shell. Consider not painting the Super Stock and save yourself a lot of problems.

CONSTRUCTION CONCLUSION

It is very important to start the construction with a focus of accuracy. The accuracy you use during construction will make your alignment and cross-bind adjustments easier.

The All-American Soap Box Derby rules change often. That means that some of the things in this book and this chapter can be outdated before you purchase this book. Stay up to date on what you can and cannot do when building your car.

If you can afford to purchase the fancy tools and trailers to race Soap Box Derby, do it. However, it is not necessary to spend that extra money to win.

To purchase Soap Box Derby tools go to this internet address. http://www.zero-error.com Derek Fitzgerald manufactures these Derby tools and he is a Soap Box Derby competitor himself.

GOOD LUCK WITH YOUR CONSTRUCTION

CHAPTER FIVE

ALIGNMENT & ADJUSTMENTS

INTRODUCTION

In this chapter, we will cover Final Weight Adjustments, Cross-Bind Adjustments, Steering Alignment, and Axle Spindle Alignment.

In Chapter 4, "Construction," we laid the foundation for most of our Alignment. Now we will make the final Adjustments to align the car to perform its best.

WINNING INGREDIENTS FOR KIT CARS

> This Chapter is for Stock, Super Stock, Masters, and Ultimate Speed Division. They all require the same alignment. The drawings and nomenclature are Stock and Super Stock car, but the process is the same for all Divisions.

There are several ways to perform the Alignments. Different tool designs can be used. This Chapter will show you how to perform the Alignment and Adjustments with the least amount of money. In this Chapter, you will learn how to make the Alignment and Adjustments as accurate as or more accurate than other methods. You can pay more for your tools than the ones used in this chapter, but you will not make you more accurate with expensive tools.

TOOLS REQUIRED

If you can afford the more expensive tools, purchase them and use this chapter to guide you in your alignment. Some of the tools can be built yourself, or with a little help from your local welder. See Chapter 6, "Tools" for more information. Below is a list of tools and items needed for this chapter.

TOOLS AND OTHER ITEMS NEEDED
1. Spindle Alignment tool See Chapter 6, "Tools" to build your own Spindle Alignment Tool
2. Torque Wrench, 0 to 200 Inch lbs.
3. 2 each Bathroom scales or purchase two calibrated scales
4. 2 Axel Spindle Stands, See Chapter 6, "Tools" to make your stands

ALIGNMENT AND ADJUSTMENTS

5. Tape Measure
6. Feeler Gauge
7. 1X8 level board 3 Feet Long, we will discuss how to make this level board in the following pages
8. Thin Boards for Shims, 1/8th to ¼"
9. Newspaper for final Shims
10. Wrenches as needed for weight bolts and kingpin bolts
11. Level 36" or longer
12. Lumber for level board

PREPARE THE CAR

The car should have all construction finished and ready to race. Weight should be installed with the car balanced close to where you want to race. The fairings do not have to be on, except when weighing for total weight, and at that time they can just be put loose in the car. When checking the car for cross-bind weight, or lateral weight, the fairings can be left off. The wheels should be in the same condition and circumference. The weight of the wheels should be about the same. Place the wheels on the spindle with enough washers to push the wheel out against the pin. With the wheels forced to the outside of the spindles, you will get the most accurate lateral weight adjustment and accurate cross-bind weight adjustment.

PREPARE YOUR SCALES

Two calibrated scales or possibly four calibrated scales with a control panel displaying the readings would be great. However, in this chapter, we will use only two scales. Later we will compare the benefits of using 2 scales, or 4 scales. Whatever your number of scales, let us check them for accuracy. Check the calibration by placing about 35 lbs. on one scale and then placing the same 35 lbs. on the other scale. Calibrate the two scales to read the same when the same 35 lbs. is placed on them. If you have 4 scales, you can check them the same way.

To perform the weight checks we will use two scales at one end of the car and a **level board 36" long** or longer at the other end. The level board will be built to the approximate height of the scales and its board to keep the car level longitudinally. See **"Make your level board"** on the next pages.

Place a ¾" X 2" board on the top of your scales as seen in photo 5-1. Also, glue two wheel stops on each board for safety. This board will spread the weight evenly on the scales and give you a good reading. In photo 5-1, you can see that from the floor to the top of the board it is 2.75". This height will be used when building the **level board**, to hold the car longitudinally level.

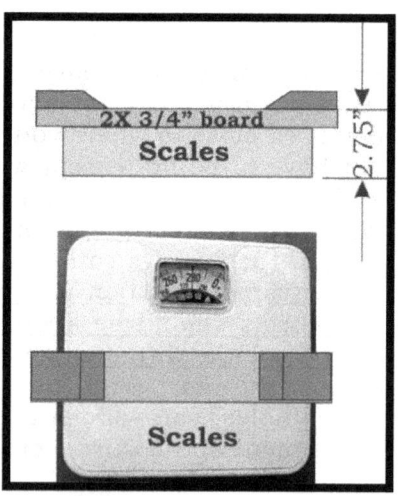

Photo 5-1

ALIGNMENT AND ADJUSTMENTS 5-5

MAKE YOUR LEVEL BOARD

The level board will follow the following rules:

1. Read all instructions before you start to build the level board. See photo 5-2 for an example of a level board.
2. The board will be at least 36" long to accommodate the length of the axles.
3. It should be made with a 1" X 8" or 2" X 8" board. Do not use a 1 or 2 X 6" because 6" is too narrow for the wheel and wheel stops combined.
4. The board should be built to the height of the scales + its wheel board on top. See photo 5-1 for an example of the height of the scales and their board.
5. If you are going to be weighing in a garage where the <u>floor is slanted as it exits the garage</u>, you will have to make allowances for this. See photo 5-3 for leveling longitudinally between the level board and scales.
6. <u>The level board will have two each 1" or 2" wide boards for the wheels to rest on with wheel stops on the ends of each wheel board.</u> *Photo 5-4 shows a side view of the level board and Wheel rests and stops.*
7. **See Figure 5-2 on page 5-9** for an example of how your scales and level board should be laid out. <u>The distance between the scales and the level board is not per scale to reduce its photo size on the page. Note the wheelbase distance written in Figure 5-2 as 61" for Stock.</u>

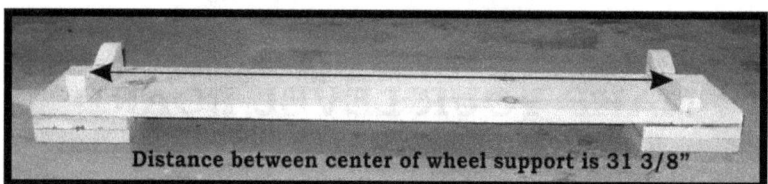

PHOTO 5-2

The level board shown in photo 5-2 is made of 1" X 8" pine board. There are 1"X 8" boards glued on the bottom to elevate the level board to the correct height. The two-wheel supports on top of the longboard are calculated in the height needed for the level board.

When the floor is not level, you will need to calculate the height required for the level board as follows. Place the scales where they will be on the garage floor on the higher side of the garage slope. **See photo 5-3** to check the level between the scales and the level board.

PHOTO 5-3

As seen in photo 5-3, place the level board at the low side of the floor slope the distance from the scales that equals the racecar's wheelbase distance (*61 inches for a Stock car.*) Place a straight board over the scales long enough to reach the level board and place a level on that board. Add shims on top of the level board under the long straight board until the level reads level. At the level board, measure from the floor to the bottom of the long

ALIGNMENT AND ADJUSTMENTS 5-7

board and shims to determine the height required for your level board.

In photo, 5-2 and 5-4 there are two boards on top of the level board that the car wheels will rest on. Their height will be included in the total height needed for the level board. Install these 1" to 2" wide wheel boards 31 and 3/8" apart on center. Glue them in place. Get a wheel to set on the center of this board and glue wheel stops in front and back of the wheels. See photo 5-4 for an example of how the level board should look with the wheel board and wheel blocks installed.

PHOTO 5-4

CHECK THE CAR TOTAL WEIGHT

PREPARE TO CHECK TOTAL WEIGHT
1. Adjust scales as needed. See **PREPARE YOUR SCALES** on **page 5-3**

2. Place the scales and level board so that the car will be level when placed on them. See photo 5-3 to check the level between the scales and the level board. The level board and the scales should be level between them by at least 1/16" to get an accurate total weight. (This will be the maximum difference in height between the front axle and the aft axle.)

3. Adjust the level of the scales and the level board **laterally**. See photo 5-5 for the Lateral level check of the scales. See the level board being leveled in Figure 5-2. Use small pieces of plywood for major adjustments, and use newspaper for fine adjustments of the level board and scales. See the newspaper under the right side scales in photo 5-5.

4. See Figure 5-2 for an example of how your scales and level board should be laid out. The distance between the level board and the scales for the Stock car is about 61". Figure 5-2 is not to scale between the Level board and scales.

WEIGHT AND BALANCE FORM

On the following pages are two forms to help you keep track of your weight and balance calculations. The forms are the same except that form labeled **Form 5-1** already has Figures and calculations entered so you can see how it works. See page 5-12 for a blank **Form 5-2** that you can copy and use for your car calculations. Follow this form to bring your car up to its proper total weight and proper tail weight.

Photo 5-5

ALIGNMENT AND ADJUSTMENTS 5-9

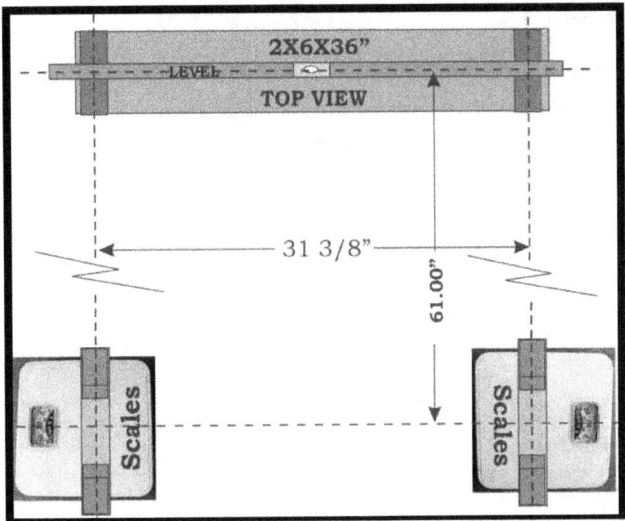

Figure 5-2

THE FORM HAS FIVE SECTIONS AND HERE IS HOW IT WORKS:

1. **(1) RECORD DESIRED TOTAL WEIGHT AND TAIL WEIGHT** in the first section. You start by entering the desired total weight of your division. The example has a Stock total of 200 lbs.
2. Next, you figure out what tail weight you want to run and record that. The example uses 13 lbs. tail weight for here at Indianapolis, although some use 15#.
3. Then you calculate what forward axle and aft axle weight would equal 13 lbs. tail. I calculated a forward axle weight of 93.5 lbs. and a rear axle weight of 106.5; the difference is 13 lbs. tail heavy. See form entries.
4. The next section is: **(2) BEGINNING WEIGHT READINGS WITH DRIVER.** The following tells you how to check the total weight of the car and driver. Record your weight on the blank form.

WEIGHT AND BALANCE ADJUSTMENTS

(1)	RECORD DESIRED WEIGHT AND TAIL WEIGHT			=	Total Wt..
Desired Total Wt..	=	200	Desired Front Axle Wt.	=	93.5
			Desired Aft Axle Wt.	=	106.5
			Desired Tail Weight =		13#
(2)		BEGINNING WEIGHT READINGS WITH DRIVER			
POSITIONS	Left Wheel Wt.	+	Right Wheel Wt.	=	Total Wt.
Forward Axle	=46.75	+	46.75	=	95
Aft Axle	=53.25	+	53.25	=	100
Total Car and Driver Wt.	-----------------		---------------------	=	195
(3)		BEGINNING WEIGHT WITHOUT DRIVER			
	Left Wheel Wt.		Right Wheel Wt.		Total Wt.
Forward Axle	31.75	+	31.75	=	63.5
Aft Axle	30.00	+	30.00	=	60
Total Wt. NO Driver	-----------------		-----------------		123.5
(4)		ADJUSTMENTS TO REACH DESIRED AXLE WEIGHT AND TAIL WT..			
Position	Add or Subtract		Adjustment Total		Total Wt.
Forward Axle	Subtract		1.5	=	93.5
Aft Axle	Add		6.5	=	106.5
Total Wt.	-----------------		-----------------	=	200
(5)		FINAL WEIGHT WITHOUT DRIVER AFTER ADJUSTMENTS			
	Left Wheel Wt.		Right Wheel Wt.		Total Wt.
Forward Axle	31	+	31	=	62.00
Aft Axle	33.25	+	33.25	=	66.5
Total Wt. NO Driver					128.5

Form 5-1

CHECK TOTAL WEIGHT OF CAR AND DRIVER

- Place the rear of the car on the level board and the front on the scales. Have the driver get in the car in driving position and <u>record the weight of the front two wheels.</u>

ALIGNMENT AND ADJUSTMENTS 5-11

- Turn the car around so you have the rear of the car on the scales and the front of the car on the level board. Have the driver get in the car in driving position and record the weight of the aft two wheels.

5. Record these wheel weights on the **(2) BEGINNING WEIGHT READINGS WITH DRIVER,** section and calculate your totals. Your cross-bind has not been adjusted yet, so your left and right wheels will not read the same as in the examples above. Your total weight and tail weight should be complete before you adjust your cross-bind.
6. Weigh just the car for total weight and record the wheel weight in **(3) BEGINNING WEIGHT WITHOUT DRIVER.** Calculate the totals.
7. The next step in the form is to adjust your weight as needed to reach the desired total weight and desired tail weight. You will do this in the forms section: **(4) ADJUSTMENTS TO REACH DESIRED AXLE WEIGHT AND TAIL WEIGHT.**
8. Now you must do some calculations as shown in the example, Form 5-1.
   a) To determine the adjustments needed look at the totals in section **(1)** where you entered the **desired weight and desired tail weight readings**. Compare those readings to the **(2) BEGINNING WEIGHT READINGS WITH DRIVER.**
   b) In the example, the desired front axle weight is 93.5 lbs. However, the front axle weight with the driver is 95 lbs. So that means to get what you desire, you **subtract** from your reading of 95 lbs. to get your desired reading of 93.5 lbs. The difference is 1.5 lbs. This is Recorded in **(4) ADJUSTMENTS TO REACH DESIRED AXLE WEIGHT AND TAIL WT.** Calculate your forward axle adjustments and enter them in section (4) of the form.

c) **Now, Figure out what you need to do to get your desired aft axle weight.** If your **desired** weight is more you will <u>subtract</u>. If the **desired** weight is less, then you will <u>add</u>. Record your calculations on your form.

WEIGHT AND BALANCE ADJUSTMENTS

(1)	RECORD DESIRED WEIGHT AND TAIL WEIGHT			=	*Total Wt.*
Desired Total Wt..	=		Desired Front Axle Wt.	=	
			Desired Aft Axle Wt.	=	
			Desired Tail Weight =		
(2)	**BEGINNING WEIGHT READINGS WITH DRIVER**				
POSITIONS	*Left Wheel Wt.*	+	*Right Wheel Wt.*	=	*Total Wt.*
Forward Axle	=	+		=	
Aft Axle	=	+		=	
Total Car and Driver Wt.	-----------------		---------------------	=	
(3)	**BEGINNING WEIGHT WITHOUT DRIVER**				
	Left Wheel Wt.		*Right Wheel Wt.*		*Total Wt.*
Forward Axle		+		=	
Aft Axle		+		=	
Total Wt. NO Driver	-----------------		-----------------		
(4)	**ADJUSTMENTS TO REACH DESIRED AXLE WEIGHT AND TAIL WT..**				
Position	*Add or Subtract*		*Adjustment Total*		*Total Wt.*
Forward Axle	Subtract			=	
Aft Axle	Add			=	
Total Wt.	-----------------		-----------------	=	
(5)	**FINAL WEIGHT WITHOUT DRIVER AFTER ADJUSTMENTS**				
	Left Wheel Wt.		*Right Wheel Wt.*		*Total Wt.*
Forward Axle		+		=	
Aft Axle		+		=	
Total Wt. NO Driver					

Form 5-2

ALIGNMENT AND ADJUSTMENTS   5-13

d) In the example for the aft axle weight, we desired 106.5 lbs. When we weighed the car and driver, we got 100 lbs. To get the weight that was desired in the example (106.5 lbs.) you must add 6.5 lbs.

e) Now Figure out whether you need to add or subtract for your aft axle weight and record it in your blank form in section (4).

9. Now you can physically add or subtract the weight to your car that you recorded in section: **(4) ADJUSTMENTS TO REACH DESIRED AXLE WEIGHT AND TAIL WEIGHT.**

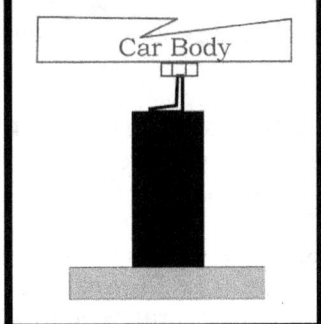

Figure 5-1

10. Reweigh your car with the driver and without the driver to make sure you have the desired total weight and desired tail weight. Record the **FINAL WEIGHT WITHOUT DRIVER AFTER ADJUSTMENTS.**

11. By recording the empty weight numbers, you can check the Total weight and tail weight in the future without the driver. Just use the Figures you recorded when you weighed the car without the driver in **Section (5) of your form.**

CHECK LATERAL WEIGHT

This check is to see if your car is balanced laterally. Your car can weigh more on one side than the other. This can more often occur when using lead for added weight. It is difficult to get the lead to have its weight distributed evenly when you pour it into molds, even when you think the mold is level. <u>This check-in was made without the</u>

5-14 WINNING INGREDIENTS FOR KIT CARS

driver. However, after the car is balanced laterally you can place the driver in the car and perform the check again. The driver's slightest move will change the lateral balance. **When the car is at the starting gate, the lateral balance should be perfect. This helps keep the same weight on each wheel when starting. This in combination with no cross-bind gives you an advantage at the start.**

ITEMS NEEDED TO CHECK LATERAL WEIGHT
1. You will need the two scales with the boards across them as in **photo 5-1.**
2. Check scales for calibration.
3. You will need something to balance the kingpin bolt-on. In **Figure 5-1,** is an axle stand that works great for Lateral Weight Check. You can make the Spindle stand in Chapter 6, "Tools."
4. The level board will not be used.
5. Install the wheels-washers to force all the wheels out. You can also force all the wheels in and achieve the same.
6. Level the two scales as shown in photo 5-5. Use a newspaper for minor adjustments.
7. Your axle kingpins should be torqued to 200-inch lbs.

Photo 5-5

ALIGNMENT AND ADJUSTMENTS 5-15

PLACE THE CAR ON THE SCALES

Place the aft wheels on the scales and the front kingpin bolt head on the spindle stand. See Figure 5-1. Record the left and right scales. Adjust the weight in your car until the scales are within .25 lbs. If you are using lead, you can shift the weight to one side or just turn the weight over sometimes. You might have to shave some of the lead off on one side.

CHECK LATERAL WEIGHT WITH DRIVER IN CAR

Checking the lateral weight with the driver is a little difficult because of the car wanting to roll off the scales and the precarious position of the kingpin. Place the driver in the car and have the driver get into the driving position. Place the rear of the car and driver on the scales. While someone holds the car on the scales, lift the front of the car, and place the front kingpin as shown in Figure 5-1, page.

With the driver in the car, you might find an unlevel lateral weight. Work with the driver to get in a position that balances the lateral weight. Sometimes this unbalanced lateral weight can make the car want to pull in a left or right direction as the car comes off the ramp. You have to reach a point where the driver is comfortable, but balanced. An unbalanced driver also contributes to more weight on the wheels on one side of the car. This can slow your car starting.

CROSS-BIND ADJUSTMENT

WHAT IS CROSS-BIND?

Cross-Bind in Soap Box Derby is when your **axles and floorboard are not parallel with one another**. It is when your car is on a flat and level spot, and two of your diagonal wheels are carrying more of the load than the other two diagonal wheels. You can see cross-bind when you lower one end of your car down to a level pavement and notice one wheel touches the pavement before the other. Along with wanting the axles to be parallel with one another, you want your floorboard to be parallel with the axles also. If you did not get everything parallel during construction, you will be able to correct it with a shim.

WHY "O" CROSS-BIND IS SO IMPORTANT

When your car is setting on the ramp ready to race all four wheels should be carrying the same load. **With all wheels carrying the same load, you have the greatest possibility of getting off the ramp first**. If you are running tail weight your two front wheels have the same load, and the aft two wheel have the same load. In Soap Box Derby, the driver who gets off the ramp first is most likely to be the winner. That is why the elimination of cross-bind is very important. "O" cross-bind is also important as you travel down the track, but not as important as when you are on the ramp.

TOOLS USED TO MEASURE CROSS-BIND AND ELIMINATE IT.

To fix a problem you need to be able to measure the problem. Throughout the years, Derby people have used numerous ways to measure cross-bind. The following are a few of the ways I have seen.

Photo 5-6

ALIGNMENT AND ADJUSTMENTS

1. **Water tube system** When 4 water tubes plumbed together are level with the ends of the axle square stock, you have "0" cross-bind. This does not work very well, because the liquid wants to wick in the tubing. This system is not accurate enough for Soap Box Derby cross-bind.
2. **Use a Transit** The car is held level; the axle ends are viewed through the transit and adjusted until the axles are level with each other and the floorboard. I have used this and it is quite accurate, but who has a Transit? See photo 5-6.
3. **Use a level spot in your garage** Use the level spot you have found on your basement or garage floor, with one end of the car on the floor, lower the other end of the car until the wheels touch the ground. Adjust until both wheels reach the floor at the same time. Many people use this system. The accuracy is questionable.
4. **Build a level table**. A level table is an excellent idea. Once you have a level table you can use 4 scales like in 7 below, or a rail system like in 6 below. This works for many Derby people. As I say below in 6 and 7, these systems win races. A permanent-level table takes up some room, you might need for something else.
5. **String or thread alignment** *Use an Aluminum Fixture* that you attach to your axle that holds a string below the car body level. In photo, 5-7 is the Aluminum Fixture that attaches to each end of the axles with a thumbscrew. Two strings are used, one from the left front to right rear axle Aluminum Fixtures, and one from the right front to the left rear Aluminum Fixtures. When the two strings contact each other you have "0" cross-bind. This does not appear like a very accurate system; however, it is a quick way to do a cross-bind check when you are away from home.

5-18   **WINNING INGREDIENTS FOR KIT CARS**

Photo 5-7

6. **Bed Rails used to check cross-bind**   Bed Rails are leveled and the car is placed on the rails near the ends of the <u>axle square stock.</u> Rest one end of the car on the bed rails and lower the other end slowly to see if the axle square stock ends touch at the same time. Adjust until both ends of the axle touch at the same time. This system is very popular, and the results are their kids are winning consistently in the All-American and National Derby Rally.
7. **Four scales are used to weigh each wheel at the same time.** The **scales are wired to a control panel** to read out the 4 scales and calculate totals. (This is like the scale system you will find at most Rally Races) Many times the **scales are placed on a large steel or aluminum frame as in photo 5-8. The frame holds the scales and can be leveled with a crank on each corner. This is the Cadillac system and works very well**. You can use it for **Lateral weight check, Total Weight, Tail Weight, and Cross-Bind.** It costs

ALIGNMENT AND ADJUSTMENTS 5-19

$1500 to $2000 for the scales system. You will have to build the structure that holds and levels the scales. I know of no one who builds this for sale. It also takes up a lot of room when not in use. Photo 5-8 below is a Level Table with the scales and adjustments to use anywhere. It was built by Don Sheets of Indianapolis.

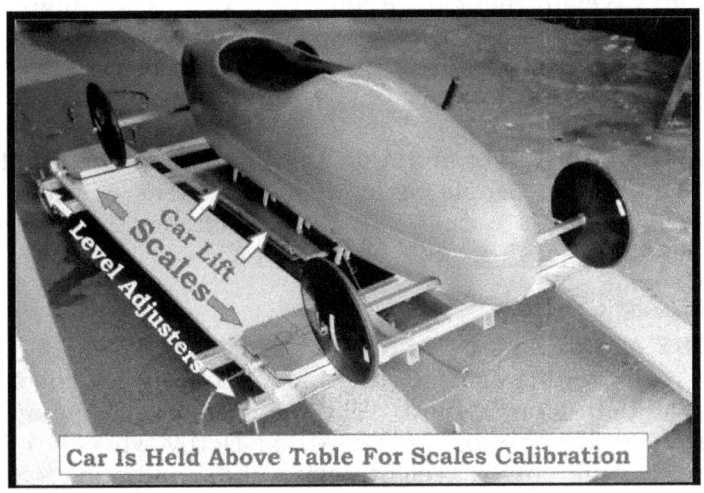

Photo 5-8

8. Last is using a level board and two scales. This system is described in this chapter. This system is low in cost. The accuracy is as high as any scales system, and the space required to store the scales and level board is minimal. This system can be used to check your Lateral weight, Total weight, and Cross-bind.

CROSS-BIND MEASURING TOOLS CONCLUSION

It is interesting to see what Soap Box Derby families come up with to measure their cross-bind, Check Lateral weight, Weigh the car, Align the axles, and Align the Spindles. Families that purchase this book are more likely to have all the latest tools money can buy.

The Total Weight and Alignment Fixture is the Cadillac of tools. Most people build their own. The 4 electronic scales can cost over $2000.00. Look on the internet under <u>racing scales</u>. See photo 5-8.

MOST ACCURATE CROSS-BIND TOOL SYSTEM
I think using scales is the most accurate for checking and adjusting cross-bind. The weakest part of the scales system is the use of the Soap Box Derby wheels. They can be different in weight, size, and condition. *Some Soap Box Derby families use 4 uniform wheel stands to support the car when checked for weight or cross-bind.*

The Bed Rail system is the second best way to check your cross-bind. It <u>cannot help you with any weight check</u>, but for checking cross-bind, it does the job very well.

ALIGNMENT AND ADJUSTMENTS 5-21

Building a level table is a good way to help with checking your weight and cross-bind. However, it takes up space that you might need.

PREPARE FOR CROSS-BIND ADJUSTMENT

Before you perform your cross-bind adjustment you must have the following completed:

- Your car is built completely. This includes the body installation.

- Install the wheels of similar weight, and use washers to force all the wheels either all the way in or all the way out on the spindle. You can use equal weighted axle stands in place of wheels, if you have them.

- The car added weight is installed and has had **Lateral Weight Checked as per page 5-13**. In addition, the total weight check must be complete, see **Check Your Car Total Weight on page 5-7**.

- Decide whether your front axle or your aft axle will be used to place the shim, <u>if needed</u>. I suggest the rear axle on the **Stock car**, because it is the easiest to reach. The front axle on the **Super Stock** is best to shim, because the aft axle is difficult to align. In the masters, it is best to shim the aft axle.

WINNING INGREDIENTS FOR KIT CARS

- Your axle mount washers should be marked for minor adjustment as needed. See Chapter 4, "Construction," page 4-9 for more information about marking your axle washers for adjustment.

- **Your kingpin bolts should be torqued to at least 200 inch-lbs. when checking cross-bind or lateral weight.** This is very important. You need to make sure your axles, washers, and floorboard are all tight against one another.

> A Derby race family was having trouble maintaining their cross-bind adjustment. The father said he would adjust it to "0" cross-bind only to have it change if he took the front axle and moved it up and down after adjustment. Come to find out he had his front axle only torqued to 100-inch lbs.
>
> For cross-bind adjustment, you must have your kingpin bolts tightened to around 200-inch lbs. With your cross-bind adjustment complete, you can torque your kingpin bolts to whatever you want for a specific racetrack.

Different racetracks need different kingpin torques to be competitive, because of track conditions. Your car will often run better with a loose front kingpin set up for rough tracks. Your car will also run better with a loose front kingpin setup if the starting ramp has cross-bind.

ALIGNMENT AND ADJUSTMENTS

CROSS-BIND ADJUSTMENT BY SCALES USING TWO SCALES AND A LEVEL BOARD

ALL DIVISIONS CROSS-BIND MEASUREMENT AND ADJUSTMENT

The Super Stock is the same except you place the front axle on the scales.

1. Level the <u>level board</u> laterally.

2. Scales are calibrated and leveled laterally.

3. The scales and level board should be perfectly leveled longitudinally to each other for the cross-bind check.

4. No matter what division racer, place the end of the car on the scales that you are going to shim.

    a) Place the end of the car on the level board that will not be adjusted and place the other end on the scales
    b) Record the right and left axle weight.
    c) The highest reading wheel is low and must be raised up with a shim (or minor adjustment of turning washer.)
    d) To install a shim, you may have to remove the weights in the front or aft of the car for access.
    e) With help, loosen *the kingpin* about a turn or two. The car floorboard will pull down and away from the axle.
    f) Place the shim between the two largest washers, on the side of the kingpin nearest the highest weight-reading wheel. See photo 5-9.
    g) Tighten the kingpin.

h) Reinstall the weight removed for access and place the axle wheels back on the scales.
i) Continue adjusting and checking until you read less than .5 lbs. difference between the left and right rear wheel. You can most likely get it on "0" difference.

You can often adjust the cross-bind a small amount by placing the shim not to the side of the kingpin, but more toward the back or forward side of the kingpin. In photo 5-9, the Stock car aft axle has a shim under the left side to reduce the pressure down from the left aft wheel reading high weight. With the shim next to the left side of the kingpin, the down pressure was reduced too much. By moving the shim slightly away from the kingpin and moving it around toward the forward side of the axle mount, the lift on the left wheel is reduced enough to equal the same on the right rear wheels. If you move the feeler gauge closer or further away from the kingpin, you can also affect the amount of lift it produces.

Photo 5-9

You can also turn your washer in conjunction with installing a shim to reach the correct amount of lift and reach "0" cross-bind.

ALIGNMENT AND ADJUSTMENTS   5-25

STEERING

Bad steering or brakes can cause you many problems. I have seen cars crash on their first trip down the hill due to steering or brake problems. Although the driver rarely gets hurt physically, his or her concentration can be affected. The driver has to have confidence in the steering and brakes.

> A new little girl had her brake pedal too far from her. She knew it was hard to reach when it was time to stop, so she planned how she would compensate for that. To compensate she started getting into position to stop before she was at the finish line. Not until a picture was taken several races later, that it was known she had been raising up before she got to the finish line to get ready to apply the brakes. No wonder she was having problems winning a race.

STEERING AND BRAKE SAFETY

- ☺ Double lock cables or double wrap as indicated in the Soap Box Derby rules.
- ☺ Tape the ends of your cables to prevent injury.
- ☺ Check your brake pad wear often.
- ☺ Check out the brake and steering with the driver on a small grade before going to the track.
- ☺ The steering wheel should be straight when the wheels are straight.
- ☺ <u>When the steering wheel is turned left, the axle should pull back on the left side of the axle.</u>
- ☺ The brake pad should extend farther than just to the pavement when applied.

FINAL STEERING ADJUSTMENT

The final steering adjustment will include the following:
1. Make sure the Steering cable is tight. This includes a way to measure the tightness. A tight steering cable is best for winning races.
2. Make sure the driver feels the steering is straight.
3. There must be a way for the car handler to determine that the steering is straight when the car is in the starting gate.

ADJUST STEERING CABLE

A. In Chapter 4, "Construction" page 4-25 through page 4-27, you installed your steering cable and put a load on it equal to about .003" Toe-Out. Check that reading now and see if the cable has stretched. Keep in mind, as you adjust the cables, to keep the reading between .003" to .005". This will keep a positive tension on your steering and you can check it with your Spindle alignment tool. <u>This is how you adjust and check the tightness of your steering cable.</u>

B. When checking the Toe-In/Toe-Out, the left and right spindle reading **will not always read the same**. This is normal. You can use whichever reading you wish to adjust the steering tightness, it will be within .002."

Photo 5-10

ALIGNMENT AND ADJUSTMENTS 5-27

C. For the eyebolts, you will need a 3/8" wrench and a tape measure. If you are going to need to adjust the plastic tube steering adjusters, you will need an 11/32" wrench also.

Photo 5-11

D. The car should be on the floor with the driver in the driving position holding the steering wheel in what he or she feels is straight. (You can use the tool on page 6-28 to hold the steering shaft) It is still best to have the driver in the car to do a final steering cable adjustment.

E. Measure from the aft axle square stock ends, to the forward axle square stock ends while adjusting the eyebolts.

F. Adjust the eyebolts until the left and right sides measure the same. If you do not have enough, or have too much travel on the eyebolts, adjust the plastic tube steering cable adjusters.

G. When the Steering is adjusted straight, secure it in that position and recheck the cable tightness with the alignment tool. The spindle should be pulled back .003" to .005".

STEERING STRAIGHT.

➢ The steering is adjusted straight and the driver feels it is straight.

➢ In photo 5-10 a squared-off piece of wood has been used to draw the vertical line on the Stock car body and a horizontal line on the axle.

➢ By viewing down the car body's vertical line, you can see where it visually intersects with the horizontal line. See photo 5-11. **The car handler needs to make sure the steering is straight in the starting gate before each race**.

➢ The lines on the side of the car and axle need not be that long. This was done to get a good picture for the book.

➢ After you mark lines on the body and axle for straight steering, *let the driver* feel what straight feels like when the lines are lined up.

> **Before each race weekend check your steering cable tension, align the steering with the marks on the body and axle, and make sure the steering wheel is straight for the driver. It will take a few races before the steering cable stops stretching.**

ALIGNMENT AND ADJUSTMENTS

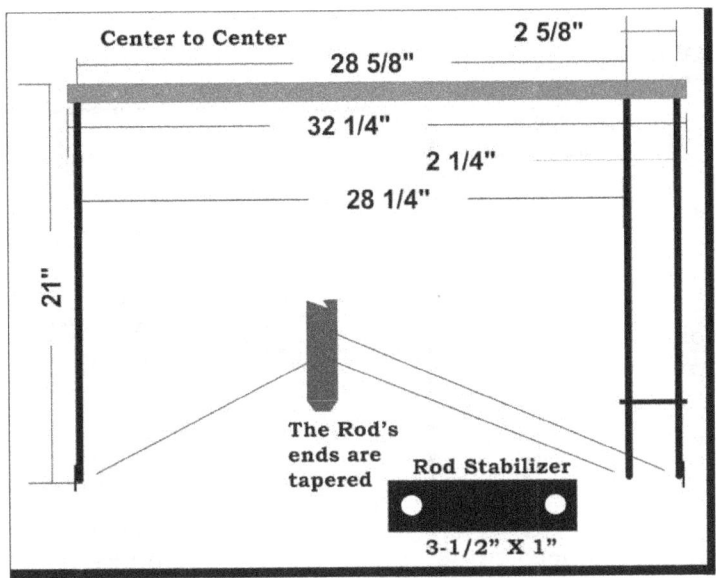

Figure 5-3

AXLE SPINDLE ALIGNMENT

The spindles on the axles are aligned to keep your wheels parallel to the longitudinal centerline of your car when going straight. Spindle alignment is desirable in all divisions. This reduces wheel-to-bearing, wheel-to-track and wheel-to-spindle friction.

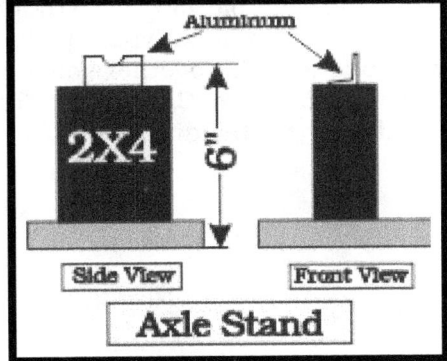

Figure 5-4

TOOLS

To align the spindles, you need an axle alignment tool like the one in Figure 5-3. There are several types of alignment tools. The one shown here is easy to make and use. See Chapter 6 "Tools" for instructions how to build the alignment tool.

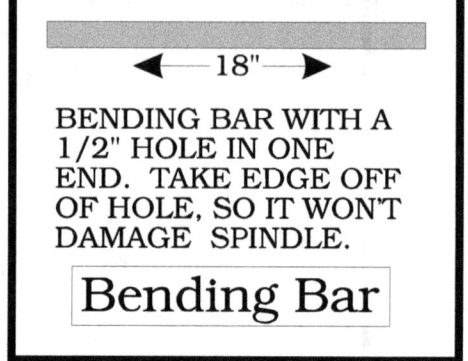

Figure 5-5

You also need two stands to set your spindles on while checking alignment. Figure 5-4 shows an axle stand made out of wood with an aluminum "L" bracket on top. See Chapter 6 "Tools," page 6-14 to 4-16 for instructions to make these Axle Stands.

You will also need a spindle-bending tool. Some use something simple like the straight bending bar in Figure 5-5. I recommend you spend a little money and get someone to weld together some bending tools as shown in Figure 5-6. See Chapter 6 "Tools" for instructions for building these bending tools.

ALIGNMENT AND ADJUSTMENTS 5-31

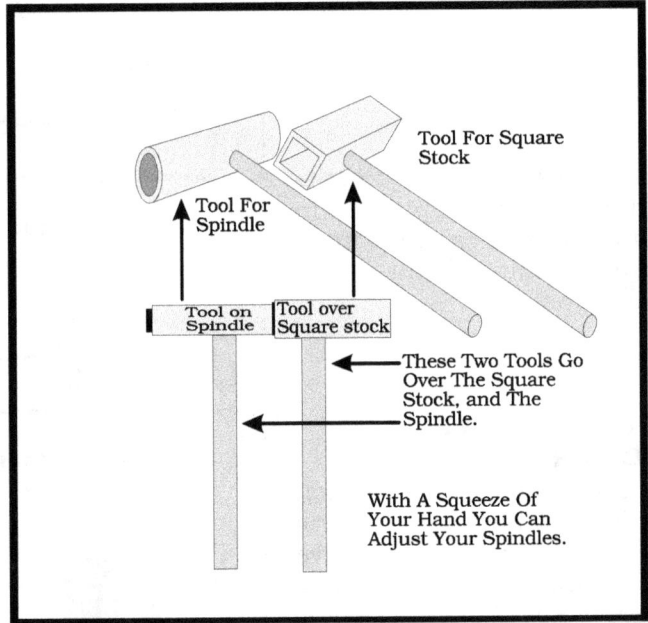

Figure 5-6

WHERE TO SET YOUR SPINDLES

Most experts feel zero forward and down is the best setting for your spindles. This will put your wheels square with the track.

Some experts feel it is better to run your spindles as much as five thousand forward and five thousandths down. They feel that the wheels are pushed back and up during the race. This might be a bit much.

Some align the spindles while the car is on an incline. The incline is usually equal to the starting ramp you are going to race on. They feel the spindles should be set at zero in this position for a faster start. I like the logic that leads to this conclusion.

Some feel the spindles should be set at zero with the car on an average track incline.

There are good arguments for adjusting your spindles in any of the ways described here. I find it difficult to fault any of their conclusions.

LEAST IMPORTANT DIRECTION

The up-and-down direction is called camber. Bending your spindle down is positive camber and up is negative camber. See Figure 5-7 for camber adjustments position. <u>Tests have revealed that more than ten-thousandths of an inch (.010") of camber is needed before you see a noticeable change in speed</u>. My experience with camber adjustment came during our first year in Soap Box Derby. We *did not align my son's spindles that year.* It was our first race and we had no knowledge of a spindle alignment tool. The car was all right on toe-in because we did not over-tighten the steering cables or radius rods. The camber was another story. After the race, I found the spindles were eighteen-thousandths of an inch up (-.018" negative camber). My son won that race! The -.018" negative camber did not hurt the car. Figure 5-7 shows a negative, positive, and zero camber.

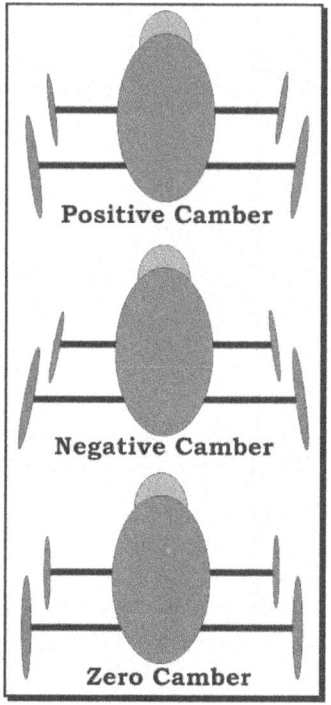

Figure 5-7

ALIGNMENT AND ADJUSTMENTS

MOST IMPORTANT DIRECTION

The toe-in is the most important adjustment of the two directions. Improper toe-in will increase the friction between the wheels, track, bearings, and the spindles. See Figure 5-8.

SUGGESTION

.000" is a good setting for all directions. One or two-thousandths forward is also an acceptable toe-in setting. Remember, alignment at the start of the race is very important. This is where you need to be the most energy efficient. To keep everything in perspective, take a micrometer and see what two thousandths of an inch (.002") looks like. Not very big, is it? Do not get picky about one thousandth. I have seen people spend time trying to get it right on the thousandths when it is not that critical. I do admire their dedication to accuracy.

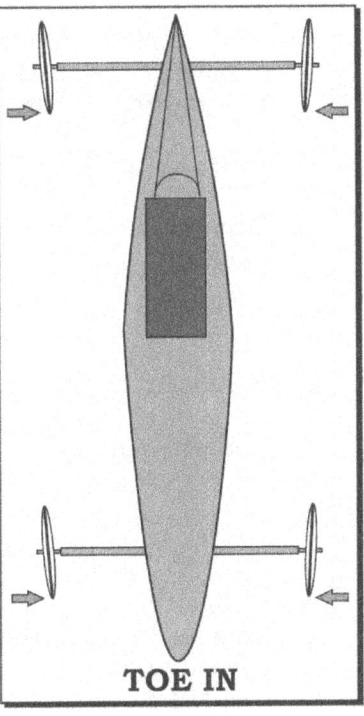

Figure 5-8

ALIGNMENT CHECKLIST

The following is one procedure for aligning your spindles.

1. Car is complete with all weight installed including added weight.
2. The weight is adjusted and ready to race.

4. Alignment is performed on level ground (Or at an angle if you prefer).

5. Place axle stands under the axle spindles to be aligned. **Place the stands between the inner and outer bearing**

6. **position**, in the middle of the spindle.

5. **Driver is in the car, in driving position for checking spindle camber adjustments.**

CAMBER ADJUSTMENTS
1. Place the tool on top of the spindle and check clearance under the inner or outer tool rods.
    a. Clearance under the outer rod indicates a down or positive camber.
    b. Clearance under the inner rod indicates up or negative camber.

2. Remove the axle stand from the spindles that need adjusting and place it under the axle square stock inboard of the spindle.

3. With the two bar system; place the square bar on the axle. The round spindle bar is slid all the way on the spindle. Bend the spindle in the opposite direction so that it is out of adjustment. You will either pull the two bars together or pull them apart to make the adjustment. After a little practice, you will know just how much force is needed to bend the spindle for a specific amount.

4. During bending, you may need someone to stand on the opposite end of the axle to keep it from moving.

ALIGNMENT AND ADJUSTMENTS

> When adjusting the spindles remember that the **steel has a memory**. This means that when you bend the spindle it remembers where it came from and wants to go back to that position. As an Example, let us say you bent the spindle forward to .001". This spindle is most likely to return to .000", or -.001". Keep this in mind when adjusting the Toe-In. Make sure the last bend is forward a little more than you desire. I generally finish Toe-In with a forward bend and leave it a +.001" or up to +.003". The Camber is not critical and can be left + OR -.005" without any effect on the car's speed.

TOE-IN ADJUSTMENTS
- A. <u>The driver need not</u> be in racing position during toe-in alignment unless you are on an incline. <u>Do have the driver stay in the car while you are adjusting the Toe-in.</u>
- B. The Alignment tool is placed behind the axle, on the rear axle alignment check. The alignment tool is placed in front of the axle, for the front axle alignment check. Check clearance under the rod on the spindle.
- C. Clearance under the inner or outer rod will determine whether you have the correct toe-in.
- D. Place the bending bar on the spindle all the way and bend the spindle to obtain the reading you desire. Recheck the spindles and bend them as required to get the correct toe-in.
- E. Repeat these steps for all spindles.

CONCLUSION

You will find yourself doing Alignment often. You are going to want to make it as simple as possible. You will want to get the tools you can depend on. You might just as well purchase them, or build them sooner rather than later.

When you get your car to the track for a race, you will be weighed again. Often the weight is different than you had. This is because of the calibration difference between your scales and the local Derby association. Just be advised. <u>Always have a plan as to what you will do if you are over or underweight.</u> Their scales will always be different from yours.

KINGPIN BOLT TORQUE
Often Soap Box Derby racers torque their kingpins above 200-in-lbs. You may have a problem finding a torque wrench that goes over 200 in-lbs. You may have to get a ft-lbs. torque wrench and convert the in-lbs. you want into ft-lbs.

To torque over 200 in-lbs. you need to go very slow from 150 in-lbs. and up. If you <u>do not</u> go slowly, either the threads will strip, or the bolt will break.

The importance of getting off the starting ramp clean cannot be overstated. The race is often won at the top of the hill in the starting gate. The following items will help you get off the starting ramp fast.

ALIGNMENT AND ADJUSTMENTS

- ❖ It is important that you do not have any cross-bind when in the starting gate.
    - o Make sure your car has "0" cross-bind when you come to the track.
    - o With your car not having any cross-bind—set one end of your car on the ramp and lower the other end slowly to see if the ramp has any cross-bind in it. All Local Soap Box Organizations should maintain "0" cross-bind in their ramp system. They should do this for their local racers as well as visitors. Often the ramps are not addressed. *Adjust your car as required* if the ramps have cross-bind. Loosening your front kingpin to 100 in-lb. or 150 in-lb. Ask the local racers what torque they use at their home track.
- ❖ As a rule, no steering is desired for the first 20 feet, or more if possible. Several things are required to do this successfully. See Chapter 10 "Practice" for more information.
    - o The car handler must be able to make sure the steering is straight with something visible on the outside of the car.
    - o The driver must know he is holding the steering straight. The car handler will adjust and tell the driver when the steering is straight.
    - o The car handler must align the car on the ramps straight each time. This requires feedback from the driver each time down the track to align the car correct.
    - o Align the spindles to .000", or + .003" for Toe-in.
    - o Spindles should be lubricated.

GOOD LUCK WITH YOUR ALIGNMENT

CHAPTER SIX

TOOLS

INTRODUCTION

In this chapter, I will tell you about tools you will need and tools you might choose to do without. This chapter has drawings and information so you can build some of these tools yourself. Included are the purpose of these tools and their important features. Some of the items listed can be purchased at your local hardware store.

Several of these special Derby tools can be purchased from a Soap Box Derby specialty tool maker, or you may choose to make the tools yourself. Make one or more of these tools yourself and you will get a better understanding of what the tool does. You will also save some money and have the satisfaction of making your own tools. Some of the tools you purchase are quite expensive and have features that are not needed. Later in this chapter, there are photos of tools you can purchase and a list of individuals you can contact to purchase these tools.

If the information on the specialty toolmakers becomes obsolete, go to the internet and look for links on the Winning Ingredients website, National Derby Rally website, or the All-American Web Site under tools. Also, search on the internet for Soap Box Derby Tools.

The following is a list of tools you need and some you can choose to do without.

TOOL LIST

1. Axle Spindle Alignment Tool 6-3*
2. Spindle bending tools (Two tools for bending) 6-12*
3. Axle Spindle Stands, used when checking spindles alignment 6-15 *
4. Alignment Table (Level Table) 6-16
5. Track Slope Test Tool 6-17
6. Fisher Gauge 6-18
7. Car Moving Tool 6-24 *
8. Trammel tool 6-24 *
9. Steering Shaft holder 6-29
10. Torque wrench *
11. Two bathroom scales, minimum *
12. Feeler gauges *
13. Small bullet level (6" long) *
14. Large level good for cross-bind alignment *

The tools that have an **asterisk** (*) next to them in the list above are the tools you will need. The tools without an asterisk you may decide you can do without.

TOOLS 6-3

SPINDLE ALIGNMENT TOOLS

The spindle alignment tool is used to adjust your axle spindle Toe-in and Camber adjustments. The Toe-in or Toe-out adjustment is bending the axle spindle forward or rearward. See Figure 6-1 for the Toe-in direction. The Camber direction is the bending of the spindle up or down. See Figure 6-2 for the Camber direction.

Figure 6-3 shows a spindle alignment tool that is accurate and costs about $50.00 or less to build. This is the type of alignment tool I use. It can be built in a short period; however, it does require some welding. After you acquire the material and have everything cut to the proper size, it will take a very short time for a welder to tack-weld the parts in place. Listed on the following page is a material list, see Table 6-1.

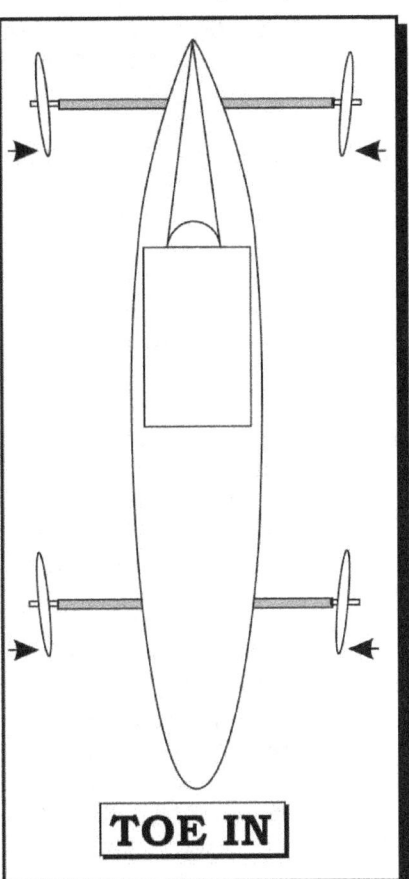

Figure 6-1

ALIGNMENT TOOL CONSTRUCTION

USE THE TYPE AND SIZE MATERIAL LISTED IN THE MATERIAL TABLE 6-1

1. Acquire the material in the material list table 6-1. Often these materials can be acquired at a junkyard, a steel fabrication company, or your local hardware store.

2. Cut and fabricate the material to the sizes shown in Figure 6-3. *See the Spindle Centering Plate in Figure 6-4.* These are welded on the rods and will hold the tool on the spindle. Note: The rods will extend into the radius area so the rods rest on the spindles while the Spindle Centering Plate holds the tool in place on the spindles.

3. *Also, see the Rod Stabilizer in Figure 6-6.* This part should be placed about 4" to 5" above the end of the two rods.

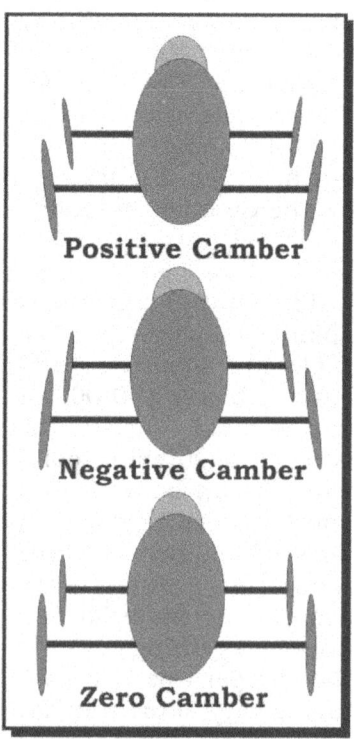

Figure 6-2

TOOLS

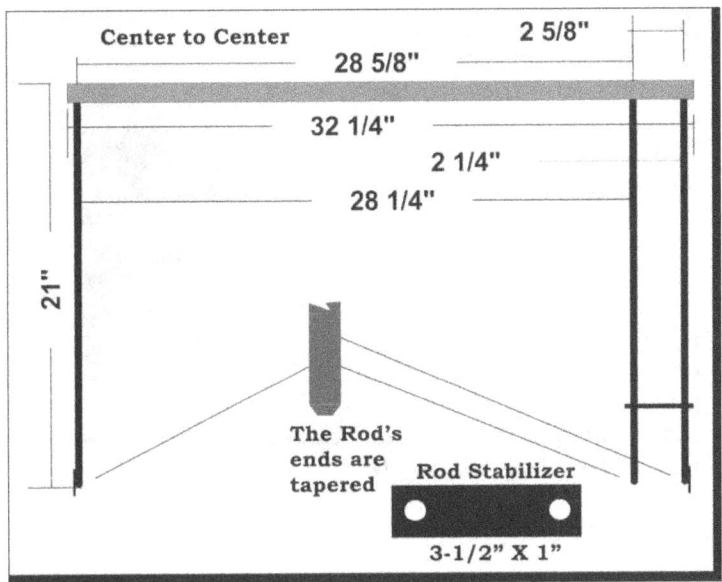

Figure 6-3

Table 6-1

MATERIAL NEEDED TO BUILD ALIGNMENT TOOL			
Item	Quantity	Size	
Steel rods	3	21" Long	Diameter 3/8"
Square Steel Tube	1	32.0" Long	1" X 1" Square Tubing
Spindle Centering Plate	2	1 3/8" long X 1" wide	1/8" Thick
Rod Stabilizer	1	3.5" Long X 1" Wide	1/8" Thick

4. Do not forget to taper the tips of the rods and knock off the rough edges of the steel parts with a file and sandpaper.

5. When the parts have been fabricated and are ready for assembly, do a dry assembly of the parts making sure you maintain the dimensions in the drawing Figure 6-3.

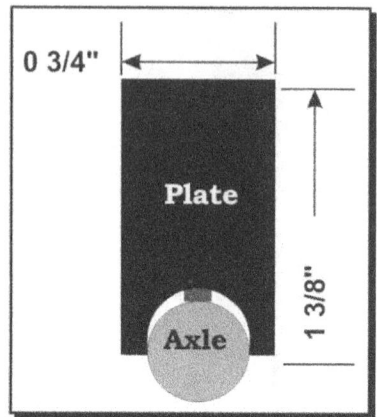

Figure 6-4

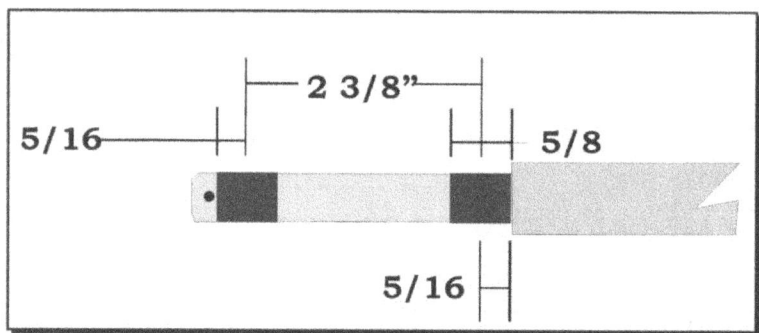

Figure 6-5

- ✓ Take your Alignment Tool parts to a welder to get the parts welded into place.
- ✓ Make sure the **Rod Stabilizer** in Figure 6-6 is attached about 4" to 5" above the end of the **rods** and that it is welded holding the two **rods** over the **center** of the **axle spindle.**
- ✓ The **Spindle Plate** in Figure 6-4 should be positioned over the ½" spindle.

TOOLS 6-7

- ✓ The Spindle Plate should be welded to the outboard rod <u>so the plate is above the spindle by about 1/32"</u>. *In other words, the rod will contact the top of the spindle and the top of the plate radius will be welded to the rod 1/32" above the end of the rod.*
- ✓ Adjust the plate against the spindle by bending the end of the plate tips in. See Figure 6-4B

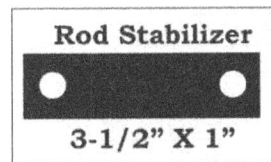

Figure 6-6

ALIGNMENT TOOL CALIBRATION

After you finish building your alignment tool, the rods should be cut to equal length and filed to a rough adjustment. Using a tape measure, adjust the length of each rod so they are even. The ends of the rods should be tapered on the ends until they have just a small contact area in the middle. Next, you will want to make a fine adjustment. Follow these steps to perform the fine adjustment.

1. Acquire a new axle that has not had its spindles bent and place it in a vice to hold it.
2. You can use an old axle that has had its spindles bent, but a new straight one is best. If all you have is an old axle that has been bent, you can place it on its side in the vice so you will be checking the spindle side (toe-in) that has not been bent.

3. Before calibrating your tool, check the spindles with a micrometer and make sure the spindles are not tapered. <u>That means that the spindle should be the same diameter throughout its length.</u> If your spindle is tapered, you will not be able to calibrate your Tool without great difficulty.
4. Have a pencil and paper available to record your readings if needed.
5. <u>In the following steps, you will adjust by only removing material from the two rods that are next to each other on the spindle.</u> See Figure 6-3. You will calibrate the tool by placing the two rods on <u>one spindle of the axle</u>. After you calibrate the tool on this spindle, then recheck the calibration using the opposite spindle on the axle.

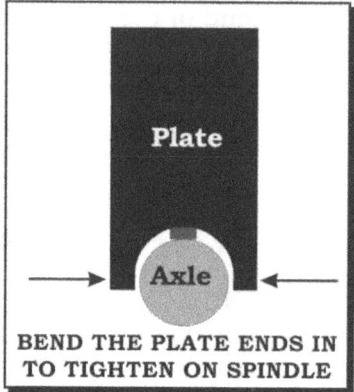

Figure 6-4B

6. Have your feeler gauges ready with sizes from .005" and smaller. You will use the .002" and .001" the most.
7. While holding the tool on the axle, place the feeler gauge under the rod that is not contacting the spindle. Record the reading, for **example,** <u>outboard rod .002" clearance = Spindle bent down by .002"</u>.
8. Now remove the tool and rotate the axle in the vice 180 degrees, so you can check the bottom side of the same spindle.
9. Checking the same spindle, place the feeler gauge under the rod that has the space under it. If the tool were in calibration, you would have a reading of <u>Inboard rod .002" clearance, = spindle bent up .002"</u>. Note when each reading is the opposite, as in this example, the tool is in calibration. One reading will

TOOLS   6-9

   be under the outboard rod, and the other will be under the inboard rod when you turn the axle over 180°.
10. Your reading will most likely be different by a few thousandths when you first test your tool. When your reading is different-- as an **example**: <u>Outboard rod reads .005" = Spindle bent down .005"</u>, and when you turn the axle over 180 °, your <u>inboard rod reads .003" = Spindle bent up.003"</u>. That is only .002" difference. That means that if you remove .001" from the inboard rod your tool will be calibrated.
11. In this example you would file or sand only a slight amount off the end of the rod at a time; it does not take much to remove .001". Recheck the tool after material is removed from the bottom of the rod. In this example, when your tool is calibrated it will read "inboard rod .004 (spindle bent up), and when the axle is flipped 180 degrees you will get a reading of .004" (spindle bent down). This is with an axle spindle that is bent .004". With a new unbent spindle you will read closer to .000" before and after rotated 180 degrees.
12. Recheck the calibration with the opposite spindle.

After you have your alignment tool adjusted, you should recheck it about once a year or after suspected rough treatment. I check mine once a year and most of the time it needs no adjustment.

PROFESSIONALLY BUILT ALIGNMENT TOOL

The following are photos of professionally built alignment tools. They are equipped with dial indicators that register to the .001". (One Thousandths of an inch) This makes the tool very expensive. This tool requires calibration each time you use it, and often must be calibrated during the process of aligning your spindles. A slight bump can knock it out of adjustment. It might be what you get used to, but I find it simpler and quicker to use the solid alignment tool with a feeler gauge.

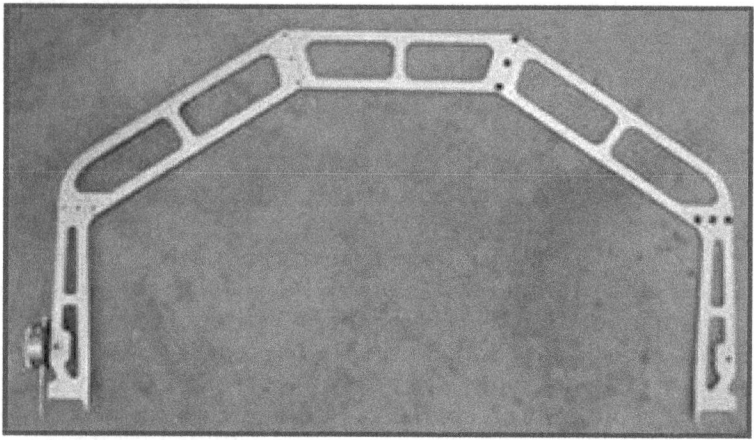

Photo 6- 1

Photo 6-2

TOOLS

Photo 6-3

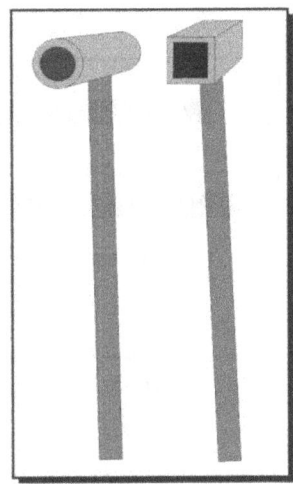

Figure 6-7

SPINDLE BENDING TOOL

After you check your spindle position with the alignment tool, you need a spindle-bending tool to make the adjustments. I have bent my spindles with a single pipe 14" long with a ½" hole drilled in its end. This is the cheapest way to go, however I do not recommend it because you have to put pressure on the entire car when you bend your spindle using one pipe. The best types of bending tools to use are ones that do not put any force on the axle mount or car in general. All the opposing force is kept at the end of the axle. Figure 6-7 and Figure 6-8 show a two-piece bending tool that is easy to build. The most important part of construction is making sure you get a good weld. You can make these handles longer for ease of use, but do not make them any shorter.

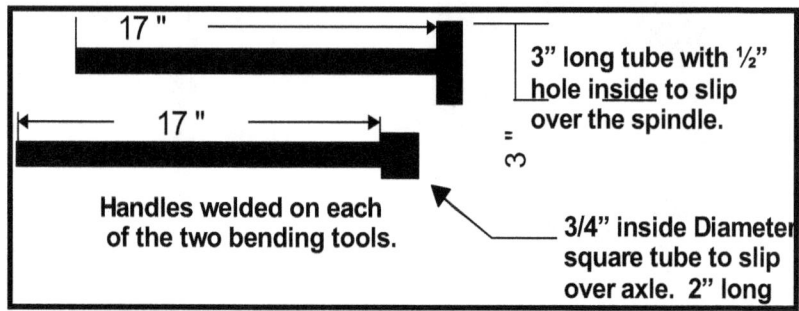

Figure 6-8

The two tools in Figure 6-7 work together. Figure 6-8 shows the dimensions to build these tools.

The square tube slips over the end of the axle about 2" and then the round ½" inside diameter tube is slid over the spindle. You squeeze the handles toward each other to make an adjustment. Sometimes you will have to force them apart to adjust the spindle. Remove the axle fairings before you can slide the square tube on the axle.

TOOLS 6-13

PROFESSIONAL SPINDLE BENDING TOOLS

The following are photos of professional bending tools you can purchase.

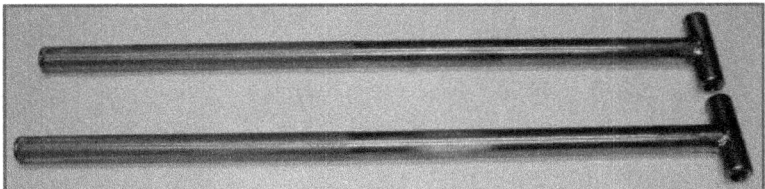

Photo 6-4

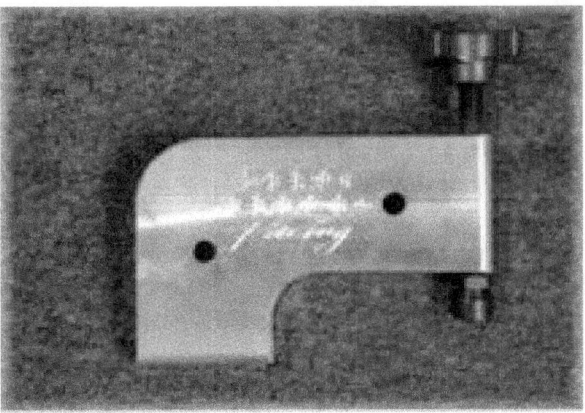

Photo 6-5

WINNING INGREDIENTS FOR KIT CARS

Photo 6-6

AXLE STANDS

Axle stands hold the car off the ground during spindle alignment. This tool is the easiest to make of all the tools. The stand drawing in Figure 6-9 is made from a 2X6 and 2X4. The bottom of the stand is 5X5" and the vertical portion is 3.5" X 3.5." The top should be made of aluminum so it will

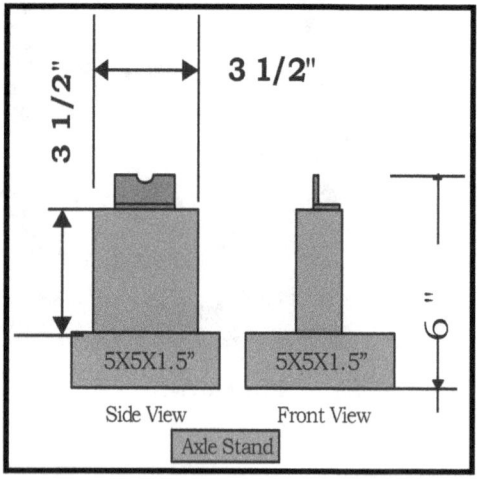

Figure 6-9

TOOLS 6-15

not to damage the spindle. Use an aluminum "L" angle. The aluminum angle should be a minimum of 1" high. If it is too low, you will pinch your fingers when you are lifting the spindle on and off the stands during adjustment. A round file was used to make the ½" round slot for the axle to rest in.

LEVEL TABLE

A level table is used to check your cross-bind, total weight, and tail weight. **See Chapters 4 and 5, "Construction and Alignment & Adjustments,"** for more detail on cross-bind adjustment. The idea is to keep all wheels on the ground with equal pressure and the Level Table is used to check that. Most of the time level tables are made by individuals and come in many different designs. Photo 6-7 below is a more complex level table that has four leveling adjustments and four digital scales on top of it. This Level Table was made by Don Sheets of Indianapolis.

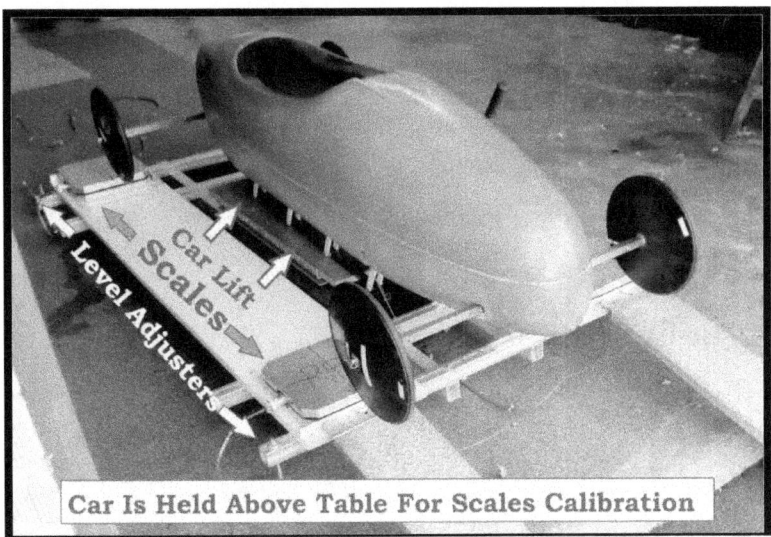

Car Is Held Above Table For Scales Calibration

Photo 6-7

TRACK SLOPE TESTING TOOL

Often it is important to drive your car in a direction on the track to catch the downhill slope. In **Chapter 10, "Practice,"** there is an illustration showing the type of sloping tracks you will encounter during your racing career. They often require you to drive from the starting gate directly to the left or right side of the track to gain the advantage of the track slope. The sooner you get to the steepest part of the track, the faster you will go.

I had made a separate Slope Tool at one time; however, I realized that my Spindle alignment tool could be used if I placed a level across the top. *All that was needed is to adjust the bottom of the two Spindle Plates (See Figure 6-4) on the alignment tool.* See Figure 6-8, 6-4. And 6-4B.

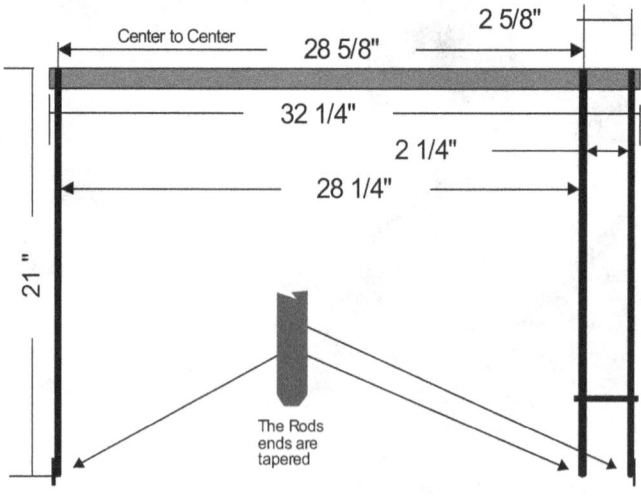

Figure 6-10

TOOLS 6-17

To level the alignment tool I first leveled a long level on my workbench. Then I placed the alignment tool on my level with a digital degree gauge attached to its top. I then adjusted the length of the spindle plates with a file until the digital degree gauge read O degrees.

HOW MUCH TRACK SLOPE IS NEEDED TO GAIN AN ADVANTAGE?

The racecar that steers the least during the first 20 feet, or more, saves a lot of energy. Therefore, steering out and back to gain a track slope advantage comes with a cost of energy. Steering at slow speeds, which is when you have low kinetic energy, costs you energy needed to speed you to the finish line. This is what we call a "trade-off."

The object is to check the track and determine the amount of slope it has and where the slope goes. Knowing how much you gain from going toward the slope can be learned from experience and testing. The following steps will help you gain the experience to determine how much slope is needed to make it worth your while to drive toward the slope.

YOU CAN HELP GAIN THIS EXPERIENCE:

- By testing your car's timing while driving different places on the track.
- Ask local competitors how they drive their track.
- On a track where the winner is determined by driving the track, watch where and how the winner drives to take advantage of the slope.
- Make the slope tool and use it to check tracks with slope. Keep a record of the amount of slope at each track and lane for future reference.

When checking a track with slope, record the track degree of drop and distance from the gates to about 50 feet down the track and record what you find. Within a short time, you will be able to Figure out where to drive and how hard to go there. Often drivers go too hard at the top and lose more energy than they gain by going out. It takes practice and experience.

FISHER GAUGE

The Fisher Gauge is used to measure the amount of flex you have in your axle Here is a photo of a professionally built Fisher Gauge.

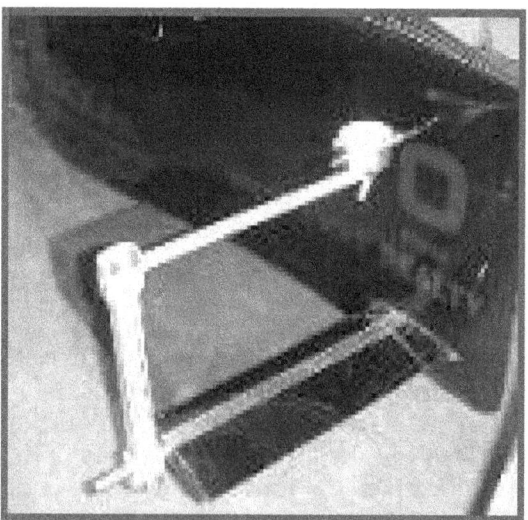

Photo 6- 8

TOOLS   6-19

A Fishers gauge comes in handy when you want to know how much movement you have at the axle mount. The fishers gauge is secured on one end of an axle. A dial indicator has its indicator touching the car about a foot above the axle. When a measured amount of pressure is put on the top of the car body you will get a reading on the dial indicator. You might tighten and loosen the kingpin until you get the dial indicator reading that you have found to be the best in the past.

STEEL CAR DOLLY

When I first got in Derby, we were always lifting the tail or nose of the cars and moving them around. That gets old very quick and by the end of the day your back is talking to you. Now days you can purchase a dolly built for around $75 to $100. However, for less than $30 you can build it yourself. The cost can rise or fall depending on your access to scrap metal and someone who will do the welding for you at a reasonable price.

YOU WILL NEED THE FOLLOWING MATERIAL TO BUILD THE DOLLY:

1. 6.25 Feet' long by 1" square outside diameter steel tubing.
2. 9" by ½" round steel bar for the axle in Figure 6-13.
3. 3" long by 1.25" X 1.25" square tubing for a pivot in Figure 6-14.
4. 3" X 3" steel plate about .100" to .125" thick in Figure 6-15.
5. An 8" to 10" long by ¾" round steel tube to attach across the top of item 1 above.
6. Two 6" diameter wheels with ½" spindle size.
7. Derby rubber brake pad.

8. <u>4 brake pad ¼" bolts</u>, with 4 locking nuts to attach brake pad to steel plate in item 4 above.
9. One 1.5" long 1/4" bolt, for 1.25" X 1.25" steel tubing in 3 above to pivot on the square tube in 1 above.
10. One flat head ¼" bolt 1/4" long, to go through the center of the plate in 4 above and center of square tube in 3 above. One self-locking nut for the bolt. See Figure 6-14.
11. Note: 6" of the 1" square tube in 1 above will be welded to the axle to support it. The 1" tube is longer than needed, see Figure 6-13.

Before you go out and purchase all the steel above, go to a steel prefab business and tell them it's for Soap Box Derby, tell them what you need, and ask if you can go through their scrap. If they do not have everything you need they might be able to recommend another business where you might look. You will most likely have to purchase the 6.25' length of 1" square tubing in 1 above. The 1/2" round steel bar 9" long for the axle might have to be bought also. However, sometimes the shorter pieces can be found in steel scrap bins and got free.

BUILDING YOUR CAR DOLLY
1. Bend your 1" square steel tubing 14.25" from one end until it is 127 degrees. Figure 6-11 shows the 1" tubing length and the proper bent angle. If you do not have access to a tubing bender, cut the tubing at an angle as shown in Figure 6-11 and 6-12. Do not cut all the way through the tube. Then you can bend it to the proper angle and weld it.
2. Next, cut the lower and upper ends of the tube to the correct length as required. The short end is 14.25" from the end to the bend. See Figure 6-11. The long end is 53". This should give you a scrap of 6" or more to use over the axle.

TOOLS 6-21

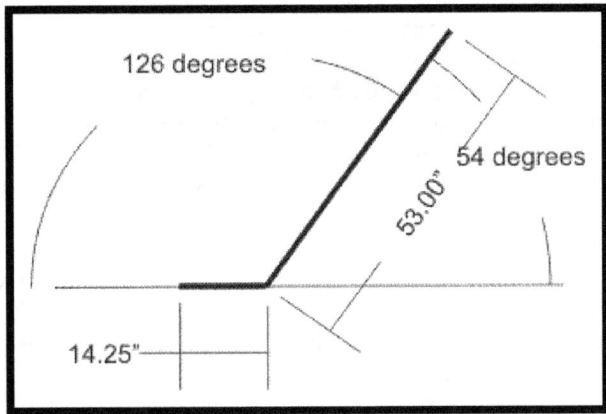

Figure 6-11

Cut "V"

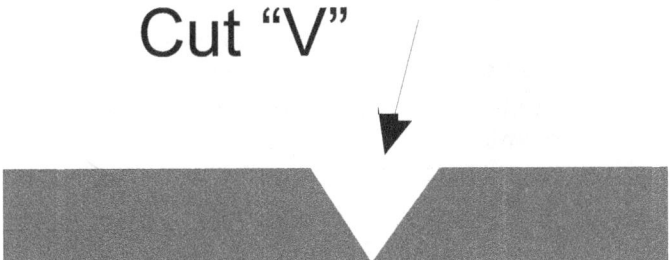

Figure 6-12

3. Drill a ½" hole in the short end of the tubing for the axle. See Figure 6-13. Drill the hole near the top of the tubing so the top of the spindle will be flush with the top side of the tubing. Drill the hole 11.125" from the forward end of the tube. Figure 13 shows just the short length of the square tube from the bend to the

end of the tube. The upper end of the square tube is not seen in this Figure.
4. Before you install the axle, you might want to drill holes for the cotter pins that hold the wheels on. This could be done later, but might be more difficult. Hold the axle, support, and two wheels together to make sure, where you want to drill the holes. See Figure 6-13. The width of the wheels you purchase will be a contributing factor. The size of the cotter pins will determine the size of the holes to drill.
5. Make sure the axle is aligned properly before you weld it in place.
6. Weld the handle in place when welding the axle and axle support.

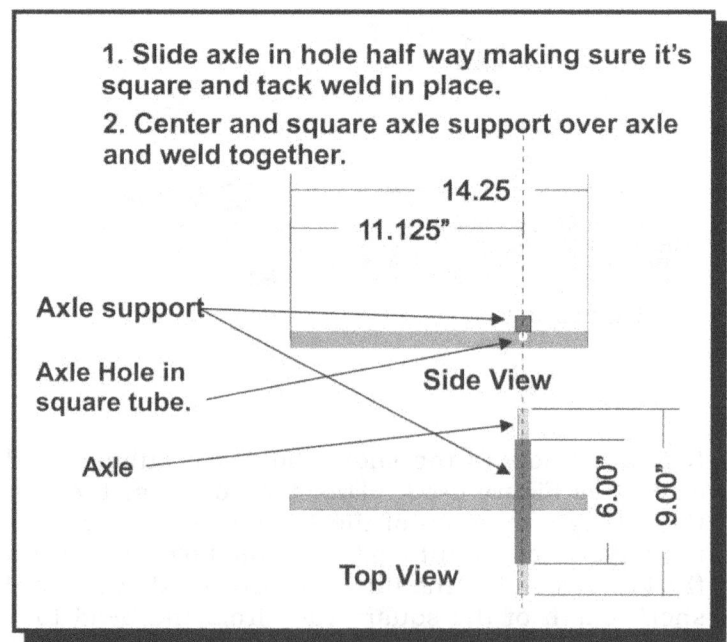

TOOLS 6-23

Figure 6-13

7. At the forward end of the 1" square stock, drill a hole horizontally as shown in Figure 6-14. The ¼" hole is .25" from the top and .75" from the forward end of the tube. This is for the pivoting action of the triangle pivot bracket seen in Figure 6-14. Also, see Figure 6-15 and Figure 6-16. Photo 6-9 can help you see and understand the final product. Cut your 1.25" tube to the shape as shown in Figure 6-14. Drill a ¼" hole in the top middle of the pivot bracket with the dimensions given in Figure 6-14.

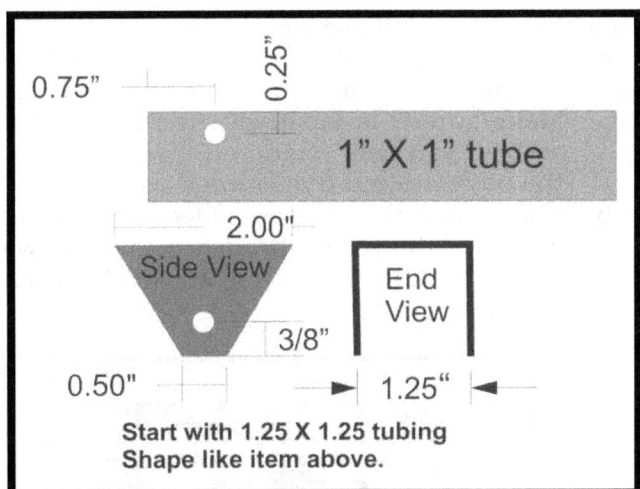

Figure 6-14

8. Figure 6-15 is the 1/8" thick steel plate used to hold the rubber pad. Cut it out to 3" X 3" sheet steel and drill a ¼" hole in each corner to match a brake pad as shown. You can use the brake plunger bolt holes, for

a pattern. Drill a counter-sunk ¼" hole in the middle for a flat-headed counter-sunk bolt.

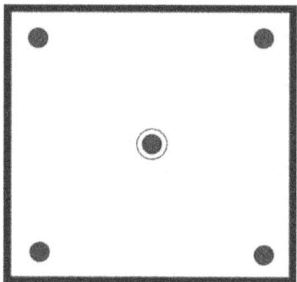

Figure 6-15

9. Photo 6-9 shows the rubber pad assembly all assembled. Follow these steps. See Figure 6-16.
   a. Place the short ¼" flat headed bolt in the center of the 1/8" plate in the counter-sunk hole. Make sure it is flush with the top of the plate as best you can. Sand off extra material from the plate around the counter-sunk hole.
   b. Continue with the flat-headed bolt through the center of the plate, through a thin flat washer, and into the top of the 1.25" modified tube as shown in Figure 6-16.

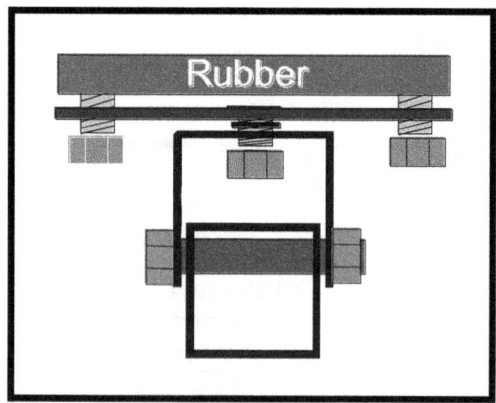

TOOLS 6-25

Figure 6-16

c. Use self-locking nuts. Tighten the center pivot bolt allowing for movement when tight.

Photo 6-9

10. Secure all the nuts and bolts. Draw bolt heads into rubber to prevent damage to your car when moving it.
11. If the center pivot bolt makes contact with the 1" tube and interferes with the movement, cut the bolt shorter.
12. Install the wheels and cotter pins and you are ready for a test drive.

TRAMMEL TOOL

The Dremmel Tool is used to adjust the alignment of the rear axle. You can purchase these at your local hardware store. They are made to attach to a long piece of wood or metal tubing. See photo 6-10.

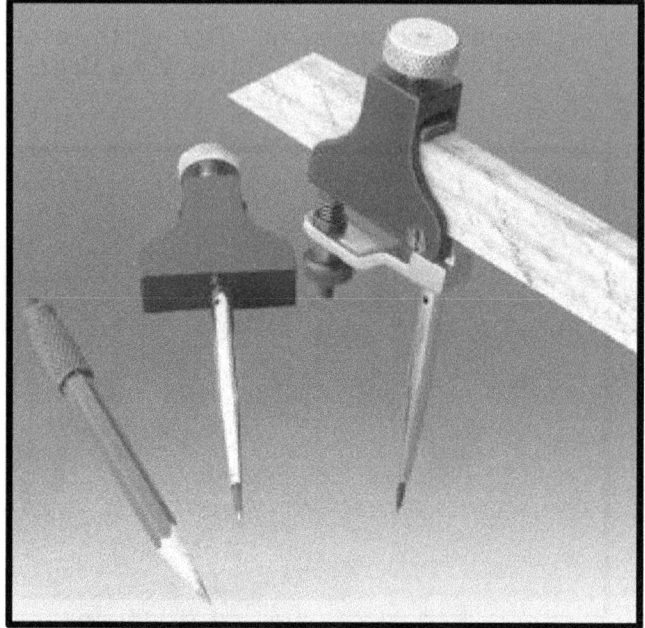

Photo 6-10

You can place a dimple in the center of the front kingpin and align the other end with the end of your square stock. This is assuming that your axle is in the proper dimension and drilled properly.

STEERING WHEEL HOLDER

Photo 6-11 shows a tool to hold your steering wheel while you install the steering cable and adjust your steering.

TOOLS 6-27

To make the Steering Wheel Holder you will need a block of aluminum as shown in photo 6-11. You can use steel if that is what you have available. The dimensions are about 1.25" square, by about 1.5" thick.

- First, drill a ¼" hole in the block on one side of the block as shown.
- Cut the block as shown so it will slide over the steering/brake assembly aft brace above the brake pulley.
- Then purchase a ¼" rod a little longer than you will need. Bend one end as shown and put it in the hole.
- With the hooked end around the steering shaft, place the block over the brace on the aft side.
- Note how much rod you will need and mark where to cut the rod.
- Disassemble, Cut ¼" rod to length, and thread it.
- Purchase a knob and you are in business.

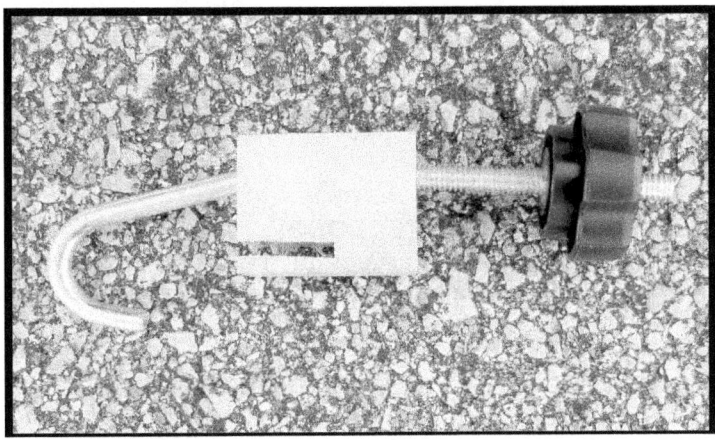

Photo 6-11

REMAINING TOOLS

The remaining tools you can purchase at your local hardware store.

TORQUE WRENCH
The Torque Wrench is needed to tighten your kingpins to the torque you have determined is the best. You will need a 1/4" drive, 200-inch lbs. torque wrench. If you can get one that goes to 250 inch-lbs. that's better.

TWO BATHROOM SCALES
In Chapter 5, "Alignment & Adjustments" I will describe how to adjust your cross-bind with two bathroom scales. Purchase the same brand at the same time for best results. You might go online and purchase two or 4 electronic scales at a good price from China.

FEELER GAUGES
The feeler gauges are needed to check your spindle alignment. In addition, they will be needed to shim an axle.

SMALL BULLET LEVEL (6" LONG)
The small bullet level comes in handy for leveling your axles to your floorboard, when you are checking the level of your floorboard with the shell on, and more.

LARGE LEVEL FOR CROSS-BIND ALIGNMENT
When I lay out my cross-bind alignment, I use a level 4 feet long. You may find that you can get along without a level this long. See Chapter 5, "Alignment & Adjustments."

TOOLS 6-29

TOOL MAINTENANCE

When you purchase a level or square, do you ever wonder if it is level or square? I do. I do not trust the tools we purchase today. We do not know where they were made nor under what kind of specifications or workmanship. Accuracy is important in Soap Box Derby if you want to come in first place. When you get a new tool, you should always test it for accuracy.

We will check a Level and a Square. First, we will check the Level.

CHECKING YOUR LEVEL
See Chapter 5, Alignment and Adjustments.

CHECKING YOUR SQUARE
First, acquire a straight edge as long as one length of your square. Secure the straight edge on a flat surface that you can draw on with a pencil. Then place one edge of the square against the straight edge and then draw a line from the straight edge along the square's perpendicular arm. Next, flip the square left to right and place the same perpendicular arm over the line you made before. Does the line you drew line-up with the perpendicular arm? If the line does not line up, then your square is not square.

SPECIAL TOOL MANUFACTURERS

When shopping for specially made tools contact one of the following.

Super Timer/Grit Timer
1228 Northgate Business Parkway
Madison, TN 37115

Zero Error Racing Inc.
251 Wheeler Street
Sharon, PA 16146
http://www.zero-error.com/

TOOL CONCLUSION

One of the keys to success in Soap Box Derby is accuracy. Make sure your tools are accurate and you will have a good start at making your racecar accurate.

I had thought of showing the many different spindle alignment tools that are used. Many are personal inventions and not available to everyone. I had trouble getting the information for all of them and showing them as I wanted.

Take the time to go to some National Derby Rally races and check out the tools used to align the spindles. Before the race, they will be out there in the pit with all their tools. Ask about their tool, who built it, and why they like it instead of something else. You will learn a lot!

TOOLS 6-31

Spindle alignment has influenced the invention of several interesting tools. The alignment tool I show you how to build is the simplest to build, the least expensive, and will give you accuracy without complication.

BUILDING YOUR OWN TOOLS WILL GIVE YOU A SENSE OF GREAT ACCOMPLISHMENT

CHAPTER SEVEN
PARTS INSPECTION

INTRODUCTION

For the first 40 years of the All-American Soap Box Derby, you received only the rules, dimensions, axles, steering assembly, and wheels; you then had the responsibility and privilege to acquire the material needed, design your car, and build it to the All-American Soap Box Derby specifications. In the 80s we had the introduction of the plastic shell. You still built the floorboard to specs and had a choice of material, but the shell (the body of the car) was plastic. In the early 90's the Stock, Super Stock, and Masters cars were developed. They are kit cars and everything needed to build your car is included in this kit except wheels and helmets.

The All-American Soap Box Derby made these changes gradually over the years. In the 80s, when the plastic shell was introduced, the All-American Soap Box Derby was trying to simplify the construction to increase participation. In the early 90's the All-American was again trying to increase participation.

In 1972, Chevrolet departed as the All-American sponsor. Since then, the All-American has been unable to find a comparable sponsor. Now the All-American is helping to support themselves with the manufacturing and distribution of Soap Box Derby parts.

With the manufacturing of the bodies, floorboards, axles, steering, and brake assemblies came a problem of duplication. At first, there were problems with the parts; however, I have talked to Joe Mazur and he said they have made great improvements over the last three years and he expects no problems with parts going forward.

INSPECT YOUR PARTS

With this book, you can make your car go fast and be competitive. To start, every family must have accurate parts. This chapter will help you inspect your car's parts to make sure you can be as competitive as anyone racing in Soap Box Derby can. It is up to you to make sure your son, daughter, or grandchild has the same chance as anyone else. That is why you have to inspect your parts.

PARTS INSPECTION

In this chapter, you will learn what makes a part good, bad, or questionable. The goal of this chapter is to make sure that these parts give your driver and family the best legal advantage you can have. This does not mean all the parts have to be perfect in every way. Some imperfections can be worked around so they do not prevent you from being competitive. Some imperfect parts may be to your advantage. Others must be replaced or repaired to make your child competitive. **Remember to get approval from the All-American Soap Box Derby in Akron for any repair you make**.

The following information will be provided to you in this chapter for each part if that information is known.

1. Part dimensions if known.
2. Part desired dimensions.
3. Note any specific problems others have found with the parts.
4. Describe what you can do to fix a part.
5. Describe what others have done to correct the part.

FLOORBOARD

In recent years, the lives of floorboards have been limited by the All-American. See the floorboard rules below taken from the rulebook, for the 2013-2014 Soap Box Derby seasons.

Rule # A-7.010   **Floorboard Phase out Revision of February 21, 2011 (update) <u>HAS BEEN RESCINDED 1-12-2012.</u>**   Kingpin replacement must meet the following placement criteria for both the Stock and Super Stock divisions.

<u>Stock Floorboards</u> – The maximum distance from the nose of the floorboard to the kingpin is 7 15/16". The distance between the kingpins is 61 1/8" +/- 1/16".

<u>Super Stock Floorboards</u> - The maximum distance from the nose of the floorboard to the kingpin is 5 13/16". The distance between the kingpins is 63 3/8" +/- 1/16".

There is no life limit on the floorboards that have a date on them at this time. The only concern is the position of the kingpin bushing and bolt. *New floorboards have a stamp on the top of the floorboards indicating the year of manufacture identification.* If you purchase a floorboard in 2014 or later, look for the date identification located on the top of the floorboard.

Figure 7-1 is a Stock car floorboard. The Super Stock and Masters are similar. You will be checking your floorboard without the hardware attached.

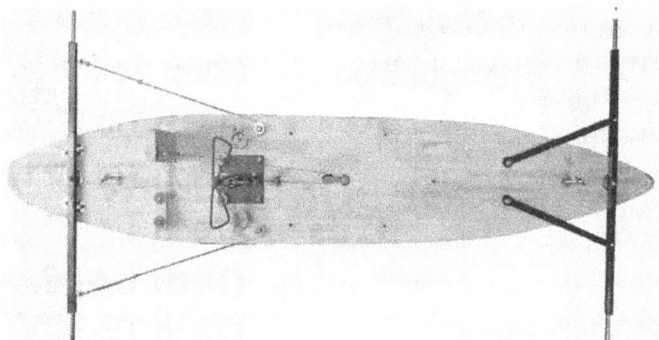

Figure 7-1

PARTS INSPECTION

FLOORBOARD FEATURES TO LOOK FOR

1. A narrower floorboard will give you less drag.
2. A floorboard that is wider at the front axle could benefit your car because the car body will cover more of the axle. The Stock car front axle fairings are often not long enough to cover the front axle to the body. See Figure 7-3.
3. The further aft your two kingpin holes are drilled, the further aft your center of gravity will be, giving your car more energy. See Figure 7-1. As previously stated, the All-American has recently given specific measurements for the distance from the front of the floorboard to the front kingpin hole and the distance between the forward and aft kingpin holes. **See Rule # A-7.010 on the previous page.**
4. Your floorboard should be the same shape on each side of the longitudinal center where the kingpin holes are drilled. See Figure 7-2 where the floorboard is divided into two halves. Also, look for divots in the side of the floorboard from being cut out incorrectly. If severe defects are found, consider replacing your floorboard. At present, the All-American is allowing the floorboards to be filled with filler if damaged. Often your floorboard will come with filler already in some defects.
5. Darker wood means harder wood. The lighter colored wood is softer. The floorboard is Aspen Pine and considered a softwood. Because the wood is soft, the kingpin bushings and radius rod bushings can become loose over time. This is less likely if the wood is harder (dark wood) in this location. Loose bushings can throw off your alignment, change your cross-bind adjustment, and cause a loss of energy. This is less likely to happen if you epoxy your bushings in place. See Chapter 4, "Construction" for bushing installation.

FLOORBOARD INSPECTION

1. Inspect your floorboard for any major warping. First, let us check your floorboard for being twisted. You can do this by securing your floorboard flat on sawhorses. Without moving your floorboard, place the level laterally at the front kingpin area, at the center of the floorboard, and the aft kingpin, noting the level indication at each position

2. Most likely, your floorboard will not read the same at these three points. With the floorboard <u>held level at the center of the floorboard</u>, place the level laterally across the forward kingpin area and then the aft kingpin area.

3. Note the amount of out of level between the forward and aft kingpin area and the center of the floorboard. *A small amount is nothing to worry about, but <u>if it is excessive</u>, you might consider replacing the floorboard.* You will have to determine if it is excessive. Go to Chapter 4, "Construction" and see if you can work around the twist and still have a competitive racer before you decide to reject the floorboard. **In the construction chapter, I address how to work with a twisted floorboard if it is not extreme. Most floorboards will have some twist in them.**

4. Inspect the drilled bushing holes in the floorboard for being centered laterally and drilled perpendicular to the floorboard.

PARTS INSPECTION 7-7

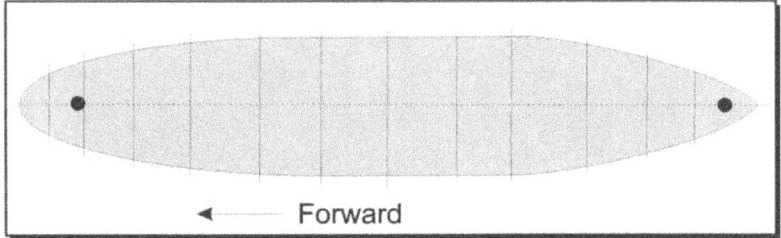

Figure 7-2

Figure 7-3

a. Start by drawing a straight line down the center of the board through the forward and aft kingpin bushing holes as in Figure 7-2.
b. Draw lateral lines across the floorboard in 5" to 8" increments from front to back. See Figure 7-2 above. From the centerline, measure left and right on each cross line to make sure the distance from the center to the sides of the floorboard is the same. Record your dimensions after measuring at each point, and check your results.
c. I hope that your bushing holes are in the center of your floorboard. If the bushing holes are off no more than 1/64", you should not have a major problem. If you feel your floorboard is off in excess, contact Akron. If your bushing holes are drilled left or right of center, it will affect weight and balance, cross-bind, alignment, and steering. You will check these things when you get to Chapter 4, "Construction" and Chapter 5, "Alignment & Adjustments."

7-8 WINNING INGREDIENTS FOR KIT CARS

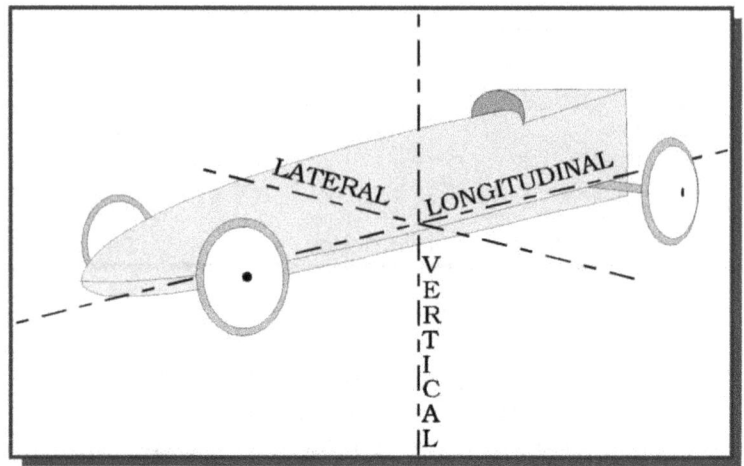

Figure 7-4

CHECK YOUR FLOORBOARD LONGITUDINALLY FOR WARPING

Check the current rules to be sure. This could be an advantage. You could use it to stress the floorboard and body when assembled. Some feel stressing parts against one another can help you gain an advantage.

Find out more on stressing parts in Chapter 4, "Construction". This warped floorboard and stressing can be taken advantage of in the Stock and Masters division because they have many body screws. However, the Super Stock car has few body screws, making it impossible to create stress and rigidity between the floorboard and the body. See Figure 7-5 for checking floorboard warping longitudinally. Use a string stretched from the front end to the aft end of the floorboard. Place a ¼" spacer at each end of the floorboard to raise the string to help you check whether it is warped up or down.

PARTS INSPECTION 7-9

Check the floorboard for warping across the floorboard laterally. If your floorboard is warped across the floorboard, placing the convex portion down is the best. If not possible to run the convex down, consider replacing the floorboard if the warp is excessive. Compare your floorboard to other floorboards. Does your floorboard have the best desirable features? Would another board put you even with your competition?

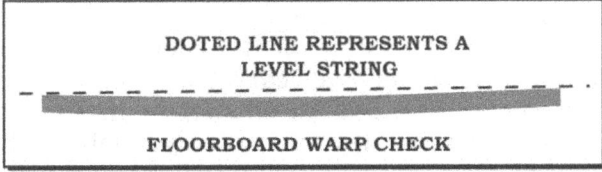

Figure 7-5

BODY

The body is very important because it plays a major role in your overall aerodynamics. I have observed car bodies that have damage in the nose and sides. Some Stock car bodies have a different height measured on each side of the cockpit. See Figure 7-6 for a side view of the Stock car shell. You want your car to be as aerodynamic as your local competitor's car and free of any mold defects.

BODY INSPECTION

1. Inspect your car body for any imperfections such as a scratch or deformity from the manufacturer. If the deformity is great enough, you might want to get a replacement. Small imperfections can sometimes be dealt with without giving you a disadvantage. A scratch can often be buffed out. The Stock body shell will sometimes crack; this can be easily repaired. Contact the All-American Soap Box Derby for instructions on how to correct any imperfection.

2. Compare your car body to others. The smallest body is the best of course. The circumference of the Stock car is measured forward of the cockpit to confirm its legality. However, a car body can meet the circumference and still be smaller in the frontal area where you want it. If your car body height at the nose is shorter than your competitor's car body, you will have an aerodynamic advantage. Some Stock car bodies can be as much as 3/8" different at the nose. You want the shortest one.

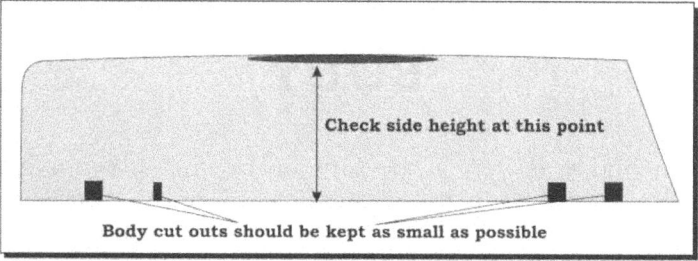

Figure 7-6

3. Inspect the body where it attaches to the floorboard for defects caused during forming. Often the body will not be dry when removed from the mold and may cause portions of the car body to become deformed. This happens most often on the Super Stock bodies.

PARTS INSPECTION 7-11

If you have a protrusion because of improper manufacturing, most of the time, you just cut off the excess material. Check with the local Director and other race families to see how they handled this problem. If needed, call the All-American Soap Box Derby in Akron for direction on removing excess material.

4. Make sure the axle, cable, and radius rod cut-out openings are not damaged and do not have sharp edges. See Figure 7-6 above. The rules have said in the past that no beveling is allowed on the edge of the cutouts.

5. If you acquired a used body, the previous owner may have enlarged the axle, radius rod, and/or steering cable openings. You want these openings to be as small as possible. See Figure 7-6.

6. Inspect how the body fits on the floorboard. Does it fit as the instructions call for? If it fits poorly, do others have similar problems? Does the body have waves down the side of the shell when attached? If you have a poor fit, you need to find out if you should consider exchanging your body, or learn whether other bodies have the same problem. It is best to mount the body shell flush with the floorboard. However, to get the minimum body dimension forward of the cockpit you may have to place the body so it is higher at this point.

7. You want your body to fit tight against the floorboard when secured properly. If you find anything you feel is abnormal or questionable during your inspection, ask your local director, Akron, All-American, manufacturer, and other Derby families for their opinion. Chances are likely that someone has run across this problem before and can help you.

8. Often a Stock car body will not fit properly at the rear where it slides over the aft end of the floorboard. This is often because some of the floorboards have straight up and downsides in the back end. This can be a problem for Stock and Super Stock cars. If your Stock car floorboard is vertical at this point, the wood will need to be tapered to fit the body. Although most Stock floorboards come tapered to accept the shell, some may not be tapered enough and you will have to do it. In the past, the rules have indicated that the aft end of the floorboard may need trimming for a proper fit; this gave you the go ahead to properly fit your floorboard at the aft end. The Super Stock body comes with two different aft ends. One may have to be cut to make it fit on the floorboard. **Check the current rules before making any adjustments; Permission from the All-American in Akron may be required.**

9. It is important to compare your car with other cars in your division. When you are at a race go around to each car and see how the body fits and if the shape is the same as yours. On the Super Stock car note if the body covers the front axles. Some Super Stock bodies do a better job of this than others do. However, keep in mind that the installation of the Super Stock body can affect how it fits at the front axles. The body that covers most of the axles gives the driver an aerodynamic advantage.

PARTS INSPECTION   7-13

AXLES

The Axles are very important to the success of your racing. Without properly made Axles, you may have problems with your cross-bind, alignment, steering, and suspension. Figure 7-7 is a drawing of the Soap Box Derby Axle and has letters representing the dimensions. In Table 7-1, there are letters on the left side of the table. Reading across from the letter you can see what the target or normal size should be, the smallest size could be, and the largest size could be.

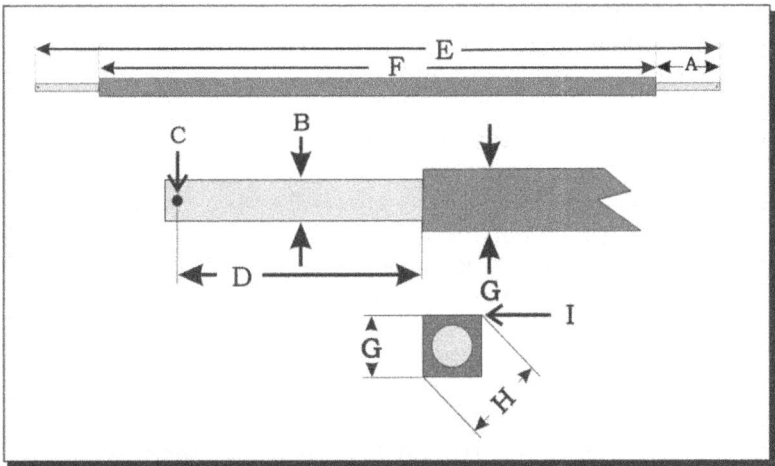

Figure 7-7

These dimensions were taken from an August 1985 Derby Tech publication, written by George Brower. George was a very great student and teacher of Soap Box Derby. I never had the privilege of meeting him; however, I am fortunate to know his brother Ollie Brower. Both brothers wrote for and published the Derby Tech during the 1980s. They distributed a wealth of information about Soap Box Derby racing in Derby Tech. I hung on every word printed in those publications. I could not wait to get my next month's issue. These two men were responsible for a lot of testing and insight into what made your Derby car fast.

Do not take these axle dimensions as the official dimensions of the Soap Box Derby organization at this time, because things change. At one time, these dimensions were the official dimensions. They may still be used today, but I have no way of knowing. **See Chapter 3, "Suspension" for more Axle desirable and undesirable information.**

AXLE INSPECTION

The following are things to inspect on your axles. The kingpin hole is the most important.

1. The ***Axle* kingpin hole should be drilled perpendicular *to the axle*.** See Figure 7-8. Use a drill bit or long bolt to check the kingpin hole. Checking this can be difficult because the bolt or drill bit may not fit snug in the hole and the bolt, or drill bit, may not be exactly straight. The object is to do the best you can to see if the kingpin hole is drilled to an acceptable condition. Try the following to check your kingpin hole.

    a. Use an 8" to 10" bolt or drill bit, inserted in the kingpin hole and a square to check this. The longer the bolt or drill bit, the <u>more sensitive (accurate)</u> your inspection will be. **Make sure the bolt, or drill bit is straight. Roll the drill bit or bolt on a flat surface making sure you do not see daylight under the bolt, or drill bit while rolling it.** See Figure 7-9.

PARTS INSPECTION 7-15

b. Make sure your square is square before you use it. Also, make sure your axle is not bent where you are setting your square. If it is, this check becomes more difficult.

c. **SOLVING MINOR PROBLEMS**
If the bolt is too small in diameter, try one layer of scotch tape wrapped around the bolt. For something thicker, use masking tape. This may make it a little snugger. With the bolt or drill bit installed, place a square against the axle and bolt. Check to see if it is perpendicular.

Table 7-1

	SOAP BOX DERBY AXLE DIMENSIONS			
ID	ITEM	NORMAL	MINIMUM	MAXIMUM
A	Spindle Length	3.250"	3.188"	3.312"
B	Spindle Diameter	.496"- .497"	.490"	.498"
C	Spindle Pin Hole Drill size	No. 36 Drill	-	-
D	Spindle Length to Pinhole	3.060"	2.969"	3.062"
E	Axle Total Length	34.75"	34.564"	34.812
F	Axle Square Stock Length	28.25"	28.188"	28.436"
G	Square Stock Thickness	.750"	.742"	.758"
H	Square Stock Diagonal	1.040"	.998"	1.072"
I	Square Stock Radius	.032	--	.060

d. Does it check good or bad? Stick the bolt or drill in the axle kingpin hole per Figure 7-8. If you do not have more than 1/32" to 1/16" gape at 10" from the axle, you are most likely OK. A small amount can be shimmed out when checking cross-bind. This is covered later in Chapter 4, "Construction, and Chapter 5, "Alignment & Adjustments."

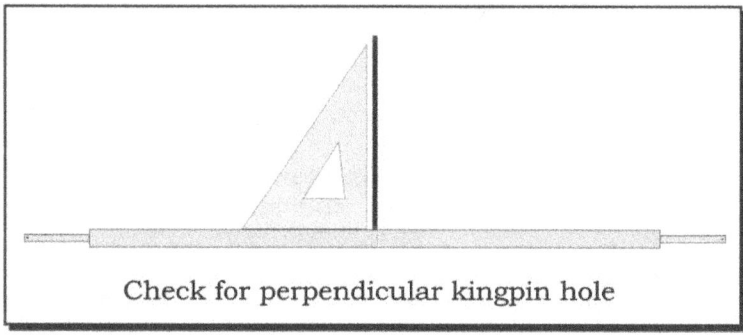

Figure 7-8

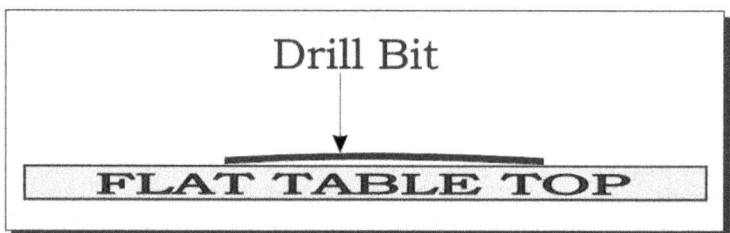

Figure 7-9

2. The **kingpin hole that is drilled off center forward and aft direction** is not a problem. It is better to have your axles further aft when building your car. Place the hole in the axle forward in the car, closest to the front of the car. Place the axle in the car as seen in Figure 7-10.

PARTS INSPECTION 7-17

3. The axle **kingpin hole should be centered left and right on the square stock** of the axle. If you have a normal 28.25" long square stock, the center of the hole should be about 14.125" from both ends. If drilled off center left or right will affect cross bind, alignment, weight, and balance. Replace this axle if off 1/32" or greater.

4. You want your **kingpin hole drilled as small as possible** to provide for a snug or tight fitting kingpin. Remember, the tighter the hole the better, because it <u>wastes less energy.</u>

5. **Check your axles for bends**. Most likely, you will have some, but not enough to be a problem. See Chapter 3, "Suspension" for how to place the bent axle.

6. The axles will often come with **_dings and sharp edges_**, so be careful. Knock the sharp edges off, <u>but do not excessively round the edges and make them illegal.</u> Look at other families' cars to see what used axles look like on the edges.

Figure 7-10

7. **Check the length of the axles**, square stock, and spindles. Of course, you want the shortest axles you can get for aerodynamic reasons. Also, check the thickness of the axle square stock and the spindle. Most likely, you will not find a problem here. I like to

have my spindles as large as I can get, but that is just a personal preference. I cannot prove it is an advantage from any testing I have done. Most of the spindles will come finished to a diameter of .496" or .498". I would not want a spindle any smaller.

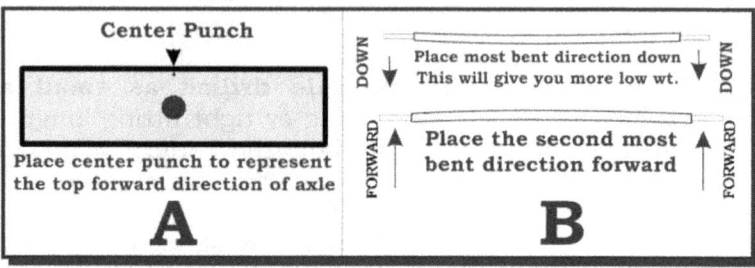

Figure 7-11

8. **Check your spindles for being uniform in diameter** its full length. See Figure 7-12. If there is more than .001" difference, make sure you consider this when you are aligning your spindles. Most likely, you will not find a problem with new axles. Sometimes older axles that have had the spindles polished often have a taper to them. Figure 7-12 shows a spindle with an alignment gauge on it. This Spindle is .003" smaller at the end than it is near the square stock. This needs to be taken into consideration when adjusting your spindles. Use a Micrometer to measure your spindles for uniform size throughout their length.

9. Check spindles for a smooth finish. **Unless it is very bad, most finishes can be polished satisfactorily.** *The underside of the spindle is the area that needs polished.* The underside of the spindle is the only part of the spindle that contacts the wheel bearing. Do not over polish the spindles and create a taper like Figure 7-12.

PARTS INSPECTION 7-19

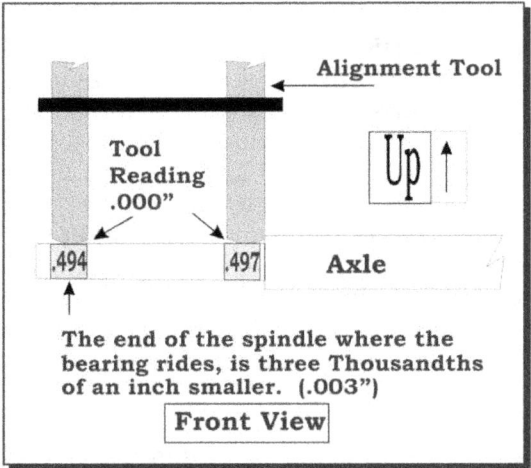

Figure 7-12

10. If you have a selection of axles, you should take the ones with the longest spindles and the shortest overall length. This assumes that a normal length axle with long spindles will have a shorter square stock and produce less aerodynamic drag.

If you find a dimension that you think will affect the car's competitiveness you should take steps to get another axle. **The most likely area of problem for your axles is;** item 1 above, having the kingpin hole drilled not perpendicular, or having the hole not centered between the spindles.

STOCK CAR RADIUS RODS

Inspect the radius rods for bends, proper thickness, drilled holes, and size.

BENT RADIUS RODS

A properly built car is said to have good or great vibration characteristics. From my very first days in Derby in 1978 I was shown how some cars reacted when they are sitting on the ground and then hit with someone's hand, down on the top of the tail of the car. The car would bounce up and down vibrating as it bounced. Everyone knew this was a good thing even if we did not know why. It is good because it indicates your car is not losing energy to improperly installed parts. The longer and greater it vibrates the better.

When I recently built my granddaughter's Stock car, I would flick my fingernail on the radius rods, listen to the vibration, and check the duration of this vibration. The left radius rod made a great sound and vibrated for a longer time, but the right radius rod did not. I took the rear axle mount and radius rods apart and put them back together several times to no avail. I eventually gave up and accepted it that way. I had mentioned the issue to my son. He was new to building Soap Box Derby cars but was hungry to learn. He spent one day trying to Figure out why the right radius rod was not giving us the same vibration as the left. Eventually, he Figured out that the right radius rod was bent. After straightening out the radius rod, he got the same vibration as the left radius rod.

So, are you wondering how much the vibrating radius rods add to the speed of the car? I do not know, but the loss of energy from loose parts is a fact.

PARTS INSPECTION 7-21

RADIUS ROD INSPECTION

DRILLED HOLES

The rear holes drilled in the radius rods should be tight. The forward end of the radius rod has a slot in it for adjustment. You want this slot narrow and rough if possible. This will keep your radius rods from slipping at the adjustment point and causing misalignment.

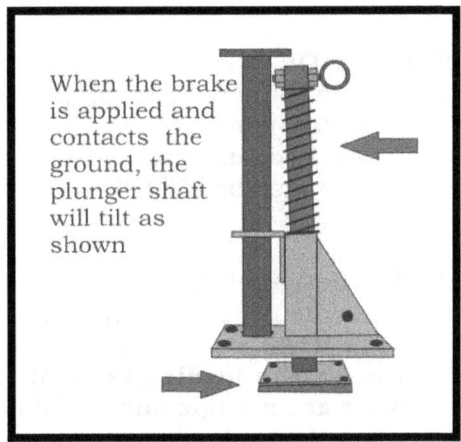

When the brake is applied and contacts the ground, the plunger shaft will tilt as shown

Figure 7-13

SIZE

The thickness of the radius rods is very important because they are in the airstream and affect the aerodynamics. There is no minimum size required by the All-American Soap Box Derby. I found there are several different sizes in use. At our next race, I went around and checked the radius rod thickness on the Stock cars. I found some as small as .118" thick. I ordered a new set and found it to be .140" thick. The set we had on our car was .127".
You want to get the thinnest radius rods possible. This will give you an aerodynamic advantage.

STEERING AND BRAKE ASSEMBLY

The steering and brake assembly is very important. It can affect your steering, braking, but also your aerodynamics.

INSPECTION
1. *On the bottom of the brake plunger, check for the proper size steel plate.* The proper size is 3" by 3". Anything larger is causing air drag. The brake pad you attach should also be 3" by 3".

2. The design of the steering and brake assembly is such that when you put your brake on, the plunger is forced back when the brake pad touches the ground. **This causes the leading edge of the brake pad rubber to wear at an angle** and might cause the brake to chatter when the brake pad is new.

3. Several things can cause this chatter:

    a. The outer square tube is being welded at an incorrect angle, not perpendicular to the mounting plate.
    b. There could be too much difference in the size of the plunger's outside dimensions and the square tube's inside dimensions.
    c. The assembly mounting plate could be bent up in the front causing the brake plunger outer square to be at the wrong angle.
    d. To correct this, bend the front end of the mounting assembly down, *if you found it bent up.* If it is a welding problem, you will have to

PARTS INSPECTION   7-23

get a different assembly or check with the All-American in Akron. I used to place two washers between the front of the mounting pad and floorboard on the two front bolts to raise the front of the brake/steering assembly. Check the rules and check with Akron before doing anything like this. However, you are responsible for the safety of your child. The front tapering of the brake pad is seen as an aerodynamic advantage. With the brake pad at this angle, the front of the brake pad gets thinner as it wears to a wedge shape. See Figure 7-13.

4. **Inspect for roughness <u>inside the outer</u> square tube** that might obstruct the movement of the plunger. Sand or file off any imperfections.

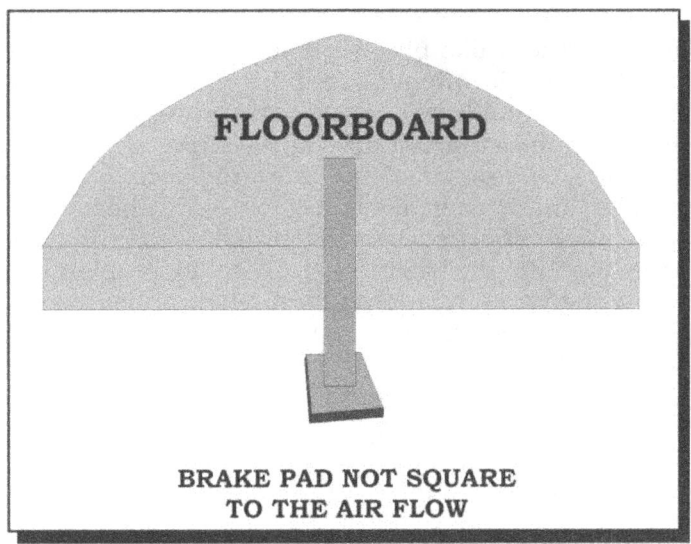

Figure 7- 14

5. **Inspect the length of the steering shaft**, including the steering handles. It should be 10.25" long minimum. This will assure the driver has clearance between their hand and the brake pedal when steering or braking. Sometimes the brake pedal can be moved to prevent this.

6. **When you have the assembly installed check that the brake pad is square with the car when stowed**. If you do have a twisted brake pad when stowed, see if the pad is welded on the shaft square. Also, check the outer square shaft for being welded square on the assembly mount pad. In Figure 7-14, you see a brake pad in a twist. This causes the cross-section of the brake pad to be larger than need be and you will have an aerodynamic disadvantage.

7. Sometimes the brake plunger will not extend and stop the car. This is often caused by a combination of things. The problem is the **brake plunger eyebolt contacting the steering shaft** preventing the plunger to extend. One or all of the following can cause the problem. The eyebolt could be too long, there could be too much slop between the brake outer tube and the inner shaft, the steering shaft could be bent, the steering shaft could be loose, and when pulled back it contacts the eyebolt. See Figure 7-13 for the eyebolt contacting the steering shaft. This problem is covered in the Construction Chapter.

MISCELLANEOUS PARTS

KINGPIN BOLTS

The kingpin bolts are grade eight. That is a high-grade bolt but not all the bolts are the same. Some bolts' diameters are larger than other bolts. In addition, when you roll the bolts on a level table some do not look straight. I do not doubt that these bolts are strong enough to do the job. As far as the bolts being out of round and having different diameters, you will have to work around these discrepancies. As far as the larger diameter bolt, you can look for the largest of these bolts and use them as your kingpin bolt inserted in the smallest bushing you can find. This will give you a snug fit, which is what you want. I often purchase 25 or more bolts and bushings to get the combination I want.

CONCLUSION

You are responsible to see that your parts are as good as you can get. To get a good set of axles, I have often purchased two sets. However, that was in the past. Today the cost of an extra set of axles is too rich for my blood.

Some travel to Akron and pick up their parts in person. If you do this, make sure you know what to look for and bring the tools to check the parts.

Most parts do not have to be perfect to make you competitive. Axles, Floorboards, and the car body are the most important parts. Where and how the kingpin hole is drilled in the axle is very important. Measure the front of the Stock shell and make sure it is not too high. The Super Stock shell can have a lot of extra plastic hanging on it after it comes out of the form and there can be a difference in size.

> Paul Gale is from Mariette Georgia. He is very knowledgeable about Soap Box Derby and has written a book called, The Science of Racing. You can download this book in PDF format by going to http://mariettasoapboxDerby.com/the-science.html.

Paul Gale has numerous drawings that show the effects of the floorboard being warped and other things that affect the speed of your car. I strongly encourage you to download this book and read it.

PAY ATTENTION TO YOUR PARTS

CHAPTER EIGHT

WEIGHT MANAGEMENT

INTRODUCTION

In this chapter, we will examine the management of Weight Placement and Car Balance. This chapter has several experiments you will perform to help you understand where to place your weight and why. Exaggerations are used so it is easy for you to see the results of the experiments. In addition, we will see trade-offs as to where you want to place your weight and where you can place your weight. We will examine types of material to use for weight and how to mold lead weight. Several experts have found interesting ways to gain an advantage with their weight and we will look at that as well.

With the Kit Car, you will not be able to take full advantage of placing your weight where it is needed. Only the Ultimate Speed Division has the freedom to place its added weight where it is needed. Proper management of your weight will maximize the energy available to propel your racer to the finish line first.

WEIGHT

The gravitational pull on you and your Race Car provides the energy to propel you to the finish line. *Weight is the measurement of the gravitational pull.*

You are not in Soap Box Derby very long, before you discover that you should race with the maximum weight allowed. The first Soap Box Derby races did not regulate the weight of the racers. It was soon discovered that a weight limit had to be imposed to make the race fair. The racer who learns how to manage this energy most efficiently will take a big step toward winning the race.

Several knowledgeable Soap Box Derby people have tested with less than maximum weight. They thought that in some conditions less than full weight might be faster. One of these men was so convinced he raced his grandson at the All-American Championship in Akron with less than the maximum allowable weight. His grandson did not win. There is still more testing on this subject to be done.

We often wonder if the max weight is too much for the Soap Box Derby wheels. My neighbor wondered the same thing. He had a friend that was an engineer and computer whiz. His friend determined the car would run faster with less than the max weight allowed by the rules.

WEIGHT MANAGEMENT   8-3

I wondered if he might have discovered something. I had never tested this and still I am not sure how to test it.

My neighbor and his nephew went out to the local race with less than max weight and <u>did not win a race all day</u>. I felt sorry for them and tried to console them as best I could. New Soap Box Derby families often feel they have an unknown edge that will help them win the race. We are all looking for the racer's edge and sometimes we find it.

Each Soap Box Derby racer is limited to a maximum weight. That maximum weight includes the driver and the racecar. If you and your racer do not reach the maximum weight, you can add lead, steel, wood, or other items to reach the maximum weight. Properly placed weight will maximize the available energy to propel your racer down the hill.

WEIGHT DENSITY

The Density of a material is the measurement of the space it takes up in relation to its weight. The densest material will take up less area for a given weight. Different materials have different Densities. To better control the placement of your weight, it is best to use the densest material you can find or afford for your added weight. Of course, you will not have access to some of the densest materials like Gold, Depleted Uranium, or Tungsten. You might be able to get Tungsten, but the cost would be prohibitive. Most Derby people use lead or steel. Lead is denser than steel and takes up less area for its weight, but steel is often used because it is felt that it will help strengthen the floorboard. This is a classic example of a trade-off. In this trade-off, you have to decide which is the most important, stiffening your floorboard, or placing your weight low in your car. In the past, weak floorboards were used which had an advantage over steel as weight. However, the Aspen Pine floorboard that we started using in the early 2000s is much stronger.

METAL WEIGHT CHART

A metal weight chart is on the next page. The heaviest items are highlighted. The listed items in the center column are Alloys, which are one or more metals mixed with the metal in the first column.

Using steel with a small driver may make you run to the maximum height allowed on the weight in the center of your car. At this time, the All-American requires the weight placed between the driver's legs to be no higher than 1.5".

WEIGHT DISTRIBUTION

It is important to carry the maximum weight because this is your car's energy. It is even more important to place that weight where the least amount of energy will be used to carry it. This refers to the basic construction weight as well as to the added weight. However, with the kit cars you have no control of the *weight of your car parts*. In addition, you have little choice where you place your weight.

WEIGHT MANAGEMENT

TABLE 8-1

Metal			
Substance		kg/m³	lbs/ft³
Aluminum		2,720	170
Brass:	- *Red*	8,720	545
	- *Yellow*	8,480	530
	- *Forging*	8,400	525
Bronze		8,800	550
Copper		8,960	560
Gold		19,280	1,205
Iron	- *Pure*	7,840	490
	- *Wrought*	7,680	480
	- *Cast (grey)*	7,120	445
	- *Malleable*	7,200	450
Lead		11,360	710
Magnesium		1,760	110
Mercury		13,520	845
Nickel		8,880	555
Platinum		21,440	1,340
Silver		10,480	655
Steel	- *Cold rolled*	8,000	500
	- *Carbon*	7,760	485
	- *Tungsten*	8,080	505
	- *Stainless*	8,000	500
Tin	- *Pure*	7,280	455
	- *Soft solder*	8,400	525
	- *White Metal*	7,264	454
	- *PeWt.er*	7,264	454
	- *Tin Babbitt*	7,520	470
Titanium		4,480	280
Tungsten		19,280	1,205
Zinc		7,120	445

As noted, exaggerations are used to magnify the results and make experiments and tests more clear. When you see the results of the experiments exaggerated, you are better able to draw the correct conclusion. The following experiments are also examples of an exaggeration to help you better see what is happening with your Race Car. This works like putting a problem under a magnifying glass or microscope. This is a valuable tool to evaluate and solve Soap Box Derby problems.

Perform the following experiments to help you understand the where and why of weight placement. You have heard that low weight is best, but do you know why? What are we trying to accomplish with low weight? Can we place the weight too low? All these questions and more will be answered after you learn how to perform the following experiments.

WEIGHT PLACEMENT EXPERIMENTS

You have to decide where to place your weight vertically, longitudinally, and laterally. These experiments will give you the knowledge to place your weight where energy is used most efficiently. Each direction has its own set of circumstances that must be considered while performing the experiments. Record the results you get in each direction along with how they relate to the direction you are testing. The first experiments are for vertical weight placement. They will give you a good foundation for the lateral and longitudinal experiments that follow. **See Figure 8-1 for Vertical, Lateral, and Longitudinal directions**.

WEIGHT MANAGEMENT   8-7

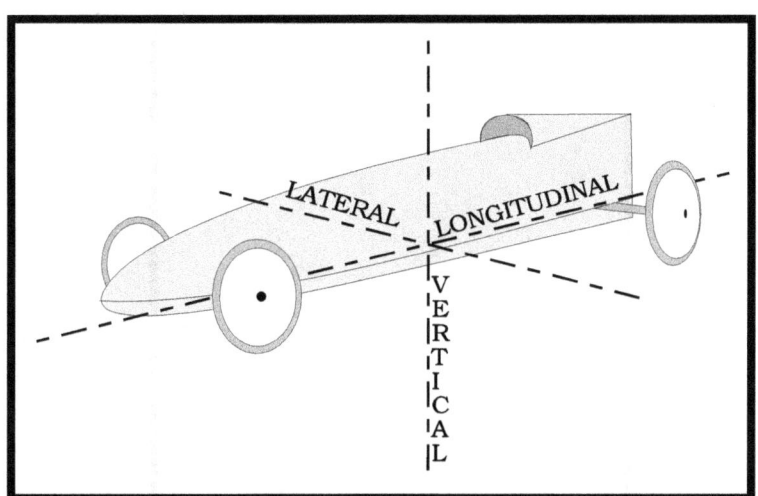

Figure 8-1

VERTICAL, LATERAL, AND LONGITUDINAL DIRECTIONS

The nomenclature used in Figure 8-1 above is used in the following experiments to identify the directions. When performing these experiments, think of the pivot point, (Where your hand is placed on the pole) as the attach point of the Derby car body to the axles, (the axle mount). See Figure 8-2.

VERTICAL WEIGHT PLACEMENT EXPERIMENT

To perform this experiment you will need a pole about 2 to 3 feet long. 2 small "C" clamps, and 2 lead or steel weights of about 1 pound each. The "C" clamps are used to hold the weights in position on the pole. A pole with flat sides will make it easier to attach the weights. See Figures 8-2 and Figure 8-3.

8-8   **WINNING INGREDIENTS FOR KIT CARS**

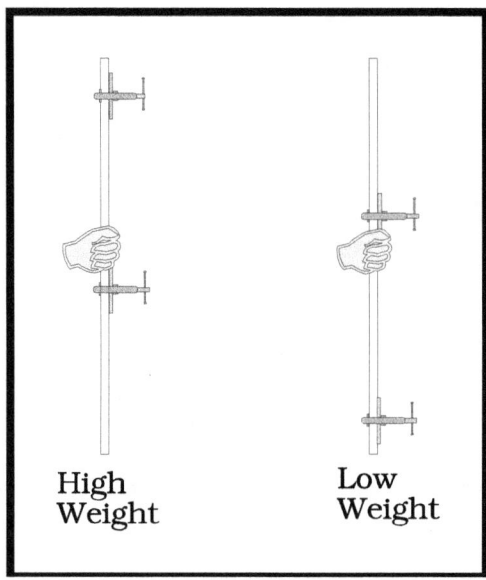

Figure 8-2

HIGH WEIGHT EXPERIMENT

As in Figure 8-2 **High Weight**, attach one weight near the top of the pole, and the other weight just below the center. Grasp the pole with one hand at its center just above the lower weight as shown in Figure 8-2**, High Weight.** Hold the pole vertically. Using your hand as the pivot point, move the ends of the pole from a dead stop to about 6 inches to one side. Do this several times from a dead stop. The high weight makes it easy to take the pole from a vertical position to a position 6" to one side or the other. Now try moving back and forth about 6 inches on either side of center. You will find you use more energy when moving back and forth the 6 inches either side of center than just to one side from a dead stop.

WEIGHT MANAGEMENT 8-9

Try moving at different speeds back and forth. Observe that even more energy is used when you speed up your movement. Kinetic energy is increased with speed, resisting a change of direction. Inertia is also increased with speed resisting the change in direction.

Now in your mind substitute the pivot point of your hand on the pole for the car body's attach point to the axle. As the Soap Box Derby car travels the length of the track, the body is constantly jolted from side to side on the axle attach point. The more laborious it is, the more energy it will use.

In the experiment, we are simulating the movement between the axle and the car's body where they meet at the axle mount. As the wheel contacts track imperfections and grade changes. This happens to your car numerous times as it goes down the track.

LOW WEIGHT EXPERIMENT
Without changing the weight positions in the previous experiment, turn the pole upside down as in **Figure 8-2 Low Weight.** Move the pole as you did in the previous experiment. Observe the effort needed to start the pole moving and the effort required to change directions.

Observe the difference between the high and low-weight tests. The force required to change directions is less with low weight. This is because of the help you get from gravity. However, note that the force required to start the weight from a dead stop is a little greater than the force required with the high-weight test. See Figure 8-2.

We are dealing with **Inertia** and **Kinetic Energy** in these experiments. The following talks about **Inertia** and **Kinetic Energy** and how it affects our experiments.

INERTIA
What is Inertia? In physics, **Inertia is an object's resistance to a change in its motion or stillness**. Things in motion want to stay in motion and those things not in motion tend to stay at rest. The more mass an object has the more resistance to change. Also, the more speed an object has the more kinetic energy it has and it is therefore more resistant to change. *See more on Inertia in Chapter 2, "Energy."*

Even an object at rest has Inertia, that is to say, resistance to change. Once an object is moving, it has a greater resistance to change because of its *kinetic energy* that increases with speed and that increases the natural resistance to change called **Inertia.**

$$KE = \tfrac{1}{2} * M * V^2$$

KINETIC ENERGY
In this formula M = mass of an object. The V = speed of an object. This equation reveals that the kinetic energy of an object is directly proportional to the square of its speed. That means that for a twofold increase in speed, the kinetic energy will increase by a factor of four. In Table 8-2 on the next page, you see how quickly the Kinetic Energy increases when going only 5 MPH to 30 MPH.

WEIGHT MANAGEMENT 8-11

The Kinetic energy numbers start at 25 and was selected at random for reference. You can understand the difference in Kinetic Energy when you try to stop a Soap Derby car at 5 MPH and then at 30 MPH. At 30 MPH you can be hurt. We have had a good intending grandmother try to stop her grandson's car when she did not think he could stop by himself. She went to the hospital with a broken leg.

Table 8-2

SPEED	KINETIC ENERGY
5 MPH	25
10 MPH	100
20 MPH	400
30 MPH	900

BALANCED WEIGHT EXPERIMENT WITH WEIGHTS NEAR THE END OF THE POLES

See Figure 8-3 "A" Place the weights near the end of your pole, spaced an equal distance from the center of the pole. Grip the pole at the center while holding the pole vertically. Move the pole with your wrist back and forth. Examine the difference between starting force, and the force required when changing directions. With balanced weight, you will find the resistance to starting movement and changing directions a lot less than high weight. You do not feel any side thrust at the pivot point. Compare this experiment to the next one.

BALANCED WEIGHT EXPERIMENT WITH WEIGHTS PLACED CLOSE TO PIVOT POINT AT EACH SIDE OF YOUR HAND

Place both weights as close to your hand as possible. Place your hand between the weights. **See Figure 8-3 "B" Repeat** the movement as before. This time you will experience the least resistance to starting movement and direction changing. Compare this experiment to the high and low-weight experiments. **From these experiments, we can see that high weight is the least desired, and balanced weight with the weight close to the pivot point is the most desired.**

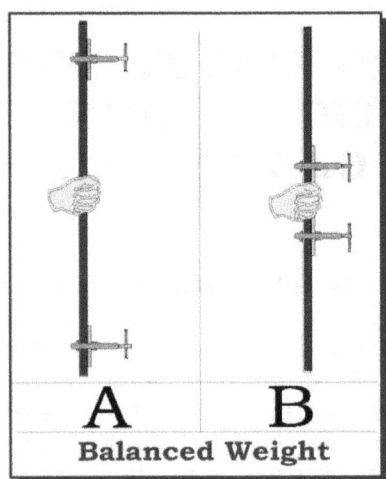

Figure 8-3

APPLICATION OF VERTICAL WEIGHT EXPERIMENT

We have found that the balanced vertical weight close to the pivot point is the easiest to move and change directions. The pivot point on your racer is where your axle attaches to its axle mount. When your racer hits a bump, the wheel moves up causing the axle to pivot (or flex) at the axle mount. When it pivots (flexes) to its limit (determined by your suspension system), the body of the car will move off center like our pole in the experiments (less exaggerated). As the wheel rolls down the other side of the bump, the body will offer the least resistance to a change of direction. This equates to the least amount of energy used to get over the bump.

If the racer is top heavy, the energy required to start the body moving may be slightly more than low weight. When the body changes directions on the other side of the bump, the energy required is greater for high weight than low weight. In addition, the body will take longer to settle down to a level position when top heavy. High weight will continue to move slightly back and forth eating up energy.

Low vertical weight will give your car body more stability. *An object is statically stable if any displacement from its position at a certain moment sets up forces to restore it to its original position.* In Figure 8-4, the Soap Box Derby racecar has a stable equilibrium. When a force displaces the car, it is restored to its original position. The arrows indicate the direction of force produced by the vertically low and laterally centered weight.

Go back to the **low-weight experiment in Figure 8-2**. This time, place the lower weight closer to your hand. About two inches below your hand should be about right. Now compare this to the extreme low weight we tested before. With a smaller amount of low weight, you have less resistance to movement, and increased stability.

Balanced vertical body weight is favored at the axle/body pivot point, but a small amount of low weight would be acceptable. The vertical center of gravity positioned just below the axle would be more desirable than above. However, a Soap Box Derby car with its axles and wheels attached is very stable.

In Chapter 8 Weight *and Balance Calculations,* **we see that getting balanced weight at the axle mount as in Figure 8-4 is unobtainable.** You will also find out that you will not be able to get low weight. In other words, you will not be able to get a Vertical Center of Gravity below the axle pivot point. If you can get your vertical center of gravity two inches above the axle pivot point, you are doing well. You might wonder why we experimented with a low center of gravity that we cannot accomplish. *Exaggeration helps us see what is desired for speed even when we cannot obtain it.* **We cannot obtain it, but we try to get as close to it as possible**. You will never experience as low weight in your car as in the experiment. I hope that you will remember the experiment and know where best to place your weight. It is important to experiment until you understand what uses the least energy. Then you put that knowledge to use placing your vertical CG as close to the axle pivot point as possible.

WEIGHT MANAGEMENT

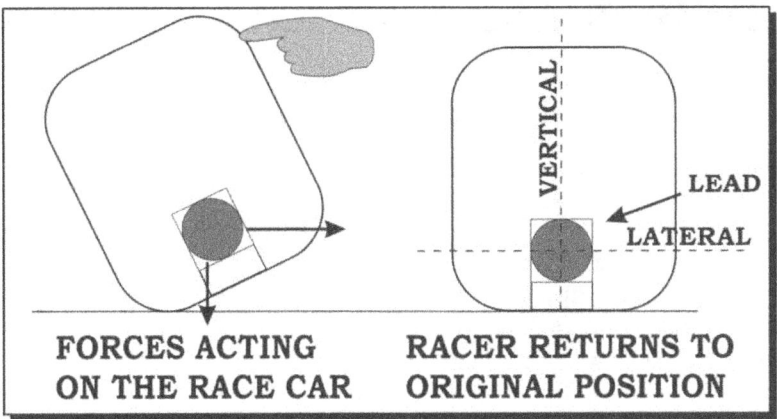

Figure 8-4

Eliminate heavy items above the floorboard during construction. **Remember, if one pound of weight is added 8 inches above the axle pivot point, you have to add eight pounds one inch below the pivot point to maintain balance.** A little high weight goes a long way. You should think twice about adding that pound of body filler to your headrest fairing.

The above experiment helps you determine the vertical placement of your added weight. Repeating the above experiments with the pole held horizontally will help you determine the lateral and longitudinal placement of your weight. Lateral is side to side, and longitudinal is lengthwise. See Figure 8-5. The vertical and lateral directions of the body both pivot at the axle mount.

APPLICATION PROBLEMS (DRIVER AND VERTICAL WEIGHT)

The driver's weight is made up mostly of water and will not react as a solid weight. Our experiments were performed with static weight, but when the racecar moves, the driver will also move. The driver's weight will not react as the weight attached to the pole. When the wheel contacts a bump, the driver's body will absorb some of the movement. This will cause your racecar to react as if it has a lower center of gravity.

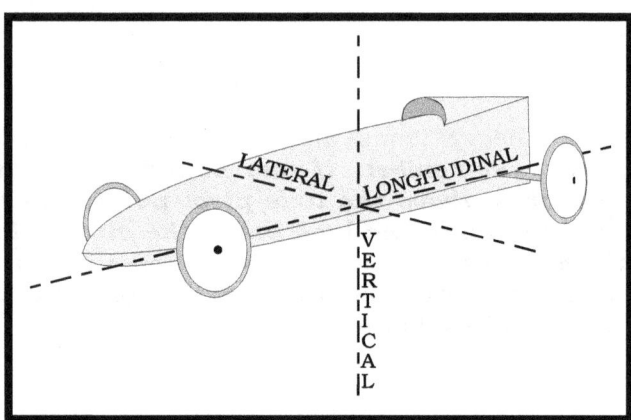

FIGURE 8-5

We can Figure the actual vertical center of gravity, but the effective center of gravity would be hard to Figure. Figure the vertical center of gravity as if the driver was a solid. Take that answer and assume your effective vertical center of gravity is about <u>one inch to an inch and a half lower</u>.

LATERAL WEIGHT PLACEMENT EXPERIMENT

BALANCED WEIGHT NOT CLOSE TO THE PIVOT POINT AND BALANCED WEIGHT CLOSE TO THE PIVOT POINT

When performing lateral weight placement experiments, you will not test unbalanced weight. You know your racecar needs to be balanced laterally. However, you do want to compare balanced weight near and far from the pivot point. You will want to know for yourself how far from the pivot point you should place your weight. In the past, I would make added weights no more than four inches wide. **With the introduction of the kit car, you have to place your weight only where the plans allow and that is wider than desired.**

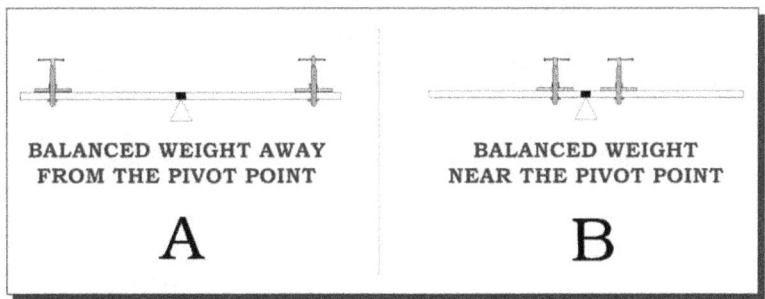

Figure 8-6

CAR BODY LATERAL EXPERIMENT

Perform the lateral experiment for the body of the car. See Figure 8-6. Grab the center of the pole while holding it level. Move the ends up and down pivoting at your hand position. <u>Perform the experiment first with the weights spaced near the ends of the pole, and then with them near the center.</u> From this and previous experiments, we see that with the weight near their center, the pole is much easier to start and change directions.

AXLE LATERAL WEIGHT EXPERIMENT

Now perform the lateral experiment for the axle. The axle pivots on the wheel at its opposite end when a bump is contacted. Figure 8-7 A, and B, shows the *axle lateral weight experiments*. The weights are equally spaced about eight inches from the center in the first experiment (A), and placed near the center on the second, (B). Make sure the weights are equal in weight and spacing in these experiments. Failure to do this could give you erroneous results. Use a spring scale to evaluate the difference. If you do not have a spring scale, you can use a spring and measure its change in distance. A weak spring will give you a more exaggerated view. As I've said before, exaggerating your experiment helps realize what you might have otherwise missed.

LATERAL WEIGHT CONCLUSION

Are you surprised at the results? *There is no difference in the energy used as long as the pole is balanced.* This shows us the importance of having our car body and axle laterally balanced at the axle mount.

Make one more comparison. Perform the experiment in Figure 8-7 (A) again, but this time use less weight! This should show the use of less energy by the less spring travel because of less weight.

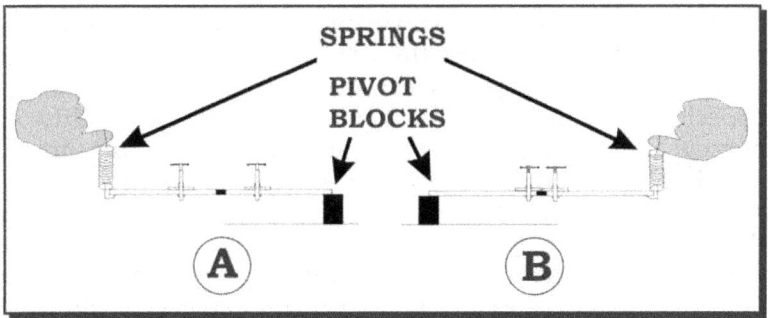

Figure 8-7

APPLICATION OF LATERAL WEIGHT EXPERIMENTS

BODY

The experiments show that lateral weight should be placed with the heaviest weight near the center of the car laterally. This gives us the least energy usage in the body movement as it pivots at the axle mount area. *(Please note that when I speak of pivoting at the axle, there may or may not be actual movement between parts. In a solid system, the body's pivot point is at the axle mount, but the movement is in part a flexing motion.)* When constructing the body, eliminate all unnecessary weight to the sides. Keep your added weight close to the center laterally. As mentioned above. With the advent of the kit cars, you have to place your weight where the plans specify.

PLACING YOUR LATERAL WEIGHT IN A KIT CAR

From the experiments, we know that the weight across the floor laterally makes the car use a lot of energy when going over imperfections on the track. At one time, I experimented with a Kit Car and made my weights as narrow as possible laterally. Of course, that was only a .5" difference on each side of the large weight in the middle. I was hoping to gain an advantage by reducing the load required to go over bumps because of the weight spread across the width of the floorboard. *I spent a lot of time re-melting the lead for this testing however, I found no advantage in doing this. If anything, I may have slowed the car down.* The conclusion is that I could not reduce the width of the weight enough to make a difference because of the location of the weight bolts.

AXLES

Because the axle pivots on the wheel at its opposite end, it reacts differently than the body. You may have heard that you should not use heavy items at the extreme ends of the axles. That is still true. The lighter an axle is the less energy will be used to go over imperfections on the track.

AXLE FAIRINGS MATERIAL

Before I wrote the first *Winning Ingredients* and up to the present time people have experimented to see what material is best for axle fairings. *Always the conclusion is the lightest material.* This goes along with the previous paragraph about axles and weight placement. Now days, your Stock and Super Stock kit car comes with plastic fairings.

The Masters Kit car has some leeway with what you can use to attach your fairings. Use lightweight materials like wood dowels, aluminum, or copper tubing to attach your airfoils.

WEIGHT MANAGEMENT 8-21

LONGITUDINAL WEIGHT PLACEMENT EXPERIMENT

The longitudinal direction is from the rear of the racer to its nose. See Figure 8-5 for the longitudinal direction. This experiment will determine whether you should place your weight in the front, back, center, or a combination of the three. See Figure 8-6 for this experiment. If you performed the previous experiments, you may already feel like you know the results. However, perform the experiment anyway. Focus on comparing the experiment with the pitching of the car body as it pivots between its axles.

Your car body moves when the grade changes in the track. When the racer goes from a level track to a downgrade, the nose of the racer will tilt down. When the grade of the track levels out again or goes up, the nose of the racer tilts up.

With the pole held as it was in the lateral experiment, space the two weights about ten inches from each side of the center. See Figure 8-6. Grasp the center of the pole, holding it horizontally. Move the pole through the air to simulate the pitching movement of your racecar as it goes over the track. Remember, the pitching motion is infrequent. A track that changes its slope three times has an unusual number of changes. One and sometimes two changes are more common.

Position the weights near the pivot point and repeat the pitching movement to simulate going over track slope changes. Compare the two experiments. *You will find the weight close to the pivot point offers the least resistance to movement.* By now, you already knew the outcome of this experiment because of your work with the previous experiments. <u>Weight placed near the pivot point is easier to move and the most desirable position for your weight.</u> If your track does not have many pitching places in the track you may not want to place your weight near the center. You may want to go spread out and low.

APPLICATION OF LONGITUDINAL EXPERIMENTS

Weight placed along the length of the racecar should be kept between the axles, and as close to the center as possible. The center is half the distance between your axles. This is usually in the small of the driver's back on the Masters car!

Because of the Kit Car set weight positions, it is often difficult to get the balance you want. Then there is the consideration of tail weight. Most tracks run best with up to 15 lbs. tail heavy. This makes it more difficult to place the weight where you want it. You have some tradeoffs to consider.

KIT CAR CONSIDERATIONS
Before the Masters Kit Car, a heavy steel plate was installed in the center of the masters floorboard. It ran from the front axle mount to the aft axle mount. This centered the weight and gave your something to mount the axles. In addition, there was great continuity between the two axle mounts. Now you cannot do that., However, it does not hurt you to hear the science of how and what to do to make your car fast if you could.

WEIGHT PLACEMENT CONCLUSION

You will do a better job of placing your weight after reading this chapter. You will understand the importance of placing your weight properly. The amount of inches you will gain from making changes you find in this chapter is difficult to determine. The characteristics of a given Soap Box Derby track will affect how much you gain. Most tracks do not have many *pitch changes* as you progress down the track, but some do and there you will gain a lot with proper *longitudinal weight placement.*

HIGH WEIGHT

In the early eighties, I met an old Derby man who was convinced that high weight was the way to go. He made a convincing argument, so I decided to test his theory.

First, my son drove down the hill with low weight as we always ran our cars. Then I moved 5 lbs. of lead weight from the floor to the top of my son's master's car and raced down the track again. The results were as if we put the brakes on. **We lost .040" with high weight**. I then placed the 5 lbs. of lead back down on the floorboard directly below where it had been attached to the top of the car. This time **I noticed a .040" to .050" increase in our speed**. I then placed the 5 lbs. weight back up on the top again and retested. Retesting showed that with the 5 lbs. attached again to the top of the car, **our time slowed down by .040" to .050"**. This was enough for me to stick with low weight. I told my old friend about this but he never changed his mind about high weight.

8-24   **WINNING INGREDIENTS FOR KIT CARS**

BALANCED WEIGHT

    Many people are convinced that balanced weight is the best way to run all the time. Each hill is different and it is up to you to find the best weight placement for a given hill. Only by testing can you be sure, or by asking someone who tests.

    As a test, Figure out which one of the wheels in Figure 8-8 is the fastest. Also, Figure out which one would come in second, and which one would come in third.

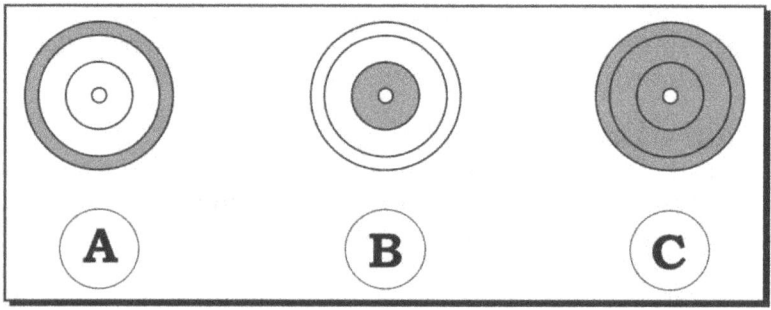

Figure 8-8

    All wheels weigh the same. **(A)** above, has 70% of its weight at the dark area, at the outside part of the wheel. **(B)** has 70% of its weight at its dark area near its pivot point. **(C)** has its weight spread out over its area equally. Which one will be the fastest wheel?

    Wheel (B) will be the fastest, because it has the lowest moment of inertia. If you <u>reduce the distance</u> the weight is from the pivot point, the wheel will accelerate faster. If you <u>reduce the weight of the wheel</u>, it will also Accelerate faster (Start rolling sooner and faster). Wheel (A's) weight is the furthest from the pivot point and <u>will be the slowest.</u> Wheel (C's) speed will be between **(A), and (B)**.

    Ollie Brower, a friend, and Soap Box Derby brain sent an article that was written by his brother George for <u>Derby</u>

WEIGHT MANAGEMENT 8-25

Tech. It makes an argument for low weight. The following is an illustration of George's line of reasoning.

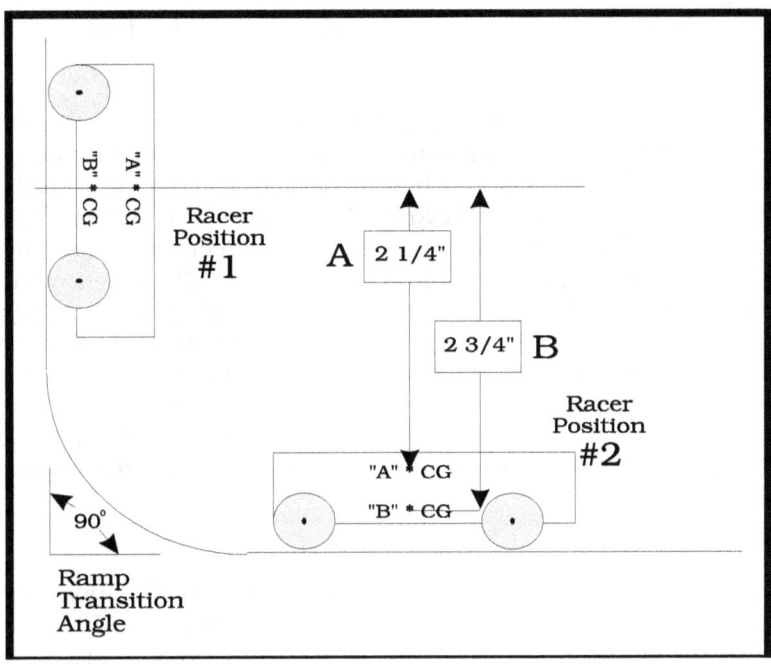

Figure 8-9

"WEIGHT A MINUTE!"

Many Derby people spend hundreds of hours building a racer and putting weight in it. However, they spend about 60 seconds deciding where to place their weight. Often the weight is placed where it can be reached fast, rather than placing it where the car can become fast.

A heavier racer is faster because it has more potential energy (PE). This PE is converted into kinetic energy, the stuff that makes your racer move. Therefore, the more PE you obtain through weight placement, the faster you go.

The formula for determining potential energy is **PE=H times W**. The total amount of PE that your racer has is found by multiplying the height by the weight. It sounds simple enough, but **"Weight A Minute!"** The height is the vertical distance that your racer's center of gravity (CG) on the starting ramp is above the CG when your racer touches the finish line. <u>This vertical distance times the racer's total weight is the PE</u>. Even though two different racers have the same total weight, they can have different amounts of PE, because of the height of the racer's CG and center of mass. One racer has the weight falling a greater distance than the other does. See Figure 8-9.

Figure 8-9 shows that the lower the CG (CG position "B"), the more PE there is to propel the racer. Although this ramp transition of 90 degrees, the low CG "B" falls 1/2" farther than the high CG. *See Figure 8-9 for the difference in the fall of weights A and B.* The lower the CG is on a transitional track surface, the more PE there is to propel the racer. The high CG "A" falls 1.82" while the lower CG "B" falls 2.17".

When you lower your CG weight or when you move weight to the extreme tail of a racer, you move the CG up a higher vertical distance from where it will be when the racer is at the finish line. This happens because the starting gate area slopes more than the finish line area. If the ramp or hill did not change, like in Figure 8-10, there would be no advantage.

WEIGHT MANAGEMENT   8-27

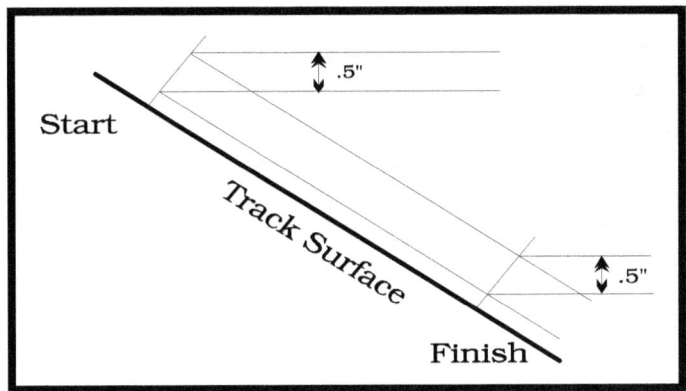

Figure   8-10

George went on to give us his thoughts on the Fort Wayne Hill. Fort Wayne's hill had a transition angle of about 4.75 degrees. The transition takes place almost immediately, becoming a major factor in your racer's speed. *Having a low CG and being tail-heavy are very important on tracks of this kind.* Not only do you get a big push off the ramp, but also you get a push throughout the track because of the concave shape of the hill. If you lower your CG by one inch, your gain would be 11.68 inches for the ramp transition and .82 inches for the hill transition. The overall gain for one time down the hill would be 12.5 inches.

At Akron, things are different. The transition at the ramp is virtually zero. See Figure 8-10. On this hill, if you lowered your CG by four inches, you would be only 2.4 inches faster. At Akron, your weight should be balanced with your weight CG at the center of all axles.

Plan the placement of your weight before construction begins. Consider the weight of everything that goes down the hill as a challenge in planning for the best CG. Place the driver low.

George Brower went on to suggest you build your car out of lightweight material to allow you to place your weight where it will have the best advantage. He also mentioned that the short wheelbase placed as far aft as possible would position your car to gain the most PE.

George's increase of energy by lowering your weight is right on track.

The Fort Wayne track George mentioned was where the National Derby Rally Championship races were held from 1982 through 1990. The track was torn down in the early 1990s to build a BMX racetrack.

CONCLUSION

Now you have a better understanding of how to place your weight to win. Your weight is your energy, but it can work against you if not placed correctly. Most Soap Box Derby families do not dissect the placement of their weight as we have done here. You can gain an advantage here that most other racers do not have.

Low weight is king. That means using Lead for your weight. It is a lot of work to melt the lead to the proper shape, but worth it. Spread your weight out to get it as low as you can.

MAKING LEAD WEIGHTS

Here is how to make lead weights.

1. Determine how much weight you need in the aft, mid-aft, mid, and forward position. You can do this by calculations or with experimentation. Using experimentation, get weights to place in the car where they are needed to bring the car and driver weight up to the maximum division weight. Keep adding and moving weight until you get it right.
2. Measure the weight in each position to determine how much lead weight you will need in each position.
3. Material needed – Lead, aluminum baking pans to use as molds, plywood to cut to the shape of the lead for each position, a Camping stove to melt lead, an iron skillet to hold the lead.
4. Cut plywood shapes for all weight positions. Round corners so as not to puncture the aluminum pan.
5. Place one wood shape in an aluminum pan and bend the pan as needed to shape around the wood. Shape the aluminum to the height you need for the weight.
6. Place the stove and pan on the ground in a well-ventilated area next to each other. Level the mold.
7. Place the weight of lead for that position, in an iron skillet on the stove.
8. Place the pan on the level spot near the stove and carefully pour the lead into the pan.
9. Repeat this for each weight position.

You can also make wood molds for your lead. If you make wood molds, line them with aluminum foil or the molds will be burnt where the lead contacts the wood.

> Hot lead is very dangerous. Be very careful melting the lead. Check on line and with others who have done this before you attempt this. Keep all children away while you are melting lead. Do not breathe the lead fumes. Perform this in a well-ventilated area. Use gloves, eye protection, and other protective gear as needed.

GOOD LUCK, AND

DON'T WASTE ANY ENERGY

CHAPTER NINE
WEIGHT & BALANCE CALCULATIONS

INTRODUCTION

I find it hard to get into performing the formulas found in some publications. I am eager to get to the meat of the subject, just give me the answer. So if you are like me, you are about to skip this chapter. If that is the case, I suggest you at least read to find out what these calculations can tell you.

The following formulas can calculate the horizontal and vertical center of gravity of your car. Working the vertical center of gravity formula gives you an idea of how low you have your weight. It will get you thinking of how you can get it lower. I was so concerned about low weight that I did not want to put too much paint on our cars. If you calculate your vertical CG and find it to be 6" above the floorboard, think of what you can do to lower that. After thinking of what you might do, (like spreading your added weight out more so it is lower), recalculate to see the new vertical CG. Low center of gravity can give you an advantage over your competition.

WEIGHT

The weight in the following formula is the weight of the car, car parts, and or the added weight in the car. This can include floorboard, brake, steering assembly, axles, mounts, and the added weight that you put in your car. For calculating weight placement, the car is weighed and the weight of the two axle positions is used, for the Weight and Arm calculations to determine the Center of Gravity before adding weight.

ARM

ARM, in the following formulas, represents the distance from the **Datum**. *The **Datum** is the "O" reference point. It is the point at which distances (ARM) is measured.* The **Datum** for the horizontal Center of Gravity is located at the nose of the car. The **Datum** for the Vertical Center of Gravity is located at the bottom of the floorboard. The distance from the Datum is the **ARM**, recorded in inches   See the vertical item column in table 9-1. All of your distances (**ARM**) will be measured from the **Datum** reference point.   See Figure 9-1

MOMENT

The moment is the product of weight times arm. See Table 9-1.

WEIGHT & BALANCE CALCULATIONS   9-3

FORMULA FOR MOMENT

Weight X Arm = Moment
(W X A = M)

FORMULA FOR CENTER OF GRAVITY (CG)

Total Moment divided by Total Weight = Center of Gravity
(TM/TW = CG)

VERTICAL CG

The center of gravity, (CG) is that point on an object where it will balance. *Ideally, we want the vertical CG to be at the axle pivot point.* That is the most desirable position. At that position, energy is used most efficiently. When a wheel hits a bump and raises one side of the car, pivoting, bending, or flexing at the axle mount, you will use the least amount of energy if the weight above that pivot point is equal, to the weight below it.

To calculate the vertical CG, the weight and position of each item are recorded before the car is built. See Figure 9-1 for a drawing reference of the positions of the items we will calculate to determine the *Vertical Center of Gravity*. (To calculate the vertical CG after the car is built takes a different formula, and it would be difficult to use for our purpose at this time.) **The wheels and axles were not** included in the vertical CG calculations. We are figuring the vertical CG of the body, floorboard, and its attachments only.

When figuring weight and balance, it is helpful to draw a sketch showing all items to be calculated. See Figure 9-1. The vertical line in Figure 9-1 represents the Soap Box Derby car. Along the right side, it is marked off in inches from the bottom of the car. On the left side of the line, items are listed across from their CG location. Some of these items will be used to calculate the vertical CG.

The weight of the items used in the following calculations is easy to Figure. The vertical position of some items is another matter. The driver position is the most difficult to calculate. I Figure the vertical CG of the driver at eight inches above the bottom of the car. That is six inches above the floorboard. The driver's vertical center of gravity is arrived at very unscientifically. Place the driver in driving position. The eyes should be at the height to see over the top of the car. That is 12" above the floorboard. Now calculate the *vertical center* of the driver's weight based on his or her position and body build. We Figured six inches above the floorboard, but everyone is built differently and positioned differently in their car. A heavy driver may have a lower center of gravity. Your 100 lbs. driver may look as if he or she has a lower or higher center of gravity.

WEIGHT & BALANCE CALCULATIONS

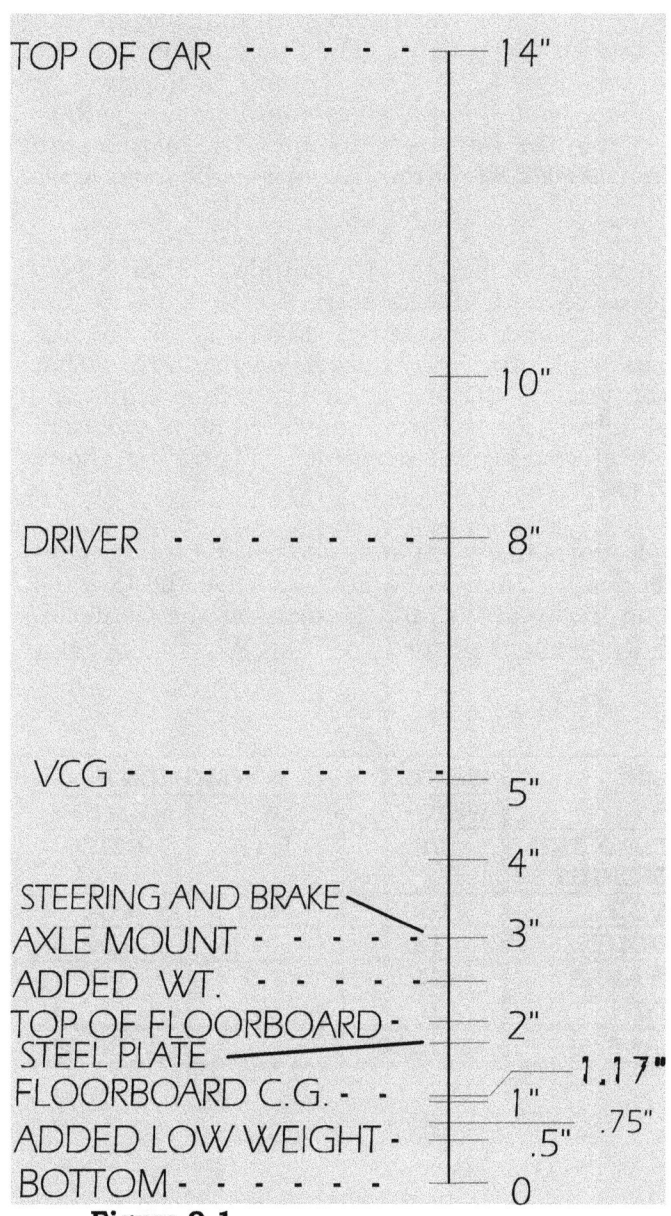

Figure 9-1

In Table 9-1, I have calculated the total weight and moment for our vertical weight. The first column lists the **ITEMS** to be calculated. The next column is their weight in pounds. The next column gives the distance, **(ARM)**. Each item is from the **Datum** "0" point. The last column is the product, **MOMENT**, *of the weight of each item, times its ARM*.

The total weight comes to 216 pounds. (*That is light because the axles and wheels were not included in the calculations*) The total moment is 1103.26. Divide the total moment, 1103.26, by the total weight, 216. That gives you the vertical **CG** of 5.1 inches. That is not the **CG** we had hoped for. Three inches from the bottom would have been much more desirable. Figure 9-1 shows the **Vertical CG** at just above 5".

Table 9-1 shows the calculations to get the total weight and total moment. Then in Table 9-2, I use the formula for converting the total Wt. and Moment to the Center of Gravity. <u>Total Moment divided by Total Weight = Center of Gravity.</u>

Table 9-1

ITEMS	WEIGHT X ARM = MOMENT		
	WEIGHT	ARM	MOMENT
FLOORBOARD AND ADDED WEIGHT	78.	1.17	91.26
DRIVER	100.	8.	800.
CAR BODY	18.	9.	162.
ADJUSTABLE WEIGHT	20.	2.5	50.
TOTALS	216.00		1103.26

WEIGHT & BALANCE CALCULATIONS

Table 9-2

TOTAL MOMENT DIVIDED BY TOTAL WT. = CG				
TOTALS	TOTAL MOMENT		TOTAL WEIGHT	CENTER OF GRAVITY
	1103.26		216	5.10768"

From the above calculation, you can see it is difficult to get your center of gravity at the axle level. You will not have to worry about getting your weight too low.

HORIZONTAL

In Figure 9-2, I have a Stock Car. *The vertical lines represent the position of the nose, tail, axles, weights attach points, and center between axles.* I wrote the distance of each item from the nose or **Datum**. The rear axle is six inches from the tail. The rear axle is 69.187" from the nose; 69.187" minus 8" inches gives you a 61.187" wheelbase. The information for the horizontal center of gravity is taken from a finished racecar.

Table 9-3 below uses the information from Figure 9-2 to calculate the total weight and moment. These calculations will be for a finished car, with the driver included. That brings us up to the total allowable weight of 200 pounds for a Stock division car.

9-8 WINNING INGREDIENTS FOR KIT CARS

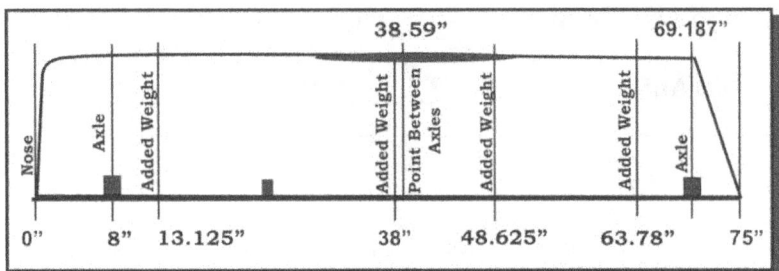

Figure 9-2

Before you can calculate your **CG**, you have to weigh your car at its front and aft axles. The first column lists the two positions where weight was taken. The second column lists the **weight** at these positions. The third column lists the distance (**ARM**) from the Datum. The fourth column has the product of the **weight times the arm, or = Moment**. Add the weight and moment to get the total weight and moment. The total moment, (7718.7) is divided by the total weight, (200) equals the **CG** (38.59"). The weight is equal at each axle in this calculation and the **CG** is exactly between the axles.

Table 9-3

ITEM	WEIGHT	ARM	MOMENT
FRONT AXLE	100.	8	800
AFT AXLE	100.	69.187	6918.7
TOTALS	200.	CG= 38.59	7718.7

WEIGHT & BALANCE CALCULATIONS

The table below gives you the CG position for different tail weights. Listed across the top are different tail weights in two-pound increments. In the column below each tail weight, you will find the weight at each axle and the distance of the center of gravity. This table can be used for any car that has a wheelbase of 65 inches and the rear axle six inches from the tail.

TABLE 9-4

TAIL WEIGHT	EVEN WT.	2 LB. TAIL	4 LB. TAIL	6 LB. TAIL	8 LB. TAIL	10 LB. TAIL
FRONT AXLE	100	99	98	97	96	95
AFT AXLE	100	101	102	103	104	105
CENTER OF GRAVITY	38.59	34.94	39.20	39.51	39.81	40.12

Now that you know the formula, you can go to a spreadsheet program like Microsoft Excel and set up a program to calculate your weight and balance and see how much weight you need in each position.

One of the most important things you need when figuring out your weight and balance is a *dependable and accurate scale*. They do not have to be expensive, just accurate. To make sure your scales are dependable and accurate, use a weight standard so you can check your scales for proper calibration before using them.

CONCLUSION

From this chapter I want you to know that low weight is king. Some still feel it makes no difference. They are wrong. Several friends and I have tested this and there is no doubt that low weight is best.

In 1980, my son won the Junior Division World Championship in Akron. It was early in my experience, but even then, I believed in low weight. After my son, Chris won the world championship, I had a friend who had 20 years of experience in Soap Box Derby tell me that he knew we were going to win when he saw the weight we had in the tail rise up aft of the axle like a mushroom.

I explained to my friend that the weight was positioned like that because that was the only way I could get tail weight, and the rules stated that the weight could not obstruct the view of the aft axle mount.

There was no convincing him that low weight was correct. He felt so strongly about high weight that I felt I needed to test his theory. We took my son and his master car out to the track and ran it down the hill about 3 or 5 times to get a consistent time. Then I took 5 lbs. from the top of the floorboard and attached it to the top of the car on the inside. The results were dramatic. It was like putting on the brakes. After a few trips down the hill, we placed the 5 lbs. back down on the floor and regained our speed.

WEIGHT & BALANCE CALCULATIONS

When you are testing or just thinking about doing something to your car to make it faster, do it with exaggeration. The exaggeration is a magnification to help you determine the correct thing to do. In this case, high weight, or low weight, the correct answer is low weight.

Soap Box Derby racing is a game of inches. If you can gain an inch with low weight, you want it. If you only learn one thing from each chapter in this book and each thing you learn is only worth 2", you want every inch.

GOOD LUCK WITH YOUR WEIGHT AND BALANCE CALCULATIONS!

CHAPTER TEN
PRACTICE

INTRODUCTION

Races are won by people who practice. Nothing can take the place of practice. It is time-consuming and a lot of work, but if you want to win, you have to practice. In this chapter, we will find out what we need to practice, whether you are a beginner or a veteran.

This Chapter covers everything involved with being out at the track **Practicing**, **Testing**, and **Drivers Education**. When you are doing one you are inevitably doing the other two.

This chapter will tell you things the driver needs to know to win. I wish we had known these things on our first trip to the track. I have seen families work as a team during the race and it gives me goosebumps. A good team is hard to beat. There is something about a family working together for a common goal that I like.

Ramp alignment is very important. It is very important that you know how to get the best start. This is the most important part of the actual race down the hill. You must understand and take every legal advantage.

As you grow in Derby, you will want to Practice and Test things. What airfoil shape is best? Does this book tell where to place my weight? How much tail weight do I use for a given track? The people who love Derby love to test. The section in this chapter on testing will help you get started on the right track.

PRACTICE

FIRST TRIP DOWN THE HILL
The first trip down the hill should start halfway down the hill where it is not very steep and you cannot get a car going very fast. The first trip down the hill should be started with a check of the steering and brake. The axle should turn left when the steering is turned left. Make sure the steering wheel is straight when the front wheels are straight.

A new driver has a lot to learn: How to steer, brake, and keep his or her head and body down. So, take it easy the first time down the hill. Start a new driver about halfway down the hill until he has the confidence that he or she can steer and brake. The driver will let you know when they are ready to go further up the hill.

I often remind my drivers that if they have any problem while going down the track, **put on the brake.** Young drivers often have steering problems, discover it is backward, or get something in their eyes and forget to put on the brakes.

DRIVER'S EDUCATION

COMMUNICATION

Communication between the driver and his pit crew is essential. Adults often misunderstand each other. Can you imagine how hard it is for young children? Adults use words in Soap Box Derby that children have never heard before. Sometimes adults will say something like, "angle to the right after you get to the tree." Angle, I am not sure what that would mean. I have heard some parents yell at their children out of frustration. That is always because the parent has not taken the time to communicate clearly on the child's level. Yelling is not the kind of communication that is helpful.

Parents should understand that communication between adults and children can sometimes be difficult. <u>Most often if a child does not know what you are talking about they will also be afraid to say anything</u>. Make sure your driver will tell you when he has a problem. "Dad! My brake feels funny." "Dad, my car goes to the right all the time." Be responsive to the driver's questions.

The driver and parent and other pit crewmember must be able to communicate. The driver should be shown what to do and told why. Just ordering the driver around is not communication. Instructions should be a team effort.

DERBY TECH

Many ideas for Driver's Education were found in <u>Derby Tech</u>, March 1985 and May 1985. The articles were written by George Brower and titled "Driver's Ed." The editor of <u>Derby Tech</u> at that time was Ollie Brower. They are used here with permission.

The driver has to be taught the driving skills he or she needs to win. The quality of the driver's education often decides the top finishers. Driving skills are best learned when the driver is told *and* shown what to do. They should also be told why driving should be done a specific way. The more information a driver has, the better driver he or she will be.

Below is a list of items that the driver should know. They are in no specific order. They cannot be learned overnight, but the sooner the better. Concentrate on the most important first, like steering and braking. Add the others as the driver's experience increases. *There is no substitute for practice.* If you do not have a hill near your house, it will be worth your time to travel a distance to use one. Plan to spend the day or afternoon and bring extra brake pads.

BE A GOOD SPORT.
This means different things to different people. To me, it means learning how to get along with people while you are under pressure. Also, shake your opponent's hand even when you lose and say something like, "Good race." This is not always easy, but a good person will always be trying to get along. Meeting new people and making new friends is one of the most pleasurable parts of Soap Box Derby.

KEEP YOUR CAR IN THE SUN
Your car runs faster when the rubber on your wheels is hot. Your suspension also works better when it is hot. For these reasons, it is best to position your car to take advantage of the heat of the sun. Some cars are affected more by the heat than others, depending on your type of construction, car color, suspension, and division.

PRACTICE 10-5

KEEP YOUR WHEELS ON THE BLACK OR DARK PAVEMENT

It is important to keep the wheels on the darkest pavement between race phases. Dark pavement exposed to the sun will absorb more heat than lighter colored pavement. The dark area will heat your tires, making them more resilient, and your car will be faster. As soon as you install the wheels, you are going to race on, get your car on the darkest pavement with the sun shining on it. Keep your car moving on the black pavement to heat your wheels evenly.

DON'T STAND AROUND YOUR CAR SHADING IT

When you are in the pit do not shade your car. Most people keep their car in the sun when not racing. I know of no one who feels a cold car runs better. During a race, make sure you do not shade your wheels. Just a little sun can heat the rubber on your wheels and make a big difference.

DON'T DRIVE ON PAINTED LINES

Your car runs faster when the wheels are hot. That is one reason why you do not want to run on the painted lines. The painted lines are lighter in color and therefore cooler. Running on the lines can result in you being as much as a foot slower. The amount of speed you lose depends on how long you run on the painted lines. The steel wheels are more affected by the heat than the plastic ones. Another reason for not running on painted lines is that the track is generally cracked where the track is painted. Driving with your wheels on cracks will waste a lot of energy and slow you down.

To see how color can make a temperature difference, try this on a hot sunny day. Place your hand on the black asphalt and then on the painted surface. Most of us are aware of these temperature differences in color, but a little experiment will help the driver remember. The largest temperature difference is between black and white colors. Temperature differences and chemical reactions are the reason for cracks where the track is painted.

STOP YOUR CAR SMOOTHLY

Apply the brakes with a steady force to prevent a spin-out. Every year at Akron, there are wrecks after the finish line because someone applies his or her brakes too hard. You have more power than you think when you put on your brake. The brake plunger can lift your car to where the wheels will start sliding, and away you go hoping not to hit anything.

DON'T JERK YOUR HEAD UP AT THE FINISH LINE

All movement should be smooth, so you do not lose control of your car and have an accident. Do not get out of driving position until you are past the finish line.

DON'T TURN YOUR HEAD DURING THE RACE

When you turn your head, you increase the frontal area of the helmet, hurting your aerodynamics. Keep your eyes forward watching where you are going. If you are looking at your opponent, you are not concentrating on your driving.

DON'T PUT ON THE BRAKES UNTIL PAST THE FINISH LINE

Often I see cars with their brakes hanging down as they approach the finish line. Make sure the brake pedal is adjusted out of the way so the driver does not rest his foot on the brake pedal when racing.

DON'T LOOK BACK AT THE FINISH LINE

After you have passed the finish line, do not look back until you and the other car have come to a complete stop. When you look back, you lose concentration and could be involved in an accident. When you turn your head, you tend to move your hands in the same direction. There are many accidents because of this.

PRACTICE 10-7

KNOW WHAT TO DO IF YOUR STEERING FAILS

If your steering fails, put on the brake! I am always surprised at how many drivers do not know this, or forget it. Often when racing, things can happen so fast you do not have time to think. You are into the guardrail before you know it. However, if you practice and discuss this possibility with your pit crew, you will be prepared.

KNOW WHAT TO DO IF YOUR BRAKES FAIL

When your brakes fail, you need to know in advance where to go. Some tracks have objects at the end of the track to stop a car without brakes. You and your pit crew may not want to run into something to stop. If there is another alternative, you need to know what it is before the first race. **Spectators should not try to stop a moving derby car with brake problems. A fast moving derby car has a lot of kinetic energy making it dangerous to try to stop by hand.**

KNOW WHAT TO DO WHEN SOMEONE DRIVES INTO YOUR LANE

During a race, if an opponent drives into your lane and interferes with your driving, he loses that heat. Therefore, you have every reason to swerve or stop to prevent an accident. Some drivers think they cannot stop or steer out of the way. If you steer out of the way or stop, the officials will declare you the winner. You will be the winner because the other driver interfered with you by coming into your lane. Remember, the other car has to drive into your lane with one or more wheels.

KNOW HOW TO SWAP WHEELS

You need to know how to do a wheel swap. You need to know where the wheels go and how to tell if they are going in the right direction. You will have to know where your washers go and how to put on your wheel safety pins. This is not easy to learn. Different tracks use different wheel swap methods. This makes it more difficult to learn. This need not be one of the first things you learn. The younger drivers have problems with the wheel pins.

THE DRIVER IS PART OF THE TEAM

The driver should be part of the team and should be expected to help with wheel changes by at least getting something to put under the car and taking it out after the wheels are changed. After the race, the driver's duties should not end until the car is properly parked back in the pit.

PAY ATTENTION WHEN YOUR CAR IS BEING HANDLED

When your pit crew is not around, you have to keep an eye on your car. If your car is damaged, you will want to let your pit crew know so they can correct any problem.

KNOW WHEN YOUR STEERING IS STRAIGHT

You should have some way of telling when your steering is straight. There are several ways to accomplish this. Do not make it too complicated or dangerous. Make sure the driver understands how it works. See Steering in Chapter 5, "Alignment & Adjustments".

UNDERSTAND WHY YOU SHOULDN'T STEER THE FIRST 20 YARDS

A lot of energy is used during steering corrections at slow speeds. Driving straight for the first 20 yards can give you an advantage over your opponent. One foot can be gained at the finish line this way. Driving is an important ingredient in winning a race.

UNDERSTAND WHY YOU SHOULD DRIVE TO THE STEEPEST PART OF THE TRACK AS SOON AS POSSIBLE

As explained earlier in the book, the first one to the steepest part of the track will go the fastest. A quick start is important for a win.

PRACTICE

ALL STEERING MOVEMENTS MUST BE SMOOTH

Smooth steering movements will keep you from wasting energy. If you have smooth steering habits, you will be less likely to over-steer.

KNOW WHAT TO DO WHEN YOU SUDDENLY FIND YOURSELF ON THE WRONG PART OF THE TRACK

An experienced driver will not drive up the highest part of the hill. If the driver finds the car going in that direction he/she should straighten the car out. Do not over-steer. Here is an example of what I am talking about. We race on a track that has a slant going down to the left as you look down the track. I always tell my drivers, "never turn right." If the car starts going left, gradually straighten it out. If the car starts going right, react more quickly to straighten the car out. Never turn right and go up the hill.

ADVISE YOUR PIT CREW OF ANY STEERING OR BRAKE PROBLEMS

If there is a change in the car's stopping or steering, tell your pit crew right away. Parents should listen to what the driver says about the car. I saw a race where a driver told his dad that his steering had been damaged during the last run. His dad replied that they would just have to drive what they had. The next heat, the steering went out and there was a wreck. The boy's car was the fastest there that day, but because he had steering and brake problems, he lost. The other driver went on to race at the All-American Soap Box Derby in Akron, Ohio.

RAMP ALIGNMENT

Ramp alignment is the positioning of the car to get to the fastest part of the track. The start is the most important part of the race. A small advantage at the start is magnified at the finish line. The following play major roles in ramp alignment:
1. Steering

2. Transition from ramp to track
3. Starting gate angle
4. Starting gate speed
5. Levelness of ramp
6. Track shape or slope.

STEERING

Steering your car off the ramp can use valuable energy. The driver should try to travel as far down the track as possible without steering. To accomplish this, place the car on the ramp in the direction you want to go. With the nose pointing in that direction, no steering should be required. In close races, steering often makes the difference between first and second place. The difference between a car that steers early and one that does not can be 6" at the finish line. You should strive not to steer your car for the first twenty yards. *Slow and smooth steering movement is best when steering is required.*

LINING YOUR CAR UP

Lining a car up the same way each time is not easy. The pit crew should do this at first, but the driver should take over as he becomes more experienced. This is important for racing at Akron, where only the driver will be allowed to align the car. (This Akron rule changes every year, so, who knows, just be <u>prepared</u>)

Lining up the car for a straight 20 yards drive without steering is not easy. The wheels should be pulled out or pushed in, to make the alignment the same each time. If you do position the wheels, make sure you rock the car to unload the wheel bearings. Rules differ from track to track on whether you can position the wheels and rock the car. It does not matter, though. If you are not allowed to position and rock, no one else is, either. Rocking the car

PRACTICE   10-11

amounts to pulling the car back off the starting gate a few inches and then easing it back on the starting gate.

TRANSITION FROM RAMP TO TRACK

Check the ramp-to-track transition area. You want to come off the ramp where it goes down smooth onto the track. You also want the track to be smooth beyond the ramp. Check the ramp for a higher transition area on one side of the ramp than the other. Check the ramps especially closely at tracks you are unfamiliar with. Move your car on the ramp so you transition from ramp to track on the smoothest pavement.

STARTING GATE ANGLE

The starting gate angle should be 90 degrees to the ramp. Most tracks will have this angle. If the gate is tilted forward, it will give an advantage to the low-nose car. If the gate is tilted back, the advantage is to the high-nose car. This is because it pushes the one car further up the hill giving it more potential energy. At Indianapolis, we Figure one quarter of an inch further up the hill is worth about one foot at the finish line! Advise the local director if you see a gate that is other than 90 degrees to the starting ramp. Sometimes people do not know the advantage or disadvantage of a tilted starting gate.

STARTING GATE SPEED

A slow starting gate can be an advantage for a high-nose car. I went to a track once that had a slow gate that caught the bottom of most cars. The cars that had a quick rounding under the nose had a distinct advantage. We were fortunate to have won that race. The locals usually have an advantage at these races because they are familiar with their equipment.

UN-LEVEL RAMP

Some ramps are higher on one side than the other. Some are in a twist. Derby organizations should keep their ramps squared away with no cross-bind. If you do come across an un-level ramp, you should start on the high side and go toward the low. The ramp is not the only consideration. You have to know where you are going after you get off the ramp and on the track.

TRACK SHAPE

The track shape has the most influence on where you want your car on the ramp. Position your car to take advantage of the downhill slope. You want to get to the steepest part of the track as fast as you can. This advantage is illustrated in Figure 10-1. In Figure 10-1, the car has three choices: 1. The **downhill** direction 2. The **straight** direction 3. And the **uphill direction**. *Our racer is smart, so he chose to take the downhill direction.*

FIRST TWENTY YARDS

After twenty yards in the **downhill** direction, the racer has four more inches of vertical drop than the **straight** direction, and eight inches more drop than the **uphill** direction. The **downhill** slope is the best choice. See Figure 10-1

Aim your car in the direction you want to go. Aim your car to the steepest spot. Do not steer your car until you start turning to straighten out at the steepest spot. Even if the track is level, try to not steer your car the first twenty feet. There are accessions when it is advantageous to steer your car out early to take advantage of a steep part of the track.

PRACTICE

Even if the hill you race on does not have a slant to it, you should practice driving as if it did. The pit crew should coach the driver in this practice. Explain to the driver that alignment consists mainly of having the steering straight and the racer's car angled toward the steepest route. Tell the driver how a quick start is the goal and why. After your explanation, show him or her what you mean, have the driver practice, and then review the progress.

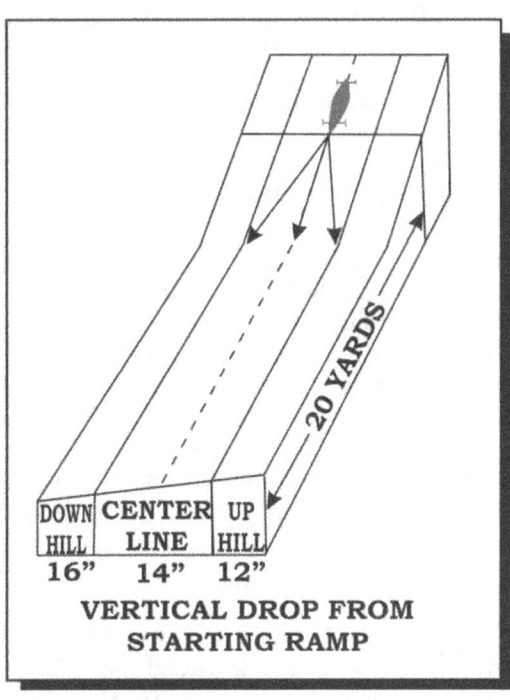

Figure 10-1

Have the driver practice getting the steering straight and keeping it straight for at least the first 20 yards. These are easy skills to learn if you practice.

USE ILLUSTRATIONS TO TEACH

Use the following illustration to show the driver how to drive a specific type of track. See Figure 10-2. Whenever you drive a track, try to keep the wheels straight for the first twenty yards. At the twenty-yard mark, you should start a gradual turn to straighten out. By twenty-five yards you should be straightened out and holding a steady course.

Figure 10-2 shows four different types of tracks. *The shapes of these tracks are exaggerated for clarity.* All the tracks shown have the racer going twenty yards in a straight line before turning. This is often the right thing to do. However, if the track has a steep side slope, it may be more advantageous to get to the outside quicker. Only practicing with a timer can tell you for sure which is the fastest way down the track. The benefit of a steep slope can often outweigh the energy loss from steering early. Use Figure 10-2 to show the driver how cars are aligned on a specific type of track and how that track should be driven.

Track "B" has a crown like a city street. This is the most common track raced on. Tracks with high crowns may require you to get to the side earlier than twenty yards down the track. Tracks "A," "C," and "D" are typical of the tracks made for Soap Box Derby. Their shapes will not be as exaggerated as they are here. Every time a track gets a new surface, its characteristics change. When this happens, we have to find the correct way to drive the track all over again.

PRACTICE

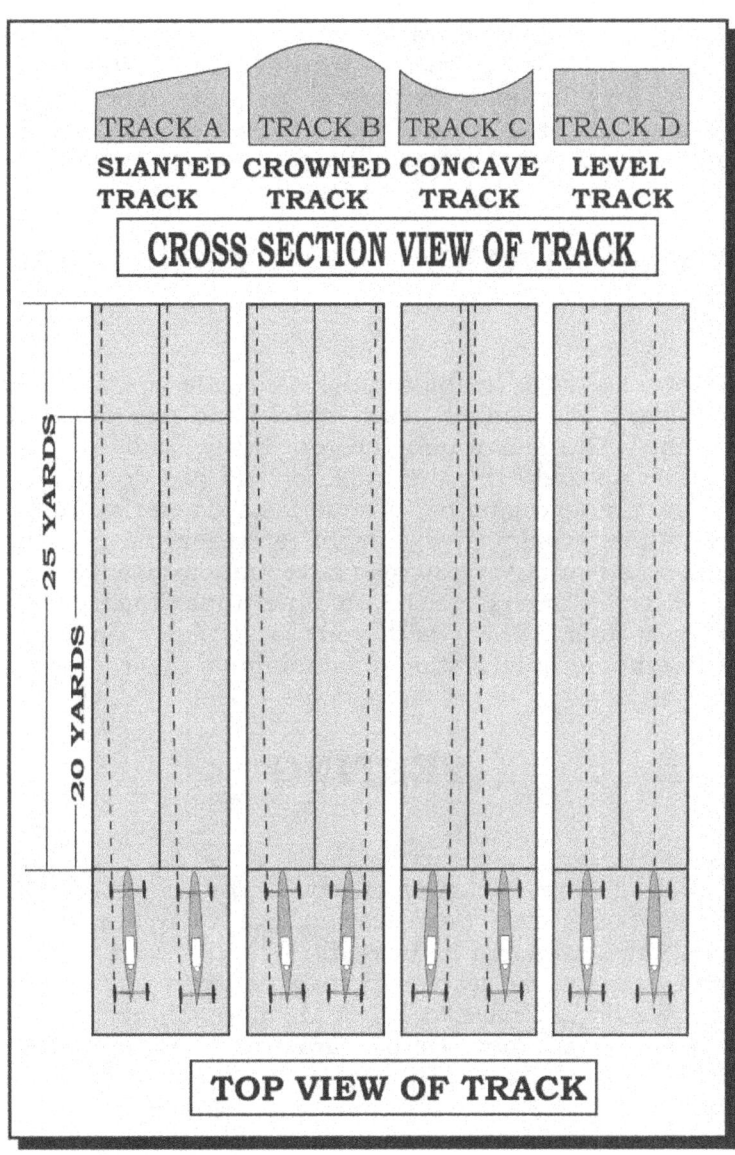

Figure 10-2

You might not have the opportunity to test on tracks other than your home track. In that case, you will have to depend on the local people for information about other tracks. At your home track, test and determine the best way down the hill. If you can, go to other tracks and test. I always liked to find my own information.

RAMP ALIGNMENT CONCLUSION

Now you have the information to decide how to line up your car. Remember, each track and its lanes are different. You can watch the top drivers and copy how they line up and drive the track, or you can do your own testing. I suggest both. If your tests do not agree with what others are doing, you might retest, or you may have found an advantage. You may have found a new "Winning Ingredient." Timers can be obtained that attach to your car for testing. Check with your local Derby Director or the internet for information on obtaining a timer.

TESTING

Testing is the backbone of good Derby people. Testing will help us grow. With testing, our thoughts on how something works can be proven. Whether we are proven wrong or right, we learn! Testing changes theories into fact. We do not have to guess anymore. When we test, we begin to see how Derby cars work and understand why.

PRACTICE

This book contains information from thousands of hours of testing. This is the accumulation of knowledge from hundreds of families in Soap Box Derby.

Misconceptions about Soap Box Derby cars happen all the time. Theories come along and everyone tries them out. If you have done a lot of testing, you will be able to judge the validity of these theories. If you cannot, you should find a quick way to test it.

There are several experiments in Chapter 2, "Energy," on "Weight Placement." These simple experiments cost you nothing but a little time. If you are a seasoned Derby participant, you may have a few theories you would like to test. If you have not already tested them, do it now.

PEOPLE WHO TEST

Many people test and my hat is off to them, but I want to mention one person who tested and has made a permanent change in Derby. The tests that he and his father performed changed our thinking on wheel placement.

> In 1967 Kenny Cline won the All-American Soap Box Derby. His car is on display at Akron, Ohio each year during Derby week. Kenny, his dad and 2 brothers gained their edge in Derby by testing. Kenny told me that when they were testing, they would be at the track almost every day.

Some of the knowledge they gained was on their local track in Midland, Texas and some were gained from tests performed on a pinewood Derby type track. The Clines were testing to see where the wheels should be placed and found that a short wheelbase placed as far aft as allowed was best. In 1967, that is how they placed the wheels on Ken's car.

They won their local race in Midland Texas, with no problem. A local radio station personality saw Ken's car and said it looked like a grasshopper! Ken was not too keen on the name, but to this day, it is still referred to as the grasshopper. Cars that were built to look like Ken's car were also referred to as grasshoppers.

While waiting for their turn to race at Akron, Ken's dad saw a grasshopper sitting on Ken's Derby car's wheel. By this time, everyone was calling the car a grasshopper, so Ken's dad wanted to get a picture, but before he could get his camera, it hopped away.

Ken went on to win the 1967 All-American and he owes it all to testing.

> Kenny and some of his friends in Chicago are responsible for the "Stock Car - kit car." Thanks Ken

TIPS ON TESTING

PROVING YOU ARE RIGHT

The most common error is to set out to prove your theory is correct. With the focus on proving your theory, you will not be able to be objective. You may ignore the test results if they do not help prove your theory. **I have seen this happen repeatedly**. To prevent this, you can have help from a friend that does not believe in your theory. You may need half of the testing team impartial.

PRACTICE

PAY ATTENTION TO THE ELEMENTS

When testing outside, pay attention to the elements. The wheels on your car are sensitive to heat and testing needs consistent outside conditions. The plastic wheels are not affected as much as the steel wheels, but they are affected. We always tried to test on a sunny day without clouds. Test when there is high pressure in the area. Testing when it is partly cloudy can be a waste of time. The second best time to test is on a day with heavy clouds all during your testing.

WIND AND SHADE

You do not want any wind while you are testing, unless you are testing the effect of wind on your car. If your track is lined with trees, you will have to pick a specific time of day to test. Can you imagine calibrating the Akron Soap Box Derby Hill? It has trees on each side of the track. It does not stay calibrated for longer than two hours.

TEST EQUIPMENT

Your test equipment has to be dependable. *If you do not have a dependable timer, you could be at the track all day and find out nothing.* I have done that before.

BUDDY SYSTEM

Use the buddy system when testing. Get a friend to help you test and share the information you get. Spend time testing each other's theories. Help each other out. You will gain more than Derby knowledge.

WHAT TO TEST

There is always something I want to test. The more I test, the more items I find to test. Test what tail weight to run, test what kingpin torque to run, and test the fastest way down the track. My testing days ended when my son grew out of his car and got other interests--to my regret--.

I have done some wind tunnel testing and other testing in my garage. I did the wind tunnel testing mainly to confirm what I was putting in my book. I learned a lot in all my testing. I kept an open mind and had to change some of my thinking to agree with my test.

GOOD LUCK,

KEEP PRACTICING

TESTING

AND TEACHING THE DRIVER

INDEX

A

Aerodynamics, 1-3
    Cross-section, 1-16
    Trailing edge shape, 1-21
    Types of drag, 1-30
    Wind tunnel test, 1-32
Alignments & adjustments, 5-1
Alignment tool 6-5
    Calibration, 6-7
    Car prep, 5-3
Apply Tung oil, 4-16
Arm, 9-2
Axles, 10
    Fairings, 1-38
    Inspection, 7-14
    Stands, tool, 6-14

B

Balanced weight, 8-16
Body inspection, 7-10
Brake cable, 4-29
    Inspection, 7-24
Brake system, 1-44
Bushing, 5-1
    Hole adjustment, 4-11
    Installation preparation, 4-3

C

Car dolly, tool, 6-19
CG, 9-3
Cockpit foam, 4-32
Construction, 4-1
    Rules, 4-3
Cross bind adjustment, 5-21, 5-15
    Tools, 5-16

D

Derby Tech, 10-3
Driver's education, 10-3
    Training, 10-1

E

Energy, 2-1
    Wheels, 2-9
    Experiment, 2-5
    Types, 2-3
Epoxy bushing, 4-14

F

Fisher gauge, 6-19
Floorboard finish, 4-16
Floorboard inspection, 7-4
Forms, weight & balance, 5-7
Formula for center of gravity, 9-3
    For moment, 9-3
Frontal area, 1-8

I

Inertia, 2-11, 8-10
Install
    Axles, 4-20
    Body, 4-40
    Brake pedal, 4-28
    Elevator bolts, 4-18
    Steering cable, 4-24

K

Kinetic Energy, 8-10
Kit car aerodynamics, 1-41

L

Lateral weight check, 5-13
Level board, 5-5
    Table, 6-15
Level,
    Check accuracy, 4-2
Longitudinal weight
Loose parts, 2-11
Lost energy, 2-4
Low weight, 8-10

M

Moment, 9-2

P

Paint, 4-44
Parts inspection, 7-1
Practice, 10-1, 10-14

R

Ramp alignment, 10-9, 10-16

S

Scales preparation, 5-3
Shimming your axle, 5-22, 24
Solid, tight, loose, suspension 3-5
Special tool Manufacturers, 6-27
Spindle alignment ck. list, 5-33
    Alignment tools, 5-30
    Alignment, 5-31
Starting gate, 10-11, 10-12
    Speed, 10-11
Steering, 10-10
    Adjustments, 5-25
    Inspection, 7-23
    Shaft holder, tool, 6-27
Streamlining, 1-6
Super Stock aft axle installation, 4-36

Super Stock aft axle, 4-38
Suspension, 3-1
Symmetrical, 1-15, 1-11

T

Teardrop shape, 1-8
Testing tips, 10-19
Testing, 10-1, 10-16
Toe-in adjustments, 5-35
Tools, 6-1
Tool list, 6-2
Tool, spindle alignment, 6-3
Tools for alignment, 5-2
Total weight check, 5-7
Track shape, 10-13
Trammel tool, 6-26

U

Un-level ramp, 10-13

V

Vertical weight, 8-12

W

Wasted motion, 2-8
Weight & balance calculations, 9-1
Weight chart for metal, 8-5
Weight, 9-2
Weight density, 8-3
Weight distribution, 8-5
Weight installation, 4-33
Weight management, 8-1
Weight placement, 8-20
Weight placement experiments, 8-6
Wheel weight test, 8-23

www.ingramcontent.com/pod-product-compliance
Lightning Source LLC
Chambersburg PA
CBHW060111170426
43198CB00010B/848